P9-CAL-960

Bob Lewis's IS
Survival Guide

Bob Lewis

SAMS

A Division of Macmillan Computer Publishing
201 West 103rd Street, Indianapolis, Indiana 46290

BOB LEWIS'S IS SURVIVAL GUIDE

Copyright © 1999 by Sams Publishing

All rights reserved. No part of this book shall be reproduced, stored in a retrieval system, or transmitted by any means, electronic, mechanical, photocopying, recording, or otherwise, without written permission from the publisher. No patent liability is assumed with respect to the use of the information contained herein. Although every precaution has been taken in the preparation of this book, the publisher and author assume no responsibility for errors or omissions. Neither is any liability assumed for damages resulting from the use of the information contained herein.

International Standard Book Number: 0-672-31437-1

Library of Congress Catalog Card Number: 98-86977

Printed in the United States of America

First Printing: March, 1999

00   99   4   3   2   1

Trademarks

All terms mentioned in this book that are known to be trademarks or service marks have been appropriately capitalized. Sams Publishing cannot attest to the accuracy of this information. Use of a term in this book should not be regarded as affecting the validity of any trademark or service mark.

Warning and Disclaimer

Every effort has been made to make this book as complete and as accurate as possible, but no warranty or fitness is implied. The information provided is on an "as is" basis. The authors and the publisher shall have neither liability nor responsibility to any person or entity with respect to any loss or damages arising from the information contained in this book.

EXECUTIVE EDITOR
Brian Gill

DEVELOPMENT EDITOR
Tony Amico

MANAGING EDITOR
Jodi Jensen

PROJECT EDITOR
Heather Talbot

COPY EDITOR
Linda Morris

INDEXER
Johnna VanHoose

PROOFREADER
Eddie Lushbaugh

TEAM COORDINATOR
Carol Ackerman

INTERIOR DESIGN
Anne Jones

COVER DESIGN
Anne Jones

LAYOUT TECHNICIANS
Brandon Allen
Stacey DeRome
Timothy Osborn
Staci Somers

OVERVIEW

CONTENTS

PREFACE

Once upon a time, when the earth was younger and I didn't, as my kids point out glee-fully to anyone within earshot, have a bald spot the size of Jupiter, I studied the behavior of electric fish.

I didn't study the electric eels you've undoubtedly read about. The fish I researched pro-duce roughly the same amount of juice as a transistor radio battery, using it to detect objects around them and to communicate with each other. They're amazing creatures.

While electric fish were my chosen animal for research during my graduate student days, my field was "ecology and behavioral biology," sometimes called sociobiology. Through my research and studies, I learned to observe and understand the behavior of animals. Part of that understanding came from learning their neurobiology. Because I studied neu-robiology I can say with confidence that management theory isn't neuroscience. Presumably it isn't rocket science either.

While the neuroscience was cool, I found the evolutionary view of behavior far more fas-cinating. The process of observing behavior and deducing how, within the physiological limitations imposed by a critter's basic biology, its behavior optimized it for its particular environment was a wonderful intellectual challenge.

I spent five years training to become a professional research scientist. Along the way I gained a treasure-trove of valuable skills: How to analyze data; how to critique the analy-sis of others; how to learn from others without blindly believing them. Most important of all, I learned the difference between genius and mere talent. Discovering I possessed the latter but not the former, I decided to change careers, earning a good living instead of becoming a professional sociobiologist.

And so I left the halls of academe to become a professional programmer. Soon afterward I had my first encounter with a different kind of critter—the professional manager. Using my cubicle as a blind, I was able to observe managers in their native habitat without scaring them off.

The tricks my colleagues and I learned studying other species came in very handy during these early days of study. For example, when studying birds, two ornithologists will enter a blind in full view of a flock. A minute later one will leave. The birds, unable to count[1], figure the blind is empty and go back to what they were doing. The same trick works with managers. Try it sometime.

---

[1]They are, after all, birdbrains.

After several years of this kind of study I became dissatisfied with the limitations imposed by my study methods. While I could observe from a distance and draw useful inferences, I couldn't get close enough to listen to managers vocalize. Worse, whole categories of interaction were hidden from me, as these strange creatures sometimes entered dark caves, known as "conference rooms" in their strange, primitive language[2]. Their interchanges in these caves were of clear importance, but I had no way of learning their nature.

With Jane Goodall's research among the chimpanzees as my inspiration, I determined to take my research to another level—I would live among them. Disguised in shirt and tie, I spent many years living as a manager, eating the manager's diet of Danishes and coffee, mimicking the manager's speech, participating in such strange management rituals as "off-site team-building exercises" and "budgeting."

Why did I write this book? More important, why should you read it? What makes me such an expert, anyway?

The sad fact is, I'm no more of an expert than you. All of the facts I know are commonplace. You've probably attended the same kinds of management seminars I have. I have no MBA. I don't even read the *Wall Street Journal* every day.

What I have done is to hold nearly every job there is to hold in the field of Information Systems. I've written programs in FORTRAN, COBOL, and another half-dozen or so languages. I've led large application development teams. I've managed network operations, application maintenance, and PC support. I spent over a year being 20% of a CIO (it's a long story). I've also been a business analyst for a manufacturing group, developed new products, and helped lead a nonprofit association through a complete change in its business model.

Most recently, I've become a consultant, helping clients integrate the use of technology into their business strategies and make their IS organizations more effective.

And, for the past three years I've written the "IS Survival Guide" for *InfoWorld*. The process of writing a column a week has a social hazard—it litters the landscape with soapboxes while worrying everyone around me that they may end up in a column sometime.

As a weekly columnist for a respected publication, I've also become a Recognized Industry Pundit (RIP) and with that status I'm at constant risk of believing my own PR, thinking I actually know something useful. Countering this risk are friends and

---

[2] *You'll find examples of this language, called ManagementSpeak, at the back of the book.*

colleagues who constantly reassure me that I don't. Even more valuable in countering the constant risk of Big Head Syndrome, I receive a constant stream of new ideas, facts, perspectives, and insights from the friends and colleagues I know and many more I didn't know I had until they were kind enough to send me a message via electronic mail in response to some column or other.

If I'm all that smart, I'd have already thought of all this stuff.

What you're about to read isn't the result of a lot of scholarly research. I haven't scoured the library, spent hours in the Internet, or interviewed dozens of industry wise-men to develop the content.

This book is nothing more than my opinion, top to bottom.

How have I arrived at these opinions? I've spent 20 years doing the job. Along the way, a lot of very smart, experienced people have shared their knowledge with me, letting me pick their brains and make use of their knowledge and experience. I've attended my share of management and technology seminars, and participated in at least my share of management fads.

And, I've read. Some of it has been about management and leadership, and while the ratio of utility to volume isn't that high, I've encountered many nuggets of pure gold this way.

More of my reading has been history. Reading history has an advantage over reading management theory, because history has already happened. When you read about great leaders and awful leaders, you get a pretty good idea of what really works with real people.

I've read huge volumes of science fiction over the years. Yes, 90% of it is junk. Of course, 90% of everything is junk: Why should science fiction be immune from this immutable law? I've read and listened to futurists, too, but as Isaac Asimov once pointed out, there are two kinds of futurist: Those who read science fiction and those who only pretend to be interested in the future. Science fiction is the literature of the future and many of its practitioners are tremendously smart, learned people.

Through total immersion in science fiction, I learned quite a bit about how technology leads to social change—enough, it turned out, that I ended up out-predicting many industry pundits regarding the success and failure of a variety of technologies and their impact on business and society. I became my own futurist. If I could only create interesting plots, I'd write science fiction for a living.

There's one other source of insight that's made its way into these pages: Stand-up comedy. Being a successful stand-up comedian requires a kind of social acuity absent from most of society. The best of the profession—people like Lenny Bruce, Mort Sahl, and Dennis Miller—spot incongruities and inconsistencies in our beliefs and opinions invisible to most of us, and describe them in pungent ways that are far more persuasive than any dry rendering of facts and logic.

You won't find much in the way of bibliography in this book. It isn't that I don't want to give credit to those who first developed the ideas I'm presenting. It's that I generally don't know. Heck, I don't even know which of the insights I think are original are really mine.

So while what you're about to read are my opinions, I don't make any claims to originality or, for that matter, validity. If you encounter an idea you find valuable, give me credit for bringing it to your attention in a convincing way. If you find you disagree with another opinion, that's fine—there's little enough in the way of universal truths, and neither Planck's Constant nor the speed of light in a vacuum have much relevance to this text.

Everything else, as Albert Einstein pointed out so long ago, is relative.

One thing I have tried to do is to make this book enjoyable to read. We're friends, aren't we? Friends don't ask friends to read boring writing. With luck, you'll at least find the contents amusing; with more luck, you'll find ideas you can use.

ABOUT THE AUTHOR

Bob Lewis writes *Infoworld*'s popular "IS Survival Guide" column that deals with IS management issues. He has held a variety of staff and executive positions in Information Systems at the Star Tribune Company, the consulting firm PSI International, and the Graphic Communications Association, as well as positions in business and product development. He currently works for Perot Systems Corporation as a consultant.

DEDICATION

This book is dedicated to Ms. Boghasen, my high school history teacher. Bogey taught a form of history rarely encountered at that level, and taught me a lot about how to probe below the surface of events to understand the motivations and interplay among those who shape events.

Even more important, she once spoke three words to me, probably meant as advice: "You must write."

It was hard to ever view anything Ms. Boghasen said as mere advice. It instantly became a command. I've tried to obey ever since.

ACKNOWLEDGMENTS

Acknowledgments are a lot like Oscar acceptance speeches: One recites a list of names, hoping nobody is left out.

Who am I to buck tradition?

First and foremost, I'm indebted to Rachel Parker, the former *InfoWorld* editor who, on the strength of a handful of guest editorials and a friendship based entirely on electronic mail, took a chance and gave me a slot in *InfoWorld's* weekly lineup. At the time I hoped to last a year without becoming repetitious. So far it's been three years of unending fun. Thanks, Rachel, and also thanks to Sandy Reed, *InfoWorld's* editor-in-chief, for keeping me in print.

I also owe a lot to Margaret Steen, who edits my column every week and makes sure I make at least a semblance of sense, and to Kristin Kueter who for several years edited an online feature called *Advice Line* which let me emulate Ann Landers.

Within Macmillan I'm grateful to a list of talented people who have helped make this book happen. Joe Wikert is the first. Although he's since moved on to a new challenge with a different publisher, Joe sponsored the idea of this book within Macmillan, defining it in a way that let me write it as "my" book with no requirement that I follow any predefined formula. Along with Joe is Brian Gill, who's been my day-to-day contact along the way. Brian's good humor and enthusiasm have had a lot to do with my ability to get this done successfully.

Who else at Macmillan? There's the whole editing and production team: Tony Amico, Heather Talbot, Linda Morris, Eddie Lushbaugh, and Carol Ackerman. If I don't write a paragraph about each of you it's only because you've made the whole process so seamless and easy.

On a personal level, I need to thank many friends who have given me aid, comfort, and encouragement throughout my writing career. Many have also reviewed this book informally, giving me comments and suggestions throughout. Steve Nazian, Alan Bose, George Columbo, Nick Corcodilos, Rich Mordhorst, and Mark Gibbs—thanks for all your help.

Then there's Larry Robbins, to whom I report in my "day job" at Perot Systems. Larry has been an enthusiastic supporter since the day I started reporting to him, viewing my peculiar hobby as something to encourage, not something that distracts me from my consulting responsibilities. During the six months it took to write this book before work and on weekends, I suspect Larry was more careful than he admits to avoid overloading me at the office. Thanks, Larry.

Larry, of course, isn't alone. It would take a small telephone directory to thank the many, highly talented people I've worked with at Perot Systems, and before that at the Star Tribune Company. Since I've learned far more by picking the brains of the experts around me who do the job every day than by reading the experts who publish, it's a literal fact that I owe my ability to create this book to the people I've worked with over the years. If you're one of them and see your ideas here … well, originality *is* the art of concealing your sources, isn't it?

I need to make one disclaimer. Throughout this book I use chief financial officers (CFOs) and Human Resources (HR) as stalking horses.

In my experience, CFOs too often focus on cost reduction rather than the creation of value. In my experience, HR often has a silent mission statement of keeping the company out of court, which supercedes any role it takes in helping the rest of the company succeed.

This doesn't mean "they're all like that." It means these are occupational hazards of these two disciplines, just as we in IS live in constant danger of becoming bureaucrats, blindly enforcing standards instead of helping the business succeed.

To every CFO and HR professional I'm about to offend … take it as an informed criticism of your specialties, not as a personal attack.

Finally, there's the personal support I've received from close friends and family. In particular, my dad, Herschell Gordon Lewis (a direct marketing industry pundit beyond anything I've ever accomplished in my own field) and his wife/my stepmom, Margo, have helped me and provided a wonderful goal for me to shoot at in the bargain.

I owe a lot to Sharon Link, whose stayed with me through all the angst of the last half-year. If it weren't for her, several thousand of these words wouldn't have happened.

And finally, to my kids Kimberly and Erin, who ended up watching a few too many cartoons while their dad pounded out "just a few more words"—thanks for all the love, all the hugs, and for being even bigger goons than your old man. You're the greatest.

TELL US WHAT YOU THINK!

As the reader of this book, *you* are our most important critic and commentator. We value your opinion and want to know what we're doing right, what we could do better, what areas you'd like to see us publish in, and any other words of wisdom you're willing to pass our way.

As the Executive Editor for the Programming Team at Macmillan Computer Publishing, I welcome your comments. You can fax, email, or write me directly to let me know what you did or didn't like about this book—as well as what we can do to make our books stronger.

Please note that I cannot help you with technical problems related to the topic of this book, and that due to the high volume of mail I receive, I might not be able to reply to every message.

When you write, please be sure to include this book's title and author as well as your name and phone or fax number. I will carefully review your comments and share them with the author and editors who worked on the book.

Fax: 317-817-7070

Email: prog@mcp.com

Mail: Brian Gill, Executive Editor
          Programming Team
          Macmillan Computer Publishing
          201 West 103rd Street
          Indianapolis, IN 46290 USA

INTRODUCTION

*"Outside of a dog, a book is man's best friend. Inside a
dog it's too dark to read."*

—Groucho Marx

MANAGEMENTSPEAK

You have to apply common sense to this problem.

Translation:

You have to think like me.

Why are we spending so much on information systems?" wailed our CFO one day in a budget meeting. "What are we going to do with all of this information anyway?"

Our CFO was given to weeping, wailing, and gnashing of teeth and eventually we all acclimated to his outbursts, but at the time he threw me for a loop. The best reply I could find on short notice was, "Our job is to manage the information. Your job is to use it. If the company doesn't need some of the systems we run, we can certainly turn them off."

OK, actually I wasn't anywhere near that clever. I wish I had been, but this was years before I learned the basics of negotiating, so offering to give him what he pretended to be asking for never occurred to me. Instead, I made the fatal mistake of trying to defend our budget, and that put me on the defensive. I should have known better.

This book is about knowing better. It's written for people who run Information Systems, want to run information systems, or work for or with the people who run or want to run Information Systems. It's a handbook on how to succeed in the day-to-day job of being a working Chief Information Officer (CIO), or at least to survive in it.

Just surviving in the job isn't that bad a goal, since according to the same kind of survey that proved nine out of ten doctors prefer Bayer[1], the average CIO only lasts about two years before getting the boot.

Surveys like this, showing that something horrible will happen to you in the near future and there's nothing you can do about it, appear in the business press all the time, which is one of the three main uses of the business press[2]. But whether the average tenure of a working CIO is eighteen months, two years, or some other number that still isn't very big, there's no question that the average CIO sits in the Desk of Death, which is why some clever soul decided that CIO really stands for "Career Is Over."

Being CIO is a tough job. It's tough because the gulf between expectations of what a company could get out from its information systems and what it actually gets is simply too immense to cross.

We've dug this chasm ourselves, of course, through years of painting pictures of the glorious day when [insert IS fad here] will transform our company into a lean, mean, highly productive competitive machine.

---

[1] *Among doctors who prescribe aspirin, for those patients who need aspirin, when Bayer is the only brand name they can remember for aspirin, and only on Wednesdays and alternate Fridays.*
[2] *The other two are to print articles proving (1) if everyone would just show a little initiative and take personal responsibility we could eliminate welfare entirely; and (2) if government would just stay out of things, the business community would rapidly create a utopia.*

The sad fact of the matter is that we could change our name from "Information Systems" to "BS Systems" and nobody would speak up in our defense (BS, if you aren't familiar with the term, stands for "BuShwah," a synonym for blarney, nonsense, and that other BS term we won't use in these pages). IS is more prone to management fads than any other discipline (according to nine out of ten hand-chosen consultants). Why is that?

THE EVOLUTION OF INFORMATION SYSTEMS ORGANIZATIONS

The reason we adopt so many fads, I think, is related to the reason we keep changing the name of our discipline. When I got my first job in the world of business computing nearly twenty years ago (before that I programmed for spare change as a graduate student while studying the behavior of electric fish[3]), we called ourselves "Electronic Data Processing" or EDP.

EDP didn't pay enough, I guess, so some bright guy decided our real job was to provide management information and *voilà*! We became MIS.

That was the worst mistake we ever made because we changed from a department that did something useful, important and understandable—processing the company's data—to something intangible, esoteric, and mystifying.

Sure, it catered to the egos of the managers running our companies. After all, we now said giving them information had a higher priority than helping employees do real work, and suggesting they'd use a lot of information made them feel smart and important. The problem, though, was that managers don't use information very often. It's too confusing. They rely on their instincts instead. If we could have provided "Management Instinct Systems" instead we'd have been far better off.

(Actually, that's not the worst problem "MIS" generated. When management information is the point, ease-of-use, process improvement, and other niceties just don't seem as important. At least, they didn't to the CIO who once said to me, about a huge development project he was sponsoring, "What I'm interested in is the database. I don't much care about the systems that feed it." Sadly but predictably, his team never finished the systems that fed it, and his tenure as CIO was shorter than the national average.)

Luckily, nobody cares all that much what we call ourselves as long as we keep our systems up and running. And when the empowerment fad swept the country, we went right along, taking "Management" out of the title and becoming "IS"—Information Systems.

---

[3]*No lie. I would lie, but I don't have the imagination to make up this kind of thing. You'll find a few electric fish anecdotes scattered through the pages that follow, along with a variety of other nonsense, largely because if I simply stuck to the subject, you and I would both be bored to death.*

Along with this evolution in purpose we experienced just two minor glitches. First, we forgot how to deliver working systems. And second, the personal computer came along to put a spotlight on all of our deficiencies.

And we did forget how to deliver working systems. I know of one company that's had two failed initiatives to replace its most important business system. These two initiatives spanned two decades and ate up over $10 million in resources without delivering a nickel in actual value.

This isn't the exception. The statistics are horrifying. Depending on which survey you read and how you interpret them, fewer than 30% of all big IS projects succeed, more than half fail completely.

Look at most IS organizations today and you'll find the major systems fall into two overlapping categories: (1) Commercially purchased systems, and (2) very old in-house-developed ones. The Year 2000 problem didn't arise because programmers thirty years ago did something stupid. It came about because the programmers who built our legacy systems in the early 1970s didn't anticipate our becoming so inept at systems development that their code would still have to support the company three decades later.

That's what makes our name changes hilarious. We call ourselves "Information Systems" but our systems date from the days we were EDP. The change has largely been in our own minds, not in the role we play. That's good, because "information," especially in this age of information glut, generally has less economic value than what we really do for a living.

And what, you're probably asking, would that be?

THE TRUE ROLE OF INFORMATION SYSTEMS

For the most part, we're process automation people. We take things the company has to do, and we help the company do them faster, better, and at lower cost (cheaper/quicker/better is the holy trinity of business). Information is a byproduct of this effort, not its focal point. Yes, we often manage the company's vital records. That isn't information management, though, it's records management—important because it's another process that would be expensive, tedious, and error-prone without our services.

Yes, we're process automation people. Most of the information our systems generate helps in managing processes, and when we do generate strategic information, it's as a byproduct of our process management systems.

Want proof? What's our rallying cry when anyone asks what we'll deliver with our Next Big Effort? Productivity! What's the big question about the deployment of personal computers? We can't find the Productivity!

And so on. As you'll read in the section on performance measures, productivity isn't always the right thing to look for, but that's not the point. The point is that we call ourselves "Information Systems" and what we promise is productivity. We're smarter than we think we are, because productivity—what we deliver with our real mission of process automation—has economic value, while information (except, of course, for this book) just sits there.

IS IT "JUST SEMANTICS"?

A word of warning. You'll run across quite a few discussions in the pages that follow that resemble the chat we just had. I can almost hear you grumbling to yourself, "That's just semantics." It is, of course, except there's nothing "just" about semantics.

Semantics, according to my dictionary, is the study of meaning. It also refers to the relationship between symbols and behavior. When you say, "It's just semantics," you're saying we're wasting time figuring out what we mean when we say something and how it affects our behavior.

Since as CIO every facet of your job requires clear communications, you'd better pay close attention to semantics. A big part of your day-to-day life is acting as a translator. You will:

- Listen to your data center manager explain why an operating system upgrade is important and then translate it into business terms for the company's executive committee.

- Listen to your application development manager explain why Use Case Analysis is the methodology that will take the company into the 21st century and translate his gibberish into CFO[4]-ese to get the cash[5].

- Listen to your PC manager explain why you have to upgrade to the next release of your office suite and translate that into CFO-ese as well.

- Listen to your company's CFO and executive committee explain to you that the company doesn't exist to subsidize fun and games in the IS department, and translate that back into geekspeak so everyone understands how they're supposed to get the job done anyway.

---

[4]*Chief Financial Officer. Sheesh, Yogi, don't you know anything?*
[5]*At least you might, until you read about methodologies later on in this book. Then you'll think long and hard before you ask for the money.*

You have two choices. You can either understand that semantics are important—that you must choose some words carefully, thinking about the experiential background of the listener as you do—or you can be widely misunderstood and stand in wonderment as your organization deteriorates into a brawl.

Worrying about words and how we use them is important. We're going to be spending a lot of time together, and it's important that we understand each other. What we aren't going to spend a lot of time worrying about is what names we should use instead of the ones we've been using. We'll keep on calling the organization IS and you the CIO (or future CIO, or victim of the CIO, depending on your role) and not spend a lot of energy developing alternatives, even though we're really process automation people at heart.

Instead, we'll worry about important questions, like: What is the role of a Chief Information Officer, anyway?

THE ROLE OF THE CIO

As CIO you spend your life herding cats, nailing Jell-O to the wall, keeping your job until tomorrow, and keeping da joint running. If you aren't careful, you'll start thinking those activities define your role.

They don't, though. Important as they are, they're merely means to an end. Your real job—the reason they pay you the big bucks—is to maximize the leverage your company gets from computing technology.

Think, for a moment, about everything you have to do to make this happen. You have to:

- Monitor the capabilities of every major technology available to your organization.
- Monitor your company's industry and its marketplace dynamics.
- Understand your company's business model—how its actions lead to the achievement of company goals.
- Gain and maintain a high-level working knowledge of the company's operations.
- Serve as the executive committee's technology consultant, participating in the formulation of the company's long-range strategy and short-term marketplace tactics.
- Manage relationships throughout the company.
- Establish IS's direction and purpose.
- Motivate everyone who works in IS.
- Decide how the company should invest a major chunk of its discretionary spending.

- Serve as a communications conduit, actively translation messages rather than passively routing them.
- Play golf with vendors.

And then after lunch…

To reiterate, your job is to maximize the leverage your company gets from computing technology. The job takes a lot of doing, and a special set of skills to succeed. This book is, in part, about helping you acquire those skills. You may think some are a matter of inborn character, rather than being learnable—you either have them or you don't.

You'd better be wrong, or all leadership training is worthless and this book is a waste of time.

CHARACTERISTICS OF A GREAT CIO

To be a great CIO you need to be

Visionary—you must be able to articulate a convincing portrait of the future and how to get there. Leadership is about change, because anyone can preside over a bunch of people milling around going nowhere. To lead change, you have to present a compelling description of the new reality and make the process of achieving it seem exciting and worthwhile.

Pragmatic—your day-to-day decision-making must be reality-based. If you tell yourself stories and believe them, indulge in wishful thinking, or, for that matter, fool yourself through excessive cynicism, your decisions won't work because they'll be based on how things work on some other planet, not ours.

Businesslike—like it or not, most business-folk distrust technologists. If you come across as a technologist, they'll distrust you, too. You must be able to interact with business people in business terms. Some of this is a matter of style—being comfortable in a suit and tie and keeping your mouth closed when you chew. It's more important to understand business at a street-smart level, because as CIO you don't make technical decisions. You make business decisions about technology.

A People Person—a lot of your job is motivation, and to motivate people you have to understand them, empathize with them, know what makes them. As a people person, you won't read a book about how to manage Generation Xers, women, minorities, or angry white males because you understand people are unique individuals and you understand them as individuals.

An Incredible Delegator—in the end, the CIO lives and dies with the delivery of working systems. This means giving people assignments and getting them to make commitments and live up to them. While it may seem basic, this ability is exceptionally rare.

Politically Savvy—doing business in a company of any size means politics. That isn't necessarily a bad thing because politics, like the Force, has both a light side and a dark side. The light side is understanding that different people have honest differences of opinion, and to get things done, you have to work with all of them. You also need to understand the dark side—backstabbing, character assassination, and other unsavory tactics, because if you don't, you'll be its victim, and you aren't paid to be charmingly naive.

Sensitive to BS—and in fact you need a state-of-the-art BS detector to wade through all the nonsense that will inundate you every day. Your BS detector must avoid what statisticians call Type 1 and Type 2 errors. You encounter a Type 1 error when you fail to recognize BS. You experience a Type 2 error when you mistake something legitimate for BS.

A Kid in a Toyshop—you personally preside over stuff that would have made Jules Verne faint dead away in astonishment. The technology we design, install, and manage, with all its faults, warts, bugs, and irritations, was unimagined when the Brady Bunch got together—only a couple of science fiction writers predicted personal computers, for example. This is really cool stuff. Your employees, or at least the best of them, get paid for their hobby. They do this stuff because it's way cool.

So should you, because otherwise why would you put yourself through this? There are easier ways to make a living, and unless you have a passion for the technology and what it can do, you'll hate your job, you'll disparage the people who make you succeed, and in a very short period of time, you'll fail.

That would be a shame, because being CIO can be just about as rewarding and fun as a career can be.

With luck, this book will help you not just survive the experience, but thrive in it.

Enjoy.

THE BUSINESS

"There must be a plan," you muse to yourself. "We could try all day, all night, and work weekends, and not get things this messed up through random chance."

Legend has it that the Biggest Problem with Information Systems is that it's off on its own doing techie stuff, ignoring what the company needs. It's a useful legend, propagated by business leaders, consultants, and CIOs alike. It probably isn't true, but it's useful, because aligning IS with company goals is much easier than fixing the real Biggest Problem with IS.[1]

That being said, many IS organizations have trouble finding the right role to play in helping the company advance its vision, mission, and strategy. Despite our strong desire to play a strategic role among the company's *dramatis personae,* it isn't always clear just what that role ought to be.

Part of our trouble stems from the silly notion, promulgated by Total Quality Management consultants who just weren't thinking straight, that we need to view other people and groups within the company as

---

[1] *Usually, its inability to deliver working systems on a timely basis. Don't worry—we'll cover this topic in Part III. You can skip to it right now if you want to. You bought and paid for it, and there are no Reading Police to stop you. I promise you won't hurt my feelings.*

our customers. The wide acceptance of the internal customer metaphor has turned many IS organizations into nothing more than passive work-order processors.

This has its good side, of course, since we can't be blamed for doing the wrong things. We're doing what our customers asked us to do, after all, and pleasing…no, *delighting* customers is what business is all about, isn't it?

Well, no it isn't, and even if it were, business certainly isn't about delighting fellow employees.

This section is about the business. Not the business of IS, but business in general. It covers the nature of business strategy, tactics, and infrastructure, and how to link your IS organization to them to make sure you're shooting at the right targets.

Linking to the business isn't a simple matter of meeting with the CEO or the executive committee, asking, "So now what do you want?" and writing down the answer. Among other complications, the business has three entirely different kinds of needs to link to: Strategic goals, tactical objectives, and requirements for its infrastructure.

You need to understand all three before you know what targets to shoot at.

Knowing what targets to shoot at doesn't make hitting them any easier—but at least you'll be pointing in the right direction.

"First Management had plans, and then strategic plans. Now we have VISION, and we're only one small step from hallucination."

—Ainsley Throckmorton, on the occasion of assuming the presidency of Bangor Seminary in Maine.

MANAGEMENTSPEAK:

Our business is going through a paradigm shift.

Translation:

We've no idea what we have been doing, but in the future we shall do something completely different.

ALIGNING WITH COMPANY STRATEGY

Back when I was a kid, Pin the Tail on the Donkey was a popular game at birthday parties. I'm still not exactly clear why blindfolding a kid, handing him a sharp object, spinning him around until he's dizzy, and telling him to stab a paper animal with the sharp object was supposed to be fun, but generally I enjoyed the process of stumbling over coffee tables and sticking holes in the wallpaper, so I suppose I shouldn't complain.

Pin the Tail on the Donkey is a wonderful children's game if you're heavily insured against property damage and personal injury lawsuits. Unfortunately, we IS professionals seem to play it a lot when trying to figure out what we ought to be doing for our companies, and that's a whole lot less fun.

Don't think so? How many times have you asked for a capital spending approval or budget increase, only to be told you haven't hit the target? "What is the target?" you naively ask. "We're not sure, but that isn't it," is a common answer.

You're still playing Pin the Tail on the Donkey, wearing a blindfold, disoriented, and trying to find the target without the help of the people who put it there in the first place.[1]

The donkey's tail you're trying to hit is the company vision, mission, strategy, and long-term goals. CIOs face two common barriers to finding this donkey. One is that the donkey isn't on the wall in the first place—that is, many corporate executives don't really understand what constitutes a strategy, and even fewer can successfully translate strategy to action.

The other barrier is the blindfold that comes from not being part of the Executive Club.

THE CLUB

Your company has a defined leadership team. Sometimes it's called the executive committee, sometimes the senior leadership team. As CIO you should be part of it.

Your company also has an Executive Club. This group isn't formally defined, but like the legendary *Illuminati*, its members recognize each other instantly, treat each other differently than mere mortals, and wield the real power. If you're part of the executive committee, you still might not be part of The Club. And if you aren't on the executive committee, you might still be a member.

---

[1]*A friend of mine, more cynical than I, describes the same process as the "Concrete Piñata". You wear a blindfold, try to whack it with a stick, and even if you do hit the thing it's designed to not release any goodies. Unless they like you, that is, in which case they pick you up and let you reach in over the top to grab what you want.*

It's very important for a CIO to be a member. That's the prerequisite for participating in the definition and execution of strategy. Succeed at this and you'll personally thrive. At a minimum, you need to recognize what's going on so you don't pin the donkey's tail onto your own backside.

Many people call The Club the Old Boy's Network, but it's no such thing. Think of The Club as the clique in high school you never became part of and you'll have a pretty good handle on the situation. This one is a bit more open than the one in high school was, but the dynamics are similar. In a high school clique, total strangers somehow instantly recognize each other as "in" or "out" without a word being spoken. Club members also know who's "one of us" and who isn't by instinct. It's a matter of chemistry, fitting into the executive culture, not being an embarrassment when introduced to members of the club who work for other companies—and by the way, having enough chutzpah to make the big plays without letting anyone else see your axillary perspiration.

The point of The Club is access. If you're a member and you see the CEO and CFO having lunch together in the company cafeteria, you can join them without anyone giving it a second thought. If you aren't a member you can still join them—that is, you can ask, "May I join you or is this a private conversation?"—but even if they invite you to sit down, it isn't the same conversation. You're an outsider.

Joining them as part of The Club is important because most of the business of most companies happens outside the documented processes. You need capital for something? You have to go through the capital approval process, of course, but if you want your proposal to sail through, you have to grease the skids by chatting up the idea with Club members. After you've socialized it, its success is a given. Otherwise (horrors!) the capital approval committee will evaluate the thing. And not on its merits alone—it will be competing for capital with other projects sponsored by Club members.

If you aren't a member and want to succeed as CIO, you either need to find one of the rare organizations run by a different sort of leader—one who recognizes you as a member of his or her club—or you need to adapt. This isn't easy, but it is possible.

The key to membership is being able to act like, think like, and comfortably socialize with business executives. It's more than wearing a suit—it's being comfortable wearing an expensive suit. It's more than reading the *Wall Street Journal*—it's reading it enough to discuss the column-one story, significant mergers and acquisitions, and otherwise participate in executive small talk-gossip about the day-to-day happenings in the business world.

Self-confidence, and sometimes overt arrogance is needed to operate in these circles. There's a lot of ego in most executive suites, and if you're easily intimidated, you will be intimidated.

No, you don't have to become an arrogant jerk to succeed as CIO. That isn't the message here, nor am I paraphrasing the guy who told a young Daniel Schorr the secret to success in broadcast journalism. "Sincerity," he said. "If you can fake that, you've got it made!"

To succeed at being CIO you must be an executive, not only in title, but in how you comport yourself, because the role of CIO is an executive one. If you're a successful executive reading this book, you already understand this part intuitively. If you aren't, and don't think of yourself as an executive who simply hasn't obtained the title yet, you have some personal changes to make.

This isn't a book about how to transform yourself into a business executive. If this section has helped you understand a barrier to your personal success, it's accomplished its purpose.

COMPANY STRATEGY

Executives have visions. No really—they do. It's part of the job, only they don't first pop a peyote button. You should have a vision too, as a matter of fact, because in business terms, it is simply a compelling[2] description of the organization's desired future state.

Leadership has many dimensions to it. Each one, though, is about making change happen, and no change happens without motivating the people who have to execute the change and embrace it when it's done. Without a vivid, exciting, persuasive picture of where you're going (in short, a vision) there's no way on earth you're going to uproot your family from its comfortable home in Peoria to follow your dream of running a lemming ranch in the Australian outback.

Of course, your CEO's vision is nowhere near as bizarre as that, is it? Probably not. It only seems that way to most of the employees who toil away in your company's vineyards, each of whom is predisposed to see the vision as just another corporate boondoggle that takes time, energy, and resources away from the real business of the company, which is to keep on doing what you've always done.

"After all," I can remember a grizzled veteran[3] commenting about a past employer's radical new direction, "we've been making this product for over a hundred years now, so we can't be all that bad."

---

[2]*Translation: Extremely complex.*
[3]*He really was grizzled, too—he had iron-gray hair, had been with the company for ages besides, and was a good guy.*

PRAIRIE CHICKENS AND OLD-SCHOOL EXECUTIVES

Modern American business executives are expected to visualize, promote, and lead change. This is profoundly different than the experience of American business even twenty years ago, when executives had a lot in common with male prairie chickens.

Let me explain.

Prairie chickens are less elaborate cousins of the peacock, living in places like the plains of western Minnesota and the Dakotas. Every spring in the hour or so around dawn, male prairie chickens congregate in areas about the size of an average lawn called "leks," claim personal territories, and do the prairie chicken dance. It's an amazing sight.

The central territory is the smallest—about three feet across. Further from the center territories get bigger but less desirable, at least as defined by female prairie chickens, which wander through the lek choosing which males will be allowed to fertilize their eggs.

Proof: The central male gets about 90% of the matings.

For as many years as biologists were aware of the prairie chicken dance, they assumed the central male was the toughest, nastiest bird for miles around. At least, they did until a graduate school buddy of mine named Henry MacDermott looked into the matter. Henry discovered something completely unexpected.

Male prairie chickens don't fight hard to carve out their territories, defending them against all comers. As the years pass, males sort of drift to the middle. There's some competition, but for the most part the males who survive long enough—those that don't die of disease or being eaten by foxes—end up near the middle.

When I left graduate school to enter the world of business in 1980, I often found myself wondering how some of the executives I encountered managed to get to their positions of influence and authority. Most of them treated important decisions the way you and I would treat a rabid ferret: something to be watched carefully and avoided while someone else foolish enough to stick his or her neck out deals with it.

One day I figured it out. In the early 1980s, American business was suffering from thirty years of complacency, succeeding more from momentum built up in the '50s and '60s than from current quality. Japan, Inc. was kicking American business in the shorts, but our executives had acquired their positions the previous decade or two.

Executives who took risks that failed were punished for their failures, and businesses succeeded nicely without taking any risks at all. Because failure was punished and success could be achieved by sitting back and watching the money pour in, the executives who made it to the top were those who avoided mistakes, not those who made bold moves.

American executives, in other words, were prairie chickens!

And you thought we had nothing to learn from the animals.

That's the attitude you have to overcome to achieve a change, and that means making the future seem worth the pain of change. The company's executives need to describe a future worth building, and that's the role of describing the company's vision.

A lot of cynicism has been expressed over this subject, most of it due to visions that aren't ("I see a future where we don't simply satisfy our customers—we thrill them!"). "Visions that aren't" come from leaders who prefer following to leading and safety to success, because a company without a vision is a company that lacks direction.

Period.

So whether you call it a vision or chicken soup, defining and communicating a clear, high-level, but unambiguous picture of where the company is going is central to leadership.

Central, but not complete because by itself a vision is nothing more than an empty promise. Vision becomes interesting when the company's leadership (and that includes you) figures out how to translate its vision into reality—in other words, when you define your strategy[4]. Many CEOs do a great job of defining the company's vision, but fail when it comes to defining a strategy. Because doing so has a lot in common with good old-fashioned top-down systems design, you should be in great shape to help lead the process. Even if you don't, you need to understand what's going on so you don't wake up one morning to discover you're running the wrong kind of IS organization for the business your company wants to become.

Creating the New Business Model

The first step in defining your company's strategy is to create its future business model. A business model is a cause-and-effect statement of how actions lead to success.

Business models are generally simple. Gillette's (give away the razor, sell the blades) was so simple and elegant that it has become a cliché, but a cliché that still works beautifully in a wide variety of circumstances.[5]

---

[4]*Words like "vision," "strategy," "mission" and so on have been used and misused so many times they've become wonderfully ambiguous. The usage in this book might not match how they're used in your company. Don't sweat it. Just pay attention to what the CEO calls things and use the same vocabulary.*
[5]*Not that many years ago, Central Point Software used a variation quite successfully: Give away the software, sell the upgrades.*

Ideally, every major activity within the company has a business model of its own that explains its role in the company's overall success[6]. IS, for example, might use this one:

> "We provide applications that help the company streamline and automate its processes, which in turn reduce unit costs, which in turn either reduce the cost of the product, therefore helping to sell more units, or increase our margins, which in turn increases our profits."

A good vision leads to redefinition of the company's business model. If it doesn't, there really isn't much point in it. If your company doesn't make creation of the business model the first step in creating its strategy, it will end up blindly wandering around the marketplace, hoping it accidentally makes some money.

Not a promising thought.

Translating the Business Model into Strategic Capabilities and Processes

Your new business model defines how you're going to make money in the future. In order to make the new business model work, your company will usually need new capabilities, often in the form of new business processes. Usually, the business model, plus a wee bit o' thought, are all it takes to make the new capabilities and processes self-evident.

To illustrate this process, let's execute our vision of becoming the leading alternative provider[7] of personal computers to the corporate marketplace.

Our focus will be on corporate customers, and our value proposition is that every PC we ship you will have only the components you've specified, including a full pre-install of all standard software.

The full business model: "We build to order instead of selling just a few standard models. Businesses choose us over our competitors because they get exactly what they want. What they want are no-hassle installations that work the same every time with no surprises due to non-standard components, and no work resulting from having to install software on-site. We sell more computers and make more money."

Hmmm. Built-to-order PCs. What will be needed to make this work?

---

[6]*For years, Lipton ran television ads showing how to use its French onion soup mix to improve the flavor of hamburgers. Their marketing followed an excellent business model: Show consumers new and innovative uses for a product, which in turn increases their consumption of the product.*
[7]*"Alternative provider" is our corporate buzzword for "Not a name brand like IBM or Compaq."*

1. A way to market built-to-order PCs so people understand why they are different and better. The head marketing weenie figures this means two new capabilities: Direct marketing so we can more efficiently communicate with our customers, and sales force automation, both to make the direct sales force more effective, and to help move the account management process from the field to the home office.

2. An efficient order-entry operation, with highly-trained order-takers who fully understand the product options so they can help callers specify their orders; an order-entry system that makes it easy to enter each order and calculate the price. We need this because the direct sales force only handles large accounts—it's too much overhead for smaller businesses, so we need a more efficient way to handle these.

3. Hey, why don't we take that order-entry system and make it directly available to consumers through the World Wide Web? Every system ordered this way will reduce wear and tear on our call center. (This works well. Reputedly, Dell sells millions of dollars worth of computers on its Web site every day.)

4. An efficient way to flow orders into manufacturing so we build exactly what we're supposed to, every time.

5. An efficient configuration testing operation to make sure customer-specified component combinations will work and be stable.

6. A manufacturing operation built around the principle of mass customization—the assembly lines or cells are designed to produce a different, custom item each time, but using the same standard process for each one to keep the defect rate low. This process must keep the order number associated with the PC from the time assembly begins until the time the PC is shipped.

7. An inventory process that accurately forecasts use of every component, both standard and custom, so we can always assemble every order without delays due to backorders, but also keep inventories low enough to avoid eating up our profits in excessive inventory costs. (This also works well. Dell is said to make money on inventory float. That is, it collects money from its customers faster than it has to pay its suppliers for every component used, so it earns interest on the cash it collects until it's time to pay.)

That wasn't hard, was it?

Turning Strategic Capabilities and Processes into Programs and Projects

Now that the executive committee has a clear understanding of what new capabilities and processes the company will need to develop in order to achieve its vision, it needs to translate that into a small number of well-defined implementation programs.

Here's where life gets interesting. Depending on the state you're in and the capabilities you've defined as critical for your future success, you might find yourself planning an easy-to-envision change, or a complex, enterprise-wide transformation.

Companies rarely succeed in achieving complex, enterprise-wide transformations. There's a point at which your transformation describes a different company that's in a different business. If the executive team is getting this frisky, it's probably better to form a whole new company, built around the new concepts, from the ground up[8]. As it succeeds and the old company falters, the new one slowly cannibalizes the old one until the transformation is complete.

Most of the time, the vision won't lead to such a radical break with the past. Change will be significant, but you'll still recognize the original company when it's done.

Whether it's building a new company or transforming the old one, translating the new capabilities and processes into implementation programs isn't a purely linear exercise. At least, it isn't for you, because there's simply no way you can manage as many major projects as there are new capabilities.

Instead, you have to find ways to consolidate the chunks of capability-creation you own into just two or three banners. There's no analytical methodology available to you here. You and your team (by all means involve your management team in this) need to apply your understanding of the problem, your knowledge of information technology, and your insights and creativity.

To illustrate, take a look at the list of capabilities and processes we developed for our hypothetical computer company. It's a big list, especially if you aren't very smart about it:

1. Customer database.
2. Sales force automation package.
3. Order-processing system suitable for call center use.
4. World Wide Web site that exposes the order-entry system to visitors.
5. Order-processing/manufacturing system interface.
6. Test lab.
7. Just-in-time manufacturing process management system suitable for mass customization.
8. A Manufacturing Resource Planning (MRP) system to handle inventory, purchasing, and receiving.

---

[8]*Except, of course, for corporate headquarters and centralized, shared capabilities like, for example, Information Systems. You want this to be a career-builder, not something that reduces your value to the company while introducing a new organizational rival.*

A lot of CIOs would cave right now, telling the executive committee it will have to pick and choose, prioritize, and wait five years to launch the new strategy. Five years is a nice safe period of time because long before then everyone will lose interest, so IS will never actually have to deliver. Five years and never are about the same period of time because there's no urgency attached to five years.

By being smarter about things you can cut the list down. This is part of the value you add—you understand the importance of systems that do double duty[9]. You come back with this shorter list:

1. Select and implement a commercial customer management system, to handle the customer database, direct marketing functions, sales force automation, and order processing.
2. Select and implement a commercial Enterprise Resource Planning (ERP) system to handle inventory, purchasing, and manufacturing. The ERP and customer management systems might be the same, but your plan is to evaluate the two sets of requirements separately.
3. Custom-developed World Wide Web site.

This is a manageable list. The three projects are big, but at least you can keep track of them and understand what's going on.

An obvious point: Just because you only have three projects to worry about doesn't mean the company only has three projects. Sales and marketing has two big worries: Learning the whole discipline of direct marketing, and cajoling the sales force into embracing sales force automation technology.

The COO has to convert the current dinky, underfunded, and demoralized call center into a state-of-the-art facility, and none of the current staff seem like the right people for the new role.

The head of manufacturing has to figure out how to convert the PC assembly area from mass manufacturing to building small batches of custom-configured systems without needing a new plant, and without losing any days of production during the transition.

The purchasing manager, who also owns inventory management…well, you don't even want to think about her headaches.

Guess what their reaction is to your list of three systems? They have plenty to worry about already, and now you're going to force something down their throats that doesn't fit their requirements, just to make your life easier!

---

[9]*Actually, you don't solve the problem in the meeting. That sets the wrong tone. You say, "Let me take this list back to my team and we'll translate it into a list of systems capabilities and projects." Being thought-leader for a team of experts is far better than just being an expert, and conveys that you're an executive comfortable in a leadership role, not an individual contributor.*

You have some selling to do. Step one: Don't make the fatal mistake of saying no. Tell the executive committee that it has two options, and although you'll be happy to accept whichever one the group chooses, it's your business judgment that consolidating functionality into fewer systems makes more sense.

If, instead, you choose to implement a best-of-breed strategy where each division of the company chooses its technology separately, you'll either have to stretch out the implementation schedule (the five-year plan) or you'll have to increase the IS organization significantly.

Now there's a threat!

Reassure everyone that their requirements will be taken into account, both during the product selection process and during implementation where these systems can be extensively customized to fit the specific requirements of each division.

The main lesson from this example is that the process of translating capabilities into programs and projects isn't difficult, but it also isn't a matter of just taking the capabilities and implementing them in a straight line. By applying some creativity you can get much more leverage out of your efforts.

Now you just have to implement, which means getting programs and projects launched. We'll deal with this in detail in a later chapter.

SIZING PROJECTS

As CIO you know by now—or should—you should never charter any project that will take longer than about nine months to complete. This means restricting the size and scope of every project.

Keeping the size to nine months is important, because anything longer than that will eliminate any sense of urgency on the part of the project team, and it's a sense of urgency that gets projects finished.

Not everything you need to do will fit into a nine-month framework. That's okay. It simply means you have to take to heart that old idea about thinking globally and acting locally. In this case it means laying out a program (a coordinated cluster of individual projects, some concurrent, some sequential all directed at the same goal).

What's that you're saying? That this is a distinction without a difference? That there's no difference between one big project and one big program?

You're wrong, bit-breath. The difference between program planning and project planning is significant. Program planning operates at a results level. When

continues

continued

> planning a program, each project's results must contribute to the whole pro-
> gram, they must arrive in time, and, importantly, they must also stand on their
> own if at all possible. In program planning you only plan the immediate pro-
> jects in detail. The rest you guesstimate and worry about the details when the
> time comes.
>
> When planning a project, in contrast, you plan all the tasks in detail before you
> launch. You have to, or you have no idea of how you're going to finish. Project
> planning happens at the task and milestone level, and neither tasks nor mile-
> stones have to provide any tangible business value. They simply have to be tan-
> gible, concrete, and designed to build the project's results.

A WORD OF WARNING

Planning corporate strategy is fun. It's exciting. It requires vision, boldness, courage, and
quite a few other self-congratulatory adjectives besides.

Implementing the strategy is a lot of hard, grinding, sometimes discouraging work.
Thomas Alva Edison once explained that invention was 10% inspiration and 90% perspiration. If implementing a new strategy is a kind of invention, Edison got the proportions
wrong: He overestimated the amount of inspiration required.

Many of the company leaders who develop exciting new visions and strategies have no
real intention of implementing them. Oh, they fool themselves into thinking they're serious, but deep down they know.

The problem with visions is that they're intrinsically risky. Fine-tuning your current
operation is safe. The risks are low and the rewards (in the form of bonuses, stock
options and other perks) are high.

To translate vision into reality requires big investments, hard work, and the intense hope
that your guess about the future will turn out to be right. Visions require a sense of
urgency. If there's no sense that something about your current business model is going to
fail pretty soon, the CEO has more prudent options than to spend a lot of money on a
risky venture into uncharted territory.

Complicating things further is business's excessive reliance on financial measures of success. No matter how poorly a company's prospects, its profit and loss statement rarely
crashes and burns overnight. Even if the airplane that is your company has run out of
fuel, a good pilot can make it glide a long way before it hits the ground. It's easy for the
executive committee to fool itself for quite a long time.

This means we've missed a key aspect of the strategic planning process in this discussion—when to drive the program to success and when to give it lip-service and wait for it to expire.

You can't apply book-learning to that charming little puzzle. It takes street smarts.

Sorry.

STRATEGY-FREE ENTERPRISES

One of my all-time favorite *Mad Magazine* pieces was called "Star Blechh." In it, the crew of the starship Booby Prize beamed down and encountered one of the natives—a character drawn by Don Martin. The planet, according to this character, had experienced numerous disasters and was pretty much in ruins. "We have no past and no future," he explained.

"What about the present?" asked Captain Kook.

"It's under the tree," was the inevitable answer.

Many companies are run like that. The past and future look just like the present, which is a money machine that somehow delivers profits.

So what do you do if your company is run as if the future will look just like the present only more so? Does having neither real nor feigned strategy relegate you to a caretaker role?

No, it doesn't. All this means is that the company's leaders expect the current business model to last for the foreseeable future[10]. Your primary job, in this situation, is helping the company get better at its current business practices—a subject covered in the next chapter.

In the meantime, you have a vital strategic role to play in your strategy-free enterprise. You're the main lookout for trouble in paradise.

Danger, Will Robinson!

So there you are, happily running IS for Will Robinson Shoes. Will Robinson Shoes has been designing and manufacturing shoes for working people for forty years now and is good at it. It has a loyal direct sales force that maintains close relationships with buyers

---

[10]*Foreseeable future, n. An indefinite period of time starting with the instant following the present moment and lasting until sometime between the end of the current fiscal year and the end of the fifth fiscal year following the current one, depending largely on the CFO's appetite for internal negotiations.*

in every major retail outlet that sells shoes, and business has been steady as a rock for twenty years or more. Whenever someone suggests strategic planning, Will Robinson Senior responds that he built the danged business without a strategic plan, grew it from nothing to a $500 million business without a strategic plan, and sees no reason he can't retire without ever having created a strategic plan.

"This is the shoe business," he's fond of saying, "not rocket science. This world doesn't change, so we don't need to change either."

What's odd about Robinson Senior is that he's proven himself open to new ideas time and again. Why he's resistant to development of a new business strategy mystifies you.

Well, it shouldn't, because Robinson Senior is right. If there's nothing on the horizon to change your business model then Will Robinson Junior can inherit the business and just keep on keepin' on.

You, however, just ordered flowers for your wife on the World Wide Web. You've also ordered every book you've read in the last year on the Web. And you just ran across a bit about a clothing manufacturer's Web site. This manufacturer gives instructions on how to take your own measurements, and sends custom-fit clothing for the price of off-the rack items, with five-day shipping and excellent quality.

You just realized that the next five years might not be like the last forty. The question is, do you bring this insight into the executive committee, aka Robinson Junior and Senior?

If not you, whom? The tooth fairy is flying from bed to bed, and Batman is too busy fighting crime to do it.

Get the picture? With almost no exceptions, what changes the market ecology in which most businesses live is technology. New capabilities enable new business models, either through new ways to create value, or through one of my favorite consulting buzzwords, "disintermediation" which means "cutting out the intermediaries[11]."

So keep your powder dry and an eye to the horizon. You're elected to watch for ways in which technological change can let a competitor...and especially competitors you don't know you have right now...get the drop on you.

---

[11]*It used to be "cutting out the middleman" but...well, you know.*

SUPPORTING COMPANY TACTICS

"You were under the impression/That when you were walking forwards/You would end up further onward/ But things ain't quite that simple."

—The Who, "I've Had Enough," *Quadrophenia*

MANAGEMENTSPEAK

I have a concern about the business need for this.

Translation:
Over my dead body.

Strategy is fun. Strategy is exciting. Strategy is about building an exciting future.

That's great, but you have to survive until the future gets here. That's why your most urgent job isn't supporting the company strategy. It's supporting the company's day-to-day tactics and operations.

How can you tell the difference between strategy and tactics? In business, strategies lead to a different way of thinking about your company. Tactics lead you to succeed within the context of the business you're in today.

Two of the nicest characteristics of strategic programs is their clarity and unity. Tactical programs, in contrast, are a hodgepodge, with each division head making plans independently and squabbling over budget, staffing, and the time and attention of IS.

Why is that?

The answer isn't hard to find. Because strategy is about the future, everyone has to figure out how the new business model is going to work, and the whole company must transform or the strategy doesn't happen.

Tactical programs are usually about improving ongoing operations. Everyone knows their role in ongoing operations, so division heads or middle managers usually charter tactical projects within the existing organizational boundaries. Usually they don't have any reason to consult each other about these projects. That's the whole point of having an organization, after all.

So Manufacturing produces goods at lower cost and with higher quality, Marketing segments the company's target audience more precisely and tailors its messages more effectively, and distribution ships product more quickly and efficiently.

The heads of Manufacturing, Marketing and Distribution don't need to consult each other when making their plans. In the end, Manufacturing will make the same products and deliver them to Distribution in pretty much the same way it always has, and Distribution will accept Manufacturing's output. Although Marketing will, with luck, generate more sales orders[1], they'll be the same kinds of sales orders Manufacturing has always had to satisfy.

---

[1] *Yes, Sales, Marketing and Advertising are separate disciplines. In this mythical test-case, the actual division is "Sales and Marketing" and it also coordinates the company's advertising. Don't be so picky!*

Then there's you. Sitting on your desk are requests from all three division heads for major systems implementations. Manufacturing wants to implement MRP/MRP2 (Material Requirements Planning/Manufacturing Resource Planning). Distribution plans to implement random-grid inventory management. Marketing's plans require implementation of a customer data warehouse and full data mining capabilities, and you're pretty sure the Chief Marketing Officer doesn't really even know what that means.

What you do know is

1. You have nowhere near the resources to handle these projects; and
2. Turning down any of these characters means career death.

What's a hapless CIO to do?

You need an effective, coordinated tactical planning process, that's what.

THE BAD NEWS: IT'S A TUG OF WAR, AND YOU'RE THE ROPE

According to your guesstimates, the MRP/MRP2 system will require five business analysts and seven developers to select the product, configure it, and integrated it into the rest of your systems.

For a variety of reasons, the random-grid inventory system has to be developed in-house, and that means committing eight analysts and fifteen programmers for two years.

Then there's the data warehouse. You've worked with Marketing before and you're pretty sure this "simple" request will end up as three entirely separate projects. Why? The "data warehouse" is supposed to support screen pops in the call center, as well as having an improved merge/purge capability. In other words, he wants a data warehouse, enhanced operational customer database, and a new call center system. Your Marketing director intends to be fully buzzword-compliant[2], regardless of what the buzzwords actually mean. Chalk up one analyst and three programmers for the data warehouse, an analyst and another two programmers to enhance the customer database, and a team of three analysts and five developers to research, purchase, and integrate the new call center system.

---

[2]*FBC, to use the acronym.*

Add up what everyone has asked for and it's pretty clear what you have to do: Hire a lot more people than you have. Across the board you need 18 business analysts and 32 programmers. With this kind of development and integration load, you also need to add a database analyst/database administrator to your Information Resource Management team.

Too bad you only have seven analysts and two dozen programmers in your division.

Each division head is trying to pull you into his or her camp. If you turn them down, you're the reason the company can't move forward. Ask for more headcount and once again IS is empire-building—didn't you just hire more people last year? Just how much technology does this company need, anyway?

THE GOOD NEWS: IT ISN'T COMPLICATED

Unlike the process for implementing the company vision, handling tactical and operational requirements doesn't call for extraordinary insights or a complex process. This is basic blocking and tackling.

You need four basic capabilities to have the tactical planning process covered:

1. Business consulting: To figure out what needs to be done.
2. Project estimation: To figure out how much effort will be needed to do it.
3. A way to set priorities: Because it's unlikely you'll have enough resources to do everything on the list.
4. Street smarts: Because nothing is ever exactly as it seems.

Think you can handle it? Good.

BUSINESS TECHNOLOGY CONSULTING

Two of the most frequent complaints leveled at IS by business users: We promote technology for the sake of technology; and we don't provide technology leadership for our companies.

Your first reaction to these two complaints is probably, "Pick one." They would seem to be mutually exclusive. In fact, it's possible to fail both tests simultaneously by buying technology that's trendy without knowing where it will provide business leverage; and by not suggesting any ways technology can help move the business forward.

One way out of this trap is to provide business technology consulting services to your company's division heads.

The goal of your business technology consulting is to work with division heads and their high-level managers to discover how they can best take advantage of technology in achieving their business goals. Depending on how your company operates, this process can be informal and staffed entirely by the CIO, or it can be highly structured and staffed by a team of professional consultants steeped in the mysteries of business consulting methodologies.

An average IS organization will succeed nicely if the IS leadership team understands business technology consulting to be a key responsibility of each team member with the CIO taking the role of thought-leader.

The process itself can look a lot like the enterprise-wide strategic planning process described in the previous chapter. As with enterprise strategic planning you begin with a vision of the future, an understanding of the capabilities needed to succeed in achieving that vision, and the projects you'll need to take on to deliver those capabilities.

The two processes aren't, however, identical. In enterprise strategic planning, part of the process is thinking differently about the business. In tactical business technology consulting, the goals and objectives[3] are more or less fixed (manufacturing, for example, doesn't get to stop assembling the product because its information-delivery business has higher margins).

At the tactical level your primary goal[4] is process improvement, and sometimes process transformation. The difference is that process improvement is incremental, finding ways to improve or eliminate steps in an existing process. Process transformation completely changes a process while still accepting the same inputs and delivering the same results.

Your consulting goal is identification of opportunities—ways new technologies and new uses of technology can be used to improve a division's core processes so it can more effectively perform its functions.

Don't make the mistake of thinking you should actually redesign processes as part of the business technology consulting role. That's the job of business analysts, and it's an early stage in the systems analysis process. Right now you're simply identifying opportunities: educating division heads about what technologies are relevant to their operations, which ones sound great but aren't yet mature enough to rely on, and what the implications are of building processes around technology instead of simply automating a manual process.

---

[3] *I have no idea what difference there is between a goal and an objective, but the two words are apparently welded together in the business consulting world. If you want to succeed in this role, never use a two syllable word when a three-syllable equivalent is available, or a single word when you can substitute a short phrase.*
[4] *I could have said "main goal" but see the previous footnote.*

In short, you're providing technology leadership while making sure all the technology you bring in has a business purpose.

Most important, you've transformed your role from passively accepting and processing work orders to active partnership in improving the business.

PROJECT ESTIMATION

There is no way for you to successfully estimate projects. Take that as a given. It can't be done, and for a very simple reason: Every one of your projects is one-of-a-kind.

The big systems integrators[5] have an advantage over you. They do lots of projects, and most resemble earlier ones. After you've installed an Enterprise Resource Planning (ERP[6])system, you're done with it, never to go through that pain again. Many systems integrators, on the other hand, have made ERP implementations a specialty. After the first few, they get the hang of it, and if they want to be both competitive and profitable, they figure out how much one of them should cost.

Even systems integrators try to avoid estimating big projects, though, and you can learn from their example. The alternative begins with the philosophy, mentioned in the previous chapter, of breaking big projects into small ones of manageable size, keeping track of them all through creation of a program management structure.

This two-layer structure reduces risk to manageable levels. That, of course, is a Good Thing (GT) because even companies that celebrate risk-taking rarely celebrate being foolhardy.

Key to your success is refusing to estimate the cost of the program. Whatever else you learn from this book, learn this lesson and take it to the bank. No matter what pressure you receive, JUST SAY NO!

---

[5]*In this book I'm going to use "Systems Integrator" to refer to any company providing a wide range of business and systems consulting, development and integration services, largely because I don't know what else to call them.*

[6]*First there was Materials Requirements Planning (MRP). Then there was Manufacturing Resources Planning (MRP2). That grew into ERP one fine day. I thought that was the end of the line. How much bigger could you get than the whole thing? A failure of the imagination, I guess, because now we have supply chain management which extends to a company's suppliers.*

THE BIG PROJECT LIFE CYCLE

If you haven't been through this fire drill before, here's what you'd face if you succumb to the pressure to estimate a big project:

1. You and your team spend an hour in fruitless argument, because you have absolutely nothing to base your estimate on.

2. One team member has learned about function points and suggests using them as an estimating tool. When you try, you find that (a) you can't estimate the number of function points in the new system any more than you can estimate the effort required; and (2) you don't know how much effort you'll need to expend in implementing a function point.

3. You scrap all methodologies and agree to a number because you have to. You pad it to be safe and call it a four-year, 25-person project. At the company's going fully-loaded rate for labor, 100 staff-years of effort turns into $10,000,000.

4. Everyone gulps and signs up.

5. Four years, 25 people, and $10 million are immediately etched in stone.

6. You form the project team, which sees that it has four years to get the job done and sets a relaxed pace. The team does not exhibit a sense of urgency but that's okay, you're told by the project manager because, "This is a marathon, not a sprint."

7. After two years you find no evidence of tangible progress, but that's okay because the project plan, although sketchy, makes it clear that tangible progress happens in Year Three.

8. Sometime in Year Three the project's main backer gets a great job with another company. Shortly thereafter, she hires away your project manager.

9. You appoint a new project manager who reviews the situation and wigs out, telling you in no uncertain terms that the project is in the ditch. The team, it turns out, has been spinning its wheels for two years—nobody even knows what work has to be done to finish the project.

10. You quietly inform your network of friends that you're ready to take on new challenges.

11. You set up shop as an independent consultant. Friends call you at your new business number to tell you the company just put a bullet in the project.

Instead of estimating the cost of the program, you charter a two-month project to design the program in detail. A small team, headed up by one of your business consultants and staffed with two or three business analysts, establishes the program's objectives and scope, recommends a management structure for the program as a whole, and maps out a logical sequence of projects to accomplish the program's goals.

The projects must have two distinguishing characteristics or the program will not work. The first characteristic is that no project can last longer than nine months or have more than a dozen full-time team members. Project managers can develop realistic, detailed plans for nine-month projects, and with only nine months from start to finish, project teams will feel a sense of urgency from the day their projects start.

The second characteristic is that every project must deliver identifiable, tangible value on its own. Even if the company pulls the plug in the middle of the program, it will have received real value for the effort expended thus far[7].

Now you have to bend and do some program estimation. The program design team should develop staffing plans for each project. It also should identify which projects will develop specifications for hardware and software purchases, and which ones will actually require the purchases.

Based on the staffing plans, you can create a reasonable estimate for the program as a whole. Do so, then add 50% to the original estimate and use it as a plug number to share with the executive committee. Every time you present the number, reemphasize that it's imaginary, and that throughout the course of the program you'll refine your estimates as you charter the individual projects.

For the hardware and software costs, once again you should simply refuse to give an estimate. Instead of providing a number, point to the program timeline and show the questioner where in the process you'll be developing the numbers. Grudgingly, you might choose to provide not-to-exceed estimates but be very careful when you do so. This isn't the time for optimism[8].

One last, key point. You've done everything you can to pad your estimates before you've provided them to the executive committee. Don't even think about sharing those estimates with the project teams and program management.

---

[7]*A later chapter will revisit this subject in more detail, but don't get your hopes up. There's no magical methodology to apply to this problem. All you can really do is tell the program design team that this is their responsibility and that they should apply their intelligence and ingenuity to the problem.*

[8]*If you're wondering, the time for optimism is when you're giving pep talks to the project team.*

Yes, open and honest communication is a Good Thing, which is why you're going to share your real, unpadded estimates with the project teams and program management. They'll do their best to hit your targets, but because you made 'em up in the first place, you need to create an environment where teams can adjust to circumstances. When a team with a nine-month project plan discovers it needs twelve months to do a quality job and clean up the rough edges, the executive committee will experience a project that's finished early, not a costly and irksome delay.

SETTING PRIORITIES

Quite a few years ago, I was part of an IS leadership team that brought in a consultant to tell us we needed a bigger mainframe. They did what we asked them to do and we got our mainframe at the regular price, plus their consulting fee.

Of course, we didn't say they were in our shop to justify the mainframe. We said we'd engaged them to assess our overall effectiveness. That meant in addition to telling the executive committee we needed a new mainframe, they also had to submit recommendations.

Their major recommendation was a Systems Steering Committee to help set our priorities. This would have been a far more interesting recommendation if we hadn't had one in place for the past five years. As it was—well, we did get the new mainframe, so it could have been worse.

IS has managed a backlog (a long list of projects it will never get to) since before it stopped being EDP. That was a long time ago, and our project lists haven't shrunk in the meantime. You'd think they'd learn to stop asking.

But they do ask, and we just described a whole process designed to encourage not only more requests, but probably more complicated ones as well.

It's time to increase the backlog, I guess.

Since I first entered IS, we've always viewed the backlog as a significant problem. That's just plain wrong-headed. A healthy company will always generate more ideas than it can use. If you didn't have a backlog—now that would be a problem.

You do, of course, need some way to figure out what work will get done and what will go on the back burner. There are three basic tools you can use. Use one, any two, or all three in combination, depending on your company. They are

1. Resource allocation.
2. Prioritization committees.
3. Staff preassignment.

Here's how each one works.

Resource Allocation

Resource allocation begins by dividing work into three basic categories. There is no way to assign relative priorities to them, so instead you divide your resources among them, fairly arbitrarily.

The first category is keeping the joint running—maintenance, making sure paychecks get printed, and so on. If you fail at these tasks, you're mortally wounded—out of business and there's no tomorrow.

The second category consists of the tactical projects we planned and estimated earlier in this chapter. These projects help improve your company's competitive position. Failure leads to a slow loss of position in the marketplace. You won't die of mortal wounds, but of starvation. Not pleasant.

Then there are the strategic programs you developed in the first chapter. These move the company into the future. Fail and you won't notice a thing in the short term, but in the long run you're a goner.

There just isn't any point in trying to set priorities among these three categories of work. They're all vital. Instead, working with the executive committee, you allocate your resources (capital and human) among them.

Although your mileage might vary, a 40/20/40% split isn't a bad starting point. In other words, allocate 40% of your resources to keeping the joint running, 20% to tactical projects, and 40% to strategic projects.

Don't worry, you aren't shorting the tactical projects. It only looks that way because you think you only have 100% to work with. It's better than that.

Although the 40% allocated to maintenance and the other 40% allocated to strategy are not-to-exceed limits, the 20% allocated to tactical projects is a floor. That's because the business sponsors for your tactical projects will usually be able to calculate a hard-dollar return on investment. Tactical projects reduce production costs or otherwise improve your company's margins or ability to sell its products and services, so you're making money on your investments.

Let's imagine the average after-tax ROI on tactical projects is 25%. The company can borrow at about 7%. That means if it doesn't have enough cash to pay for all its tactical projects it will make money by borrowing more.

What CFO will turn down a proposal that makes 18% after paying taxes and servicing the debt?

So that 20% you've reserved for tactical projects is your starting allocation, not your total allocation. You're probably best off contracting with a systems integrator for the remaining tactical projects. This is as much a political issue as anything else: If you staff up to handle them, the following year you just have more people, and then it might look like you're trying to find work for them all.

Prioritization Committees

Except for highly politicized companies, a Systems Steering Committee is a great idea, although you're probably best off if you don't form one.

That is, you're better off asking the executive committee to take on project priority setting as one of its regular agenda items instead of forming a separate committee. You'll most likely be dealing with the same players—the CEO, COO, business unit heads, CFO, and HR-meister—so why have all of them attending two different committee meetings?

Although to some CIOs it might seem that using a Systems Steering Committee (or the executive committee) to set your priorities is either abdicating responsibility or giving away power and authority, smart ones understand that this is your best opportunity to gain acceptance and broad ownership of the value you provide. Involve people in a process and they own the results. Present the results of a process to the same people and they critique.

Which do you prefer?

Either annually as part of the budgeting process, or quarterly (far better), meet with this group. Confirm your 40/20/40 split (or whatever percentages you've chosen). Then present them with the list of projects and available resources you can take on during the next planning cycle. Your job is to facilitate the discussion. Their job is to figure out which projects to fund. That means deciding which ones fit within your existing resource structure and which ones to provide additional funding for.

You'll have several interesting discussions in these meetings. For your strategic programs, the committee will have to figure out whether the 40% you've allocated gets the company where it's going fast enough. If it doesn't, that's fine—these are exactly the right people to bump up your funding for strategic programs.

For tactical projects, each committee member will find herself having to sign up for the claimed benefits of their projects. When you claim hard-dollar savings that means you have to be able to see them on the profit-and-loss statement. You have one key role in this conversation: Don't participate!

The last thing you want to do is position yourself as an advocate. As much as you might want to be the driver on one of these projects, in the end it's the business unit heads who have to take ownership of the results. Let them sponsor their projects, promote them, and make the key commitments. You'll have enough work delivering the systems they need to achieve their results.

The maintenance budget is the easy discussion. Simply present your best numbers and wait it out. All you have to explain is that the numbers are what they are. The specific decisions regarding how the money and staff time will be spent will be made at lower levels.

Forming a Systems Steering Committee (or co-opting the executive committee) is merely the most obvious prioritization committee you should form. The same idea works at every level of your organization, so your Information Center manager should form a key users group, the network manager should form a network steering committee, and so on.

At every level the advantages are the same. You create allies, you establish open and sympathetic communication channels for your messages, you find out how the rest of the company really perceives your organization, and you set better and more realistic priorities.

You'd better take two key success factors into account or your efforts will flop. First, every participant must perceive membership as status-enhancing. They gotta wanna, and in part, that means fostering the idea that this is an exclusive club you've formed.

Second, every member must leave each meeting thinking the experience was personally value-adding. That means organizing agendas and running meetings so those in attendance think they learned something important, participated in decisions of some significance, and helped set the direction for building the future.

That, of course, means that while project prioritization is an important goal for these groups, you need to involve them on a broader front so they understand, and eventually help direct, the overall context for their decisions.

It's heady stuff, and after you get past the notion that you're giving up control of IS to the business side of the organization, you'll realize you've done the exact opposite. You've taken a leadership role within the organization, instead of acting as an external service provider.

Now that's a great thing to do.

STAFF PRE-ALLOCATION

In Western society we equate altruism with virtue. In Darwinian terms, though, altruism is maladaptive. In other words, a gene that promotes true altruism—one that encourages behavior benefiting other genes at its own expense—will, over time, vanish from the species through its own actions. What looks like altruism always turns out to be some form of *quid pro quo*, or a case of the gene actually helping itself.

Business, Darwinian to the core, isn't an environment where altruism thrives, so don't expect members of your Systems Steering Committee to make serious personal sacrifices for the good of the company. Nobody in the executive ranks has much incentive to think about the long-term good of the company.

WHO CARES ABOUT THE HEALTH OF THE COMPANY?

Business schools spend lots of time teaching budding MBAs how to make companies succeed.

Business, however, isn't about the success of companies. It's about the success of a company's stock. And although the two are often related, the relationship is tenuous enough that a lot of what business schools teach is irrelevant to the kinds of decisions made in the executive suite.

Here's the problem. In theory and in law, a certificate of stock confers a share of ownership in the company. In practice, most shareholders view a stock certificate as one of the company's products, and themselves as buyers of that product.

Given a choice between the company succeeding and the stock going up, stockholders will choose elevation of stock price over company success every time.

In the case of most publicly held companies, it's even worse. Stockholders don't even make their own buying and selling decisions. Instead, by investing in mutual or pension funds, they've delegated their stock trading decisions to the fund manager.

continues

continued

> And that means that the people who can vote the board of directors in and out of office aren't the owners at all—they're the fund managers, who are paid based on the performance of the fund they manage, and only the performance of the fund. If you give a fund manager a choice between a good long-term decision, and one that will generate explosive growth for a year followed by explosive decompression, he'll choose the latter every time, as long as he thinks he can sell before the stock price plummets.
>
> The company's top executives get stock options, they receive bonuses based on how the stock performs, and they receive golden parachutes, so whatever happens, they leave with no financial concerns.
>
> Contrast them with line employees. Employees only receive raises when there's enough money left over at the end of the year to give raises. They're laid off when the financial results aren't strong enough, when sales diminish, or when the company restructures itself to keep the numbers looking good so the stock price doesn't drop after a year or two of poor performance.
>
> Employees have much stronger ties to company success than executives, or the board of directors.
>
> Is this a great country or what?

Instead, like members of Congress, they need to bring back a share of the bacon for their own constituents—the people who work in their business unit. These folks, who can't vote the business unit head out of office, will instead find lots of reasons to work less hard, less accurately, and less diligently than before.

This is human nature. Employees constantly generate ideas—good ideas—to help the company. The company either expresses interest in those ideas and takes action on them, or it shuts off all hope of incremental improvement while simultaneously demotivating its employees.

Take this up one level and you'll see that your attempt to remove politics from the process of setting IS priorities—creating a Systems Steering Committee—can easily backfire because each committee member has a career to pursue and only succeeds in that pursuit by achieving highly visible successes.

Do you really think George, your COO, is likely to say, "Okay, for the next two years, Julia will get most of our discretionary resources to build her marketing database while we limp along with what we have?"

He might, but only if you provide a framework where George isn't cutting his own throat.

What's a poor CIO to do? Preallocate your developers among the business units, allocating them in proportion to the relative size or significance of each one.

Imagine you have 125 developers in your organization, and the Systems Steering Committee has bought into the 40/20/40 split. That means 50 programmers are assigned to strategic projects, leaving 25 for tactical projects and the remaining 50 for maintenance.

Now imagine human resources receives 2% of the company's overall budget. It gets 2% (or one) of the 50 maintenance programmers. No, that isn't a lot. Depending on what HR needs, though, and the decisions made by the Systems Steering Committee, HR will also get as many of the 25 programmers reserved for tactical projects as makes sense.

HR can also get more resources, simply by signing a check. You need to be very good at engaging contract programming resources, because the right answer to any question is never "No." The right answer is, "We can do that. Here's what it will cost. If you'll sign up to the cost, we'll get it done."

Sometimes, staff pre-allocation is the whole story. In highly politicized companies, or companies with no central strategy, Systems Steering Committees just don't work. They can't, because there's no framework for making enterprise-level decisions.

And if a Systems Steering Committee won't work, don't form it. Why would you sponsor an idea you know in advance will fail?

A FINAL THOUGHT: LEVERAGE

We've been talking about the company's tactical programs as if each business unit's tactical requirements were entirely separate, both from each other and from the company's strategic programs. In fact, one of your most important tactical responsibilities is finding opportunities for leverage.

COMPANY INTEGRATION: A KEY IS ROLE

There are only four places where the whole company comes together. The CEO's office is one of them, of course. So is the Accounting Division, but only for budgeting and financial reporting, and Human Resources, from a staffing and organizational development perspective.

Then there's you. IS gets inside the operations of the entire company. That means you, more than anyone else in the company, has a chance to know everything.

continues

continued

> Used wisely, that puts you in a position of incredible influence, but only if you're smart enough to take advantage of the situation.
>
> One way, the obvious one, is to use your position to help satisfy your formal responsibility to maximize the return on the resources your company puts into its information systems. By putting together all the information at your disposal, you can find ways to achieve multiple ends with each effort.
>
> You have a more subtle opportunity as well. By putting together what each business unit does and wants to do, you know better than anyone else in the company who should be talking to whom about their plans. Every time you say, "That has a lot in common with what we're hearing from Distribution. Why don't the three of us get together and see if there's a way we should combine our efforts," you gain stature, credibility, and influence.

Leverage[9], in this case, means achieving more than one end with a single effort. That means collecting everyone's tactical requirements, merging that information with what you know about the company's strategic programs, and finding ways to consolidate them. Ideally, you'll find you can construct a single set of programs that achieve the company's major tactical goals, while simultaneously advancing its strategy.

You might not achieve the idea, but if you don't set it as your goal, you'll waste a lot of time and effort on a bunch of disjointed activity.

And the sense that you're herding cats will increase.

---

[9]*Many consultants would use the term synergy here, but we're friends, so I won't. This is one of the few places where synergy would be used appropriately, though, because it refers to times when the whole is greater than the sum of the parts. If you can make an investment in one system that satisfies HR, Manufacturing, and advances the company strategy, rather than having to execute three independent projects to achieve the same results, the whole really is greater than the sum of the parts.*

SUPPORTING THE INFRASTRUCTURE

"They say I should've been here/Back about ten years/Before it got ruined by folks like me."

—James McMurtry, "I'm Not From Here," *Too Long in the Wasteland*

MANAGEMENTSPEAK

I didn't understand the email you said you sent. Can you give me a quick summary?

Translation:

I still can't figure out how to start the email program.

The personal computer is about two decades old. Business, and especially IS, tried hard to lock the doors. PCs were toys, we said. They lacked the storage and processing power needed for serious business computing. We already had millions of dollars invested in our mainframes, we said. Why don't people use those instead of being renegades?

While IS was busy missing the point entirely, end-users bought more PCs, hidden in their office equipment budgets like contraband hidden in luggage linings. Armed with PCs and electronic spreadsheets, accounting departments soon looked like little silicon gardens because so many PCs had sprung into place.

Make no mistake about it, the PC has changed business far more than any other invention since the telephone. Because of the PC, IS has changed from a mysterious priesthood to a business partner. Because of the PC, we have employee empowerment. Because of the PC, we have removed layer upon layer of management and replaced it with high-yield communications in the form of ubiquitous electronic mail.

The PC first led executives away from the obvious trappings of status (secretaries who took dictation and typed correspondence) because today, an executive who can't type his own emails is just another old fossil that hasn't noticed its own extinction yet.

The PC is just the latest in a long line of personally empowering technologies that have driven major cultural shifts in America[1].

And here's the most exciting part: Not only are you responsible for the PC, you're responsible for most of your company's transformational technologies, and you probably figure every single one of 'em is a colossal pain in your backside.

Corporations have infrastructures. Some of the infrastructure consists of bricks, mortar, plumbing, and glass. More of it consists of telephones, PCs, networks, and email. You own the latter.

You might as well enjoy it.

Infrastructure has a problem: Nobody knows how to figure its value, except, perhaps, for its original purchase price and liquidation value. Try to determine what it does for the company, though, and you quickly figure out the limits to financial reporting and analysis.

---

[1]*No, this isn't too strong. Imagine life in America without the automobile and telephone. Both your personal and professional life would be so different as to be unrecognizable.*

Face it—you just can't compute a return on investment for an upgrade to your email system, your telephone system, your PC operating system, networks, or any other piece of the company infrastructure you provide.

But you have to manage it anyway, so let's figure out the best way to handle this unpleasant task.

INFRASTRUCTURE—OUR DEFINITION

The first synonym listed for "infrastructure" in the Microsoft Word thesaurus is "foundation." The way we're using the term right now fits that usage. We're talking about the stuff that forms the foundation for all the work that happens in the company.

The key distinction to keep straight in this chapter is that we're dealing with the company's infrastructure, not your computing infrastructure. You're responsible for the technical components of the company infrastructure—the technical infrastructure, which includes the telephone system, electronic mail, word processor, and spreadsheets.

We'll talk about your computing infrastructure in Chapter 6, "Platform Layer—What You Have."

IT AIN'T STRATEGIC

The first thing to understand is that these technologies aren't strategic, any more than plumbing is strategic. If the pipes break, you're out of business until they're fixed, but that doesn't make plumbing strategic. Important yes[2], but not strategic. Not even tactical. These are general-purpose utilities, and you need to manage them as such.

How should you deal with them? As CIO, *you* should deal with them as little as possible. Your attention should be focused on all sorts of stuff, but not this. This you want to delegate except for a couple of minor matters.

WORK-STYLE

There's a basic question about the company's technical infrastructure that can only be handled in the executive suite, and that's the question of work-style—the workplace equivalent of lifestyle.

---

[2]*One of my favorite Isaac Asimov-isms was his comment about who is more important: a nuclear physicist or a plumber. "Now before you answer," he'd say, "ask yourself this: When was the last time you woke up at 3 a.m. and said, 'I need, immediately, a nuclear physicist!'"*

Work-style is what determines whether employees have cubicles or offices, and of what size. It determines whether the furniture is real wood, Formica, or government surplus.

It also determines whether the telephones have actual hold buttons, or whether the user must be trained in an arcane combination of keystrokes; whether you keep PCs running for five years or get rid of them after three; and whether the food in the company cafeteria has actual flavor, or just calories and enough nutrients to prevent malnutrition.

Somehow, you need to structure an annual conversation on this subject so you don't end up sticking your neck out when the time comes to spend money on it. If at all possible, get the rest of the executives to start thinking of this stuff the way they think about employee benefits.

This might seem wild, but it makes sense. There's no tangible return on the money spent on employee life and health insurance, a subsidized cafeteria, or the other expenditures that fall into the benefits category. You spend the money anyway, because otherwise any employee worth keeping will immediately leave your employ to work for a more generous competitor.

The question you need to ask in the executive suite is, "What's standard issue for every office employee?" Telephone? Check. PC? Check. Word processor, spreadsheet, email client? Check. Personal Digital Assistant? No, not this year.

Okay, you've managed to get the executive committee/Systems Steering Committee to agree to the basic employee toolkit. What's your next step?

BUDGETING

Here's where it usually falls apart. Especially if PCs are still considered capital expenses in your company, things can get ugly. What you want to do is divide technical infrastructure into two categories: central facilities and desktop facilities. You include the central facilities (the PBX, email servers, networks, and support staff) in your budget. Every cost center manager has to include the cost of new PCs, telephones, long-distance, and local service if your telephone company charges on a per-call basis.

That gets you out of the role of sponsoring this technology for individual employees. If it makes employees more effective, their managers ought to be willing to pay for it and if it doesn't, well, why are you sponsoring it?

You get a fringe benefit. Most of your costs are variable costs. They're demand-driven. And you've just moved the demand side of the equation to the cost center managers. That means your budget is easy to defend. You either satisfy demand or you don't. You're just multiplying unit costs times volume to develop your budget numbers, and if the company wants to buy all these expensive PCs without training the users, that's OK. We'll just get more calls to the Help Desk.

PRODUCTIVITY, AND THE TOTAL COST OF OWNERSHIP

We've promised productivity so often people are starting to wonder when it will show up. You don't have to worry about the telephone—nobody asks if the telephone increases productivity because they "know" the opposite is true, but they still just assume there will be a phone on every desk. The PC, on the other hand, is still in the cross-hairs, even though its presence is also assumed. And the plain fact is, productivity is the wrong thing to ask for.

Productivity counts how many identical units of work an employee produces in a standard unit of time. Widgets per hour is a measure of productivity.

PCs generally don't make employees more productive, because PCs are used mostly by knowledge workers and knowledge workers don't spend their days stamping out lots of identical units of work. We'll cover this topic in more detail in a later chapter. For now, take this to the bank: PCs make employees more effective, not more productive.

And effectiveness can be awfully hard to measure.

This will be a hard conversation, because it sounds awfully academic. Somehow you'll need to get the point across, and the best ways can make people pretty uncomfortable. For example, asking members of the executive committee to demonstrate their productivity certainly will illustrate the point, but it won't make you any friends.

Best suggestion: Say something like, "I don't call it productivity because I don't know how to quantify it. We couldn't measure their work output before we had PCs, we can't measure it now, and besides, the PC has changed the nature of the job so it would be an apples-to-oranges comparison anyway. It's pretty clear PCs make our employees more effective, though—just imagine what we'd have to do if we tore them all out and went back to the old ways of doing business."

If you manage to put the productivity issue away, you'll almost certainly get nailed by the Total Cost of Ownership (TCO)—a highly publicized red herring promulgated by some of the big research companies.

According to these pundits, the TCO for a PC—that is, the fully loaded cost taking all factors into account—ranges from $11,000 to $13,000 per year. What's amazing isn't the number itself. It's how many people have fallen for this bushwa.

The TCO calculation, as formulated by the pundits, has so many problems it's hard to keep track of them all. You'll need a lot of ammunition if TCO fever has

continues

3

SUPPORTING THE
INFRASTRUCTURE

continued

taken hold in the executive suite, so here are a few bullet points to get you started:

- $13,000 per year per employee? That's higher than our after-tax profit per employee! These guys just want us to pay them a lot of money so they can give us a bunch of worthless advice. That's why they publish ridiculous numbers like this.

- The way TCO is calculated, the more benefit we get from a PC, the higher its TCO. That's because it includes non-overhead costs like training, supplies, and the cost of time spent using the PC. According to the accounting methods these guys use, a day planner costs us at least five grand a year.

How does it get that high? Start with a standard $40 per hour fully loaded labor rate and 48 productive weeks per year.

Now add the cost of the day planner itself—maybe $150. Using it properly isn't self-explanatory, so you'll need a time management course: Probably another $150. You'll lose the time your employee spends in the course, and at $40/hour times 8 hours that's $320. "Installation" cost: $620.

On to the ongoing costs. Here's the first: Every year after the first, you buy refills for about $50—$200 over five years.

Now, add up the 15 minutes every morning you're supposed to spend planning your day. Over five years, $12,000 in lost time accumulates. During the day, you may spend 10 minutes putting things on your to-do list and scratching them off. Chalk up another $8,000. Then, just before leaving the office you're supposed to spend another five minutes recapping your day. There goes $4,000 more.

Then there's the time you spend fiddling with refills, because every so often you have to take stuff out of the book and put new stuff in. Add another $600 for the time you spend doing that.

Add it all up and the TCO for day planners is just as ridiculous as the TCO for PCs: $25,420 over five years.

- TCO purports to measure the cost of a thing, but modern management accounting focuses on the cost of processes, not things. That's why Activity Based Costing (ABC) has become popular—it tells us what our processes cost us. Every PC in the company is used in several different processes, so TCO just doesn't mean anything.

- In IS we worry about keeping overhead costs as low as we can, not TCO. We want to encourage employees to get maximum use and value out of their PCs. And we're doing everything we can to keep our overhead as low as we can. I'd love to tell you about it in more detail some time…

Of course, you can't just toss these around like hand grenades and figure the explosions will do the job for you. You'll have to be more subtle, dropping them into conversations as the opportunity presents itself. It's important that you remain above the fray.

DEVELOPING AN INFRASTRUCTURE PLAN

Okay, they've bought the work-style approach, and you know what's in and what's out. You've divided budget responsibilities, which means each cost center manager signs up for the benefits and drives your demand.

How do you translate all this into an infrastructure plan?

You don't.

Instead, you delegate the rest to your loyal telecommunications manager, network manager, PC manager, and Information Center manager. However you've organized this work, ask your managers to figure it out based on the work-style and budget constraints established with the executive committee.

As they develop their plans, ask for a few key elements:

- *Training and Support:* This falls into three major categories:
    - *Training for major implementations*, in which large numbers of employees will need training in a new technology.
    - *Upgrade, or "delta"[3] training.* Typically, just enough changes in an upgrade to be really, *really* irritating. Also, upgrades allegedly have new and nifty features everyone will want to take advantage of. Rather than asking every user to figure it you explain what's changed and what's stayed the same.
    - *Discretionary training, also known as your standard curriculum.* These are the classes you provide on a regular basis, like Voice Mail for Fun and Profit, Intro to Word Processing—How to be Bold in Print, and Spreadsheets for the Mathematically Challenged: Just Say No.
    - *One-on-one Support.* Whether provided through a help desk, information center, mentor program, end-users need some personal support from time to time.

---

[3]*From the Greek letter Δ, which in algebra means "change." This is one of the few bits of jargon we have that isn't an acronym, so we'd better use some ingenuity to fix it. I propose "Dang! Everything from Last Time is Altered!". Or maybe, "The Dopes changed Everything we Liked, Transforming them into something Awful." Okay, so maybe these aren't great. Let's see you do better.*

- *Upgrade Policy:* When do you buy and implement upgrades? This doesn't have to be consistent[4] across every technology in the company infrastructure, but it should be a matter of policy, not improvisation. The obvious options:
  - *Keep Current:* This approach works when upgrades are included in a mainte- nance fee, products are rapidly evolving and past upgrades have added valu- able new features, or there's risk associated with skipping an upgrade (for example, it will be impossible to apply the upgrade after this one if you haven't kept current).
  - *Upgrade When You Have To:* "Have to" can be an interesting phrase to define. In most circumstances, though, it's clear you don't want to build the company's infrastructure on an unsupported product, so when the release you use is no longer supported by the vendor, it's a good sign you should move to a newer one. Or, a release might be unsupported but might not run on newer versions of hardware or operating systems. Or…
  - *Upgrade When the File Formats Change:* Especially when you exchange information electronically with other businesses, you want to make sure you can read and process what they send you. (Reminder: Figure out whether you're going to convert the old files to the new format or not. Even if the new software can read the old formats, there's no guarantee that the next release will still be able to do so. So if there's a good conversion utility avail- able now, you might want to take advantage of it.)
  - *Upgrade When You Want the New Features:* That's pretty self-explanatory, isn't it?

  Regardless of the policy, upgrading rarely means being the first on your block. Let someone else sail on the shakedown cruise so you can learn from their experience.

- *Product Life Cycle Management:* It's just too easy to coast along with a product while the industry has moved in whole new directions that can confer real advan- tages for your employees. Sometimes you have to change horses, so you want to make sure the responsible managers know part of their job is to keep track and rec- ommend a change when the time has come.

---

[4]*After all, "A foolish consistency is the hobgoblin of little minds," according to the famous philosopher Ralph Waldo Emerson. Because he was a buddy of Henry David Thoreau, we should pay attention to him, even though he didn't live by a pond.*

- ***Opportunity Identification:*** Okay, so "opportunity" is frequently used as a synonym for "problem." The fact is, every year brings new possibilities. Right now you have telephones, PCs, email, word processing, spreadsheets, PDAs, cellular phones, and pagers. Next year you might want to look at unified messaging[5] and roaming phones[6]. You ignoring these opportunities is a luxury you don't have, and thinking of them as headaches doesn't get you anywhere.

So you might as well have fun with them. Whoever you put in charge of this category of *stuff* needs to keep an eye out for the new and cool stuff, meet regularly with user groups, and let you know when there's enough demand for you to raise the question with the executive committee.

Just remember, you want to be a reporter, not an advocate.

OH YEAH, ONE MORE THING

At the beginning of this chapter, we established that just because the infrastructure isn't strategic, that doesn't mean it isn't important. We also discussed the transformational effect PCs have had on business.

That's a good lesson to learn. The technologies managed under the "infrastructure" umbrella are personal technologies. You might or might not manage them centrally, but they're used as individual tools.

That makes them subversive in the best sense of the word. Every new tool you bring in has the potential for reworking the corporate culture. It's doubtful you will successfully predict just how they'll rework it—only a handful of science fiction writers have ever been really good at that black art, and the two best (Robert Heinlein and John W. Campbell) have long since passed on.

Whatever you do, don't discount them. Remember: IS barely survived the PC.

3

SUPPORTING THE INFRASTRUCTURE

---

[5]*Exceptionally Cool Item (ECI). It's like email, only you see your voice mail messages and inbound faxes in the same inbox as your email messages.*
[6]*Another ECI. The industry hasn't converged on a name yet. We're talking about a telephone that acts as a portable phone in your building and a cell phone outside.*

THE IS MISSION

"Do not ascribe to malice that which is adequately explained by incompetence."

—Napoleon

MANAGEMENTSPEAK

There are larger issues at stake.

Translation:
I've made up my mind, so don't bother me with the facts.

"We gotta have a Mission Statement!" exclaimed a colleague, shortly after our annual IS reorganization.

I hadn't read about that amendment passing Congress and there were no Mission Statement Police milling about, so I wondered out loud about the "gotta" part of the statement.

According to someone or other who had studied such matters, my colleague explained, every successful organization has a Mission Statement. The "logical" conclusion: If we wanted to be successful, we'd better craft one too[1].

Let's see now:

Premise: All successful organizations have Mission Statements.

Premise: We want to be a successful organization.

Conclusion: We need a Mission Statement.

It sounded convincing, although we never did learn how many unsuccessful organizations also had Mission Statements[2]. Quite a few, I suspect.

Anyway, I'd grown up as a Cub fan, so I knew that although managers can't win games, they can contribute a lot to losing them. I figured the time we spent developing a Mission Statement was time we didn't spend interfering with Getting The Work Done, so it seemed like a harmless enough idea.

So we toiled, argued, and sweated, and in the end we'd wordsmithed a typical example of the genre: An eloquent, information-free declaration.

That's the problem with most Vision Statements, Mission Statements, Value Statements, and the other intellectual rubbish foisted upon us by the experts in organizational development.

It isn't that having these statements is a bad idea or that they can't provide any value.

It's that we're told having one is what's important. A good Mission Statement (or Vision Statement, or nearly any other statement) is a byproduct, not the main event. What's important is a broad and deep understanding of your mission permeating your organization. Having a formal Mission Statement is merely a means to that end.

---

[1] *Did you take Logic 101? Spot the flaw in this non-syllogism before reading on.*
[2] *The logical flaw, of course.*

As evidence, I offer the manufacturing division of a company I once worked for. It never developed a Mission Statement. I never even participated in a "what's our mission" conversation. Through three successive leaders I knew of personally, spanning at least two decades, this organization made use of an exciting alternative: The leader communicated the mission, in uncomplicated terms, whenever the point of it all served to clarify a conversation.

Had we bothered to develop a Mission Statement, it would have been, "We produce the goods while constantly reducing production costs—but whatever else happens, we never miss a ship date."

Here's how well the mission pervaded this group: When I first started working in this group (as a business analyst), I toured the manufacturing facility. A member of the manufacturing crew—a union member—saw me and asked me my business. I explained my role, which largely involved budgeting and capital cost justification, and why I wanted to learn the facility first-hand.

"Well, you can tell them to buy us some new equipment," he growled. "How do they expect us to deliver quality on this old junk!"

And this from a union guy. I guess nobody told him he's supposed to be worried only about working as little as possible so he can spend as much time as he can on his boat. Nope. He was focused on the mission.

Which brings us to our first big insight.

WHY IS A MISSION STATEMENT IMPORTANT?

Why do so many organizational development consultants start with the Mission Statement? Because they've been taught to by other organizational development consultants, of course, all of whom charge you big bucks so they can tell you, "First of all, you need a new Mission Statement."

Despite all the cynicism that's developed on this subject, though, there's a kernel of real value in worrying about missions. The mission is a focal point. It directs everyone's energy on achieving a goal, which in turn means that energy isn't squandered on useless minutiae.

As a consequence, mission-driven organizations tend to have less in the way of dysfunctional office politics than unfocused organizations. In an unfocused organization, the managers generally figure that if the person in charge isn't focused on achieving a well-defined goal, well, it's everyone for themselves.

Note, though, that it's not the Mission Statement itself that leads to the benefit, and that brings us to:

Rule #1: Understanding the mission is important. Crafting the Mission Statement is an afterthought.

The Mission Statement is simply one vehicle for communicating your mission, and it isn't even the most important vehicle. Think, for a minute, about how you can use the mission statement itself. You can:

1. Make posters and hang them on the walls at strategic locations.
2. Print wallet cards to hand out to everyone who works for you.
3. Incorporate it into a memo to the CEO, so she knows you have a new Mission Statement.
4. Recite it instead of the Pledge of Allegiance at meetings.

The plain fact is, *telling* is an awesomely ineffective method of imparting information[3]. Discussing works much better, and discussing before you've made a decision is far more effective than discussing it afterward, because people are energized by helping to shape results far more than by learning of them.

There's also the little matter of making sure you need to go through this. Not every organization needs to develop a new Mission Statement, after all.

So your first step should be a pulse check: Does everyone understand the mission already?

Start with yourself. What do you consider the mission of your organization to be? And how do you tell? That brings us to:

Rule #2: The mission defines the end or ends—the point of it all. Everything else is means to the end.

The question you need to ask yourself is, what are you really here for? Is it process automation, as asserted in the Introduction? Is it acting as steward for the company's information resources? Keeping the computers running? Or something else?

Whatever the answer, though, your Mission Statement must connect the work of IS to the company's success. It must make everyone in IS feel important to the company.

---

[3]*Except, of course, for the things I'm telling you in this book. Of course, by buying the book you—the information recipient—initiated the transaction. When you recite your Mission Statement, you—the teller—initiated the exchange. That makes all the difference.*

There's no right Mission Statement for IS. No textbook solution fits every business situation. What's important is choosing a focal point, because when your mission becomes a bulleted list you aren't making choices anymore—you're simply describing the current mess, whatever it happens to look like. And that insight leads to:

Rule #3: Good missions, and Mission Statements, exclude alternatives.

Good Mission Statements, in other words, make it clear that you've rejected some goals, activities, plans, and actions. Useless ones try to express everything you might ever want to do.

"We develop or install high-quality software," has no place in a Mission Statement, for example, because what other choice might you have expressed? The alternatives:

- "We develop or install mediocre software."
- "We develop or install awful software."
- "We refuse to develop or install any kind of software."
- "We'd really like to develop and install software, only we've forgotten how."

All are non-starters. Because the only statement you can make about software is that it will be high quality, don't waste the paper and toner.

Besides, software is the means to an end, isn't it? If your mission is to develop and install software, or some similar nuts-and-bolts declaration, you've mistaken means for ends, or else you've just decided to let someone else worry about whether what you do is worthwhile.

Good Mission Statements contain information. Sadly, relatively few IS professionals know anything about information theory, though, so it might not be obvious when a Mission Statement (or any other statement) is a collection of words that conveys no information.

4

THE IS MISSION

WHAT CONSTITUTES INFORMATION?

Information is the reduction of uncertainty.

If you watch someone flip a coin but don't see the result, you have no information regarding which way it landed. Your uncertainty is at a maximum—each of two possible outcomes (ignoring landing-on-the-edge) is equally probable. After you're told it landed on heads, you're no longer uncertain.

continues

continued

> The amount of information needed to resolve a coin toss is one bit. In other words, any time an event has two equally probable outcomes, it contains one bit of information—one bit of uncertainty.
>
> Now you watch someone toss a coin twice. You're told the first toss came out tails, but you don't know anything about the second toss.
>
> You still received one bit of information, but the double-toss contained two bits of uncertainty, and you're still a bit short.
>
> Information resolves uncertainty. If your Mission Statement resolves some uncertainty about what your department is and does, it contains information. Otherwise, it doesn't.

Okay, you've finished checking your own pulse[4]. You have, at least in your own mind, decided what your mission really is. The point of it all is, for the sake of argument, supporting process automation throughout the company. What next?

Check everyone else's pulse, of course.

Start with your leadership team. Ask in your regular one-on-one meetings (you do hold regular one-on-ones, don't you?). When you're done, you'll probably feel like the elephant who's just been poked and probed by all the proverbial blind men, but you'll have a pretty good idea of how well or poorly aligned your team is.

If everyone seems to be pointed in the same direction, you can probably stop. Everyone already understands your mission, and you don't need to worry about it any more.

More likely, though, your application development manager said something about delivering new functionality, your data center manager focused on keeping da joint running, your software support manager talked about supporting the company's information systems, your database administrator thought IS maintains the security and integrity of the company's vital information, and your PC support manager figured your department is all about improving individual productivity.

You have work to do.

---

[4]*If you can't detect it, stop reading immediately and dial 911.*

Discuss the mission in your leadership team meeting one day. And whatever you do, *don't* start with your idea. You have three important roles in this discussion, but Imparter of Wisdom isn't any of them. Your roles are to:

1. Prevent anyone from trying to develop a Mission Statement, and
2. Ask pertinent questions.
3. Participate.

The third role is the least important of the three.

For the first point, you want everyone to focus on what the mission is, not on how to clearly state it using the minimum number of words.

Personally, I discourage formal brainstorming techniques in this kind of discussion[5]. A free-for-all is much healthier. If Julie thinks Fred's idea is all wet, don't you think it would be refreshing for Julie to say, "Fred, that idea is all wet. Here's why I think so, here's what I think is better, and here's why."

If your team has that kind of conversation and nobody takes offense, you have a healthy team. Otherwise, it's time to figure out how to fix your team.

In any event, when the discussion turns to phrasing, blow your facilitator's whistle. The right conversations center on what an idea means, its implications, why it might be a good idea, and why it might be a bad idea. Figuring out how to make the point more clearly can wait until the whole team has settled on the idea it likes best.

For the second point, you want to hold off presenting your ideas until a healthy discussion is under way, but that doesn't mean your ideas have no place. By asking pertinent questions, you can help everyone think through the issues more effectively.

For example, if your DBA suggests "stewardship of vital information" or something like that, and everyone simply nods, you might ask, "Let's poke at that a bit. How does the information add value?"

Somewhere in the ensuing melee you can then ask, "Is this an end, or is it a means? Fred, what do you think?"

Asking questions can be far more enjoyable than presenting your opinion.

4

THE IS MISSION

---

[5]*Of course, I discourage formal brainstorming techniques in all kinds of discussions because psychologists proved a long time ago that brainstorming is no more effective than having the same number of people develop ideas independently. Honest!*

Once the discussion is off and running, and after several other people have presented ideas, you're in a position to offer your own. Just don't be too certain. You may be off-base, so you want to encourage criticism, not solicit rubber stamps. You also want to get your idea on the table before the team seems to be coalescing around a different notion, unless you like their concept better than the one you started with.

Timing, as always, is everything.

One way or another, you and the team get to a decision (if you're not clear on the best way to do this, it's covered in Chapter 10, "Making Decisions"). Now is the time to craft the Mission Statement.

PROMOTING THE RESULTS

After you've completed your shiny new Mission Statement, remind everyone that it was the process, not the writing, that mattered. Now it's time to spread the word.

Depending on your leadership style, you'll either join your direct reports at their staff meetings or simply let them do the job themselves. Regardless, they need to host similar discussions at their staff meetings, except their discussions are to clarify and understand your Mission Statement, not to redevelop it.

Most importantly, you, your direct reports, and everyone else must find their understanding of the mission useful when making decisions. You need to get them in the habit of asking, "Is this consistent with our mission?" whenever you're faced with a difficult choice.

If you treat your mission as a checklist item, rather than as a valuable part of your leadership role, nobody else will pay any attention to it either, and you're better off not wasting your time.

JUST ONE MORE THING

It's important for you and your team to develop your Mission Statement. It's equally important to make sure it's not way out of sync with what the rest of the company expects of you.

At some point in the process, you and your team will want to review your Mission Statement with people throughout the company who are likely to care. They'll want to understand how the stuff they need you to do fits into your mission. Your job is to demonstrate how it does—or, in some cases, to tell them frankly that a pet requirement of theirs won't be your primary focus.

Handle this last situation very, very carefully. Remember that turning down a constituent is political nitroglycerin, so you need to develop well-honed mechanisms for substituting, "Here's how we'd handle that kind of request," to "That isn't consistent with our mission."

You can end up in the same place. It will just be a safer drive.

LOOSE ENDS

This chapter has focused on Mission Statements. The same process and thoughts apply to the other directional statements you might choose to encode…Vision, Values, Style, Charters, and the rest.

You might, however, be confused as to which is which, and which ones you need to deal with. Here are the definitions I use, which you might find helpful:

Mission	What you do, why you do it, how it fits into the company's business model.
Charter	An assigned responsibility. While you define your own mission, you charter someone else's project or department.
Vision	A directional picture of the future, painted in primary colors. Whereas missions are about the job you have now, visions are about what you want to become.
Values and Style	Your ethics, level of formality, and other intangibles. Pool values and style together.

There are probably other directional statements as well. Define them as you like. Just keep them from overlapping as much as possible, and don't hesitate to not bother with any one of them if it appears you have the topic under control.

YOUR ROLE IN THE BUSINESS

"My problems start when the smarter bears and the dumber visitors intersect."

—Steve Thompson, wildlife biologist at Yosemite National Park

MANAGEMENTSPEAK

All our customers are satisfied.

Translation:
Our former customers, on the other hand...

When I was a kid growing up in Highland Park, Illinois, my world view was just a wee bit distorted. Geographically, Highland Park surrounds another Chicago suburb named Highwood. Oversimplifying a bit, Highland Park is Jewish; Highwood is Italian. Until the first grade, I thought the entire United States of America was composed entirely of Jews and Italians. And because Jews and Italians pretty much speak and gesticulate with similar exuberance, and cook with similar seasonings as well, my world enjoyed a comforting uniformity.

Imagine my surprise.

Anyway, Highwood was the source of all good pizza in the universe back then, so my family frequented several restaurants there. In one of them hung a sign that said, "If you don't like our food, tell us. If you do, tell your friends."

You've probably encountered this slogan or a similar one in your travels, and if nothing else, it proves that garden-variety restaurateurs anticipated modern consultants by at least several decades[1].

Despite a decade's emphasis on the importance of customers, though, the nature and importance of customers is still widely misunderstood. Many businesspeople, for example, think the customer is the person who writes the check, and many of the rest think the customer is the person who receives their products and services.

Business strategy is a whole lot easier when your customers also write the checks and receive your products and services, but neither of those characteristics make someone a customer. No, a customer is someone who is in a position to make a buying decision about your products and services.

This realization explains all sorts of annoyances in modern life. For example, the reason air travel has become so awful is that the people making most of the buying decisions aren't travelers, but purchasing agents. Purchasing agents care about shaving a few more bucks off the cost of travel, so airlines do everything they can to cut costs, like reducing seat size and legroom so as to cram more passengers onto every flight.

Happily ignoring the true definition of "customer," a generation of consultants, trained in total quality management and process redesign techniques, have taught us that what's true for the company is also true for every department—your goal must be to please, or maybe to delight, your customers.

---

[1]*Need more proof? Tom Peters discovered the importance of service and turned "delighting customers" into a trend in the late 1980s. Restaurateurs discovered, with no consulting help, that service—that is, ambiance, the demeanor of the waiters and waitresses, décor, table spacing and so on—determined what they could charge for food far more than portions and flavor. And they discovered it centuries ago.*

Your "internal customers", that is, incorrectly defined as the recipients of your department's products and services.

Internal customers have gotten entirely out of hand, which I discovered years ago talking to an accounts payable manager who proudly explained her organization's cultural shift to a more customer-pleasing model. Her customers, she explained to me, were the company's suppliers.

Yes, that's right. The accounts payable department inverted the supplier/customer relationship, so our suppliers became our customers.

Don't you hate when that happens?

Internal customers have gotten entirely out of hand, which I discovered while placating a new executive who "needed" both a different brand of personal computer and a different electronic spreadsheet than our corporate standard. "I'm your customer," he told me sternly. "You have to satisfy me."

"Do you also want a different voicemail system than our company standard?" I asked in reply.

WHAT'S WRONG WITH INTERNAL CUSTOMERS

Internal customers have all the undesirable characteristics of Real Paying Customers (RPCs) while lacking every desirable one. Internal customers, in other words, are fully capable of acting unpleasantly, making unrealistic demands, and requiring the delivery of your products and services.

RPCs pay money in exchange for all this, which provides the wherewithal to renew your supply of products and services. Assuming a business has priced everything to turn a profit, this means no customer demands are unrealistic. You pay enough, you'll get whatever you ask for.

Internal customers are like hungry lumberjacks at an all-you-can-eat buffet. They have no incentive to regulate their appetites.

Some companies try to fix it all by instituting a charge-back system. This means you do get to charge for your goods and services, so your internal customers are paying customers, you get to staff for demand, and everything's right with the world.

Or it would be, if it weren't for a few minor glitches in the system.

Most companies with charge-back systems simply add IS to the overall General, Administrative, and Overhead line item, which is tacked onto the departmental income and expense statement as a surcharge, calculated on a percentage basis. Congratulations: The strategic role you've been wanting has been exchanged for "part of overhead."

The companies that do let IS charge back on a unit-cost basis (when IS does charge for what it actually delivers) find IS embroiled in endless negotiations about the exact amount it charges for each item in its repertoire. IS pricing becomes a drain on IS leadership, and the IS strategy gets lost, replaced by creation and maintenance of the IS goods-and-services catalog.

Companies that have instituted extensive charge-back systems have a lot of trouble achieving any strategic focus, in fact, because every cost center manager, determined to make a "profit," engages in all sorts of behavior that's dysfunctional when viewed from the perspective of enterprise-level goals[2].

The internal customer metaphor is the starting point, and charge-back systems the worst manifestation of a business philosophy that ignores one of the great rules of leadership: aligning everyone to a common purpose. It takes companies to the opposite extreme, inducing severe myopia. When employees believe in internal customers, and cost center managers worry about internal cash flows, they look no further than the needs of the next person in line. Only a few employees worry about the needs of real paying customers.

And that, in the end, is why the whole idea is so awful. Yes, it's better than a company with internal charge-backs but no notion of internal customers. That's a prescription for disaster, because it pits every team in the company against every other team in the company in financial competition for whatever rewards are available.

It's still awful, though, because if your concern is satisfying your internal customers, your concern isn't satisfying the company's external customers. It's that simple. In companies with internal customers, maybe one in ten employees ever thinks about the company's customers. The rest are focused internally.

There's a simple, mathematical expression that captures the essence of this problem:

Internal Focus=Bad.

---

[2]*The problem in microcosm: A fellow manager once pointed out to me that some minor purchase or other—about twenty-five bucks in total—had accidentally been charged to his cost center instead of mine, so he was about to journal over the costs. I pointed out to him that the cost of transferring the charge from one cost center to another exceeded the amount being transferred. (I also solved his problem—I picked up the cost of his next $25 purchase.)*

You Do, However, Have Internal Customers

You have three, more or less. These are the people who make buying decisions about your products and services. They are:

- The boss you have today.
- The person you want to report to tomorrow.
- The CEO.

They are your personal internal customers. Keep them happy and your career thrives. Tick them off, disappoint them, or just make them nervous, and your career vanishes.

INTERNAL CUSTOMER=BAD, VALUE CHAIN=GOOD

An early lesson we're all taught (and that some of us learn) is to never point out a problem without also suggesting a solution. So if internal customers are a bad idea, what's a better alternative?

Business theorists like to talk about "value chains." It's a useful notion. It's easiest to understand using a manufactured product as an example, so let's use everyone's touchstone of niftiness, sliced bread.

Sliced bread begins with raw materials. The brand I buy uses ground whole wheat, water, enriched wheat flour [flour, malted barley flour, niacin, reduced iron, thiamin mononitrate (Vitamin B1) riboflavin (Vitamin B2), folic acid], high fructose corn syrup, partially hydrogenated soybean oil, salt, yeast, and vinegar.

The raw materials for a 1 lb., 8 oz. loaf probably cost no more than 20¢, but somehow I ended up paying $2.29 for the last loaf I bought.

Whereas a process analysis would consider the steps needed to convert the raw materials to finished product, value chain analysis describes the steps through which 20¢ of stuff was transformed into $2.29 worth of stuff.

In practice, businesses almost never try to figure out just how much value each step adds, of course. It's not only impossible, but probably meaningless to figure out whether mixing adds more value than baking, baking than packaging, packaging than marketing, and so on. About the only thing everyone agrees to is that slicing is the most important link in the value chain, because nobody ever says, "That's the niftiest thing since unsliced bread."

Your company has a value chain, too, and you aren't part of it. At least, there's no link in your company's value chain labeled "Information Systems."

Instead, you'll find that IS permeates each link in the value chain, and that's the message you need to convey to everyone in your organization. Their role isn't to satisfy your internal customers. They need to understand the value chain. That way they will understand how the people and departments they help add value to the company's products. With that knowledge, they can help everyone else in the company succeed.

THE RIGHT ATTITUDE

"Internal customer" is a metaphor, and, although metaphors can be helpful in illustrating a concept, eventually they get us into trouble because we expect every last attribute of the metaphor to have a parallel in our real-world situation. The solution is to stop using the metaphor and simply describe the behavior that's desirable.

Contrast the hideous phrase, frequently uttered to internal customers, "We're here to help you, the customer[3]," with "We're here to help you succeed in providing value to our customers," or more simply, "We're here to help you succeed."

Internal service organizations, like IS, human resources, and finance, all live in day-to-day danger of becoming bureaucracies. The difference? This book proposes that we help the rest of the company succeed. A bureaucracy tries to prevent the rest of the company from failing.

Finance often becomes the one foot on the brake while the rest of the company is the other foot on the gas pedal and hands on the steering wheel. It's unstated mission: "No."

Human resources usually ends up turning the employee handbook into the company rulebook, operating under the unstated mission of "Keeping the company out of court," whatever its claimed purpose.

And IS? We're at risk of becoming the "standards police," regulating how, where, and why employees are allowed to use technology because our own unstated mission has become "Avoid headaches." If you disagree, look at how most IS departments have dealt with the personal computer.

---

[3]*If you absolutely must call them "customers", at least replace "...you, the customer," with "...you, our customer." Trivial as it seems, the word "our" changes the service provider's attitude from rote recitation of a catch phrase to ownership of the relationship. Can you imagine a more energizing thought?*

Most IS organizations spend a lot of time and energy making the PC as impersonal as possible. We forbid the use of all software not on the "approved for use" list, which usually contains no more than five items—word processor, spreadsheet, presentation package, email, and personal information manager. We even enforce the standard screen resolution.

A personal DBMS? Forget it. I've lost track of the number of IS leaders who actually believe a workgroup or department is better off doing without automation entirely than suffering with an application that's "poorly designed by an end-user who doesn't know the first thing about data modeling."

IS has become the software police in most companies, and it's a shame. If we, HR, and finance all took "helping the rest of the company succeed" as our basic responsibility, we'd transform the place.

YOUR ROLE

In this section, we've mostly talked about executive suite relationships: helping develop the company's strategy and riding shotgun in the corporate pickup truck with your eyes peeled for strategic threats and opportunities, while building technology into the company's core processes.

This is heady stuff.

It's important stuff.

It isn't, however, where most of the time goes.

Most of your time and the time of your leadership team goes into handling the minor crises, irritations, and situations that make up a day in the life of the American manager. And as the old saying goes, when you're up to your eyeballs in alligators, it's hard to remember your original goal was to drain the swamp.

So here's a quick bedtime story to remind you.

Once upon a time, your loyal author led a team of network professionals on a contract to manage the local area networks of a government agency. It was a good agency, composed mostly of smart, hard-working, mission-driven professionals.

And they really and truly were, despite what you think of government workers and agencies.

One day, a manager in the agency, who had managed to destroy his file server by being too smart for his own good, called to ask why we hadn't fixed it yet. I explained that this repair was taking us into uncharted territory, but that we'd be able to fix it quickly if we could simply wipe the hard drive and start over.

Because he hadn't backed up his server (a departmental responsibility in that agency) in a very long time, data loss was unacceptable, but so were additional delays, as he explained at high volume and with exceptionally unpleasant phrasing.

As I held the phone away from my ear I said to myself, "I'm not paid to take this crud."

Then I smiled, because I realized…yes, I was being paid to take exactly that crud.

A career in IS provides more fun than should be legal in a career. It's also filled with the kind of frustrations and annoyances that can lead to a terminal migraine. And so, as the great guru of your IS organization, here's the mantra you should repeat to yourself, and that you should encourage everyone in your cult…uh, department…repeat to themselves as a calming transition to alpha state:

"I'm paid to have headaches. I'm paid to have headaches. I'm paid to…"

MANAGING TECHNOLOGY

PART II

Quite a few years ago, the time had come to replace our mainframe with a bigger model, which also meant disposing of the old one. The machine in question—an IBM 3033, if memory serves—was in excellent working order and had served us faithfully throughout its tenure in the company. We'd simply outgrown it.

Our data center manager was a pretty good negotiator and knew the market well, so he was able to sell our old mainframe for enough money to cover all packing and shipping costs. I managed PCs, networks, and telephones at the time, so I found it especially amusing that our old mainframe was worth only about a quarter the cost of a single new personal computer.

The CFO wasn't happy about the transaction. "When do we get to say, 'We have enough technology?'" he asked us, using the tone usually reserved for parents lecturing a boy who has squandered his allowance on junk and is now asking for lunch money.

"Anytime you want," we answered[1]. We probably used the same inflection as a car dealer who has just been asked if it's possible to buy a new Lexus by a prospect who's on a Yugo budget; in any event our CFO made it clear he categorized us with car salesmen.

---

[1]*As with most repartee reported in these pages, in the actual dialog your loyal author was neither this self-possessed nor this snappy. One advantage of writing a book is the chance to set things right.*

Such are the hazards of managing technology. The company's requirements change, new opportunities and technologies present themselves, and old ones disappear or become obsolete. In order to respond to changing circumstances, we need to invest and reinvest in technology.

Back in the Good Old Days[2], when vendors defined our computing architectures, our investments and reinvestments were a matter of upgrades and expansions. IBM issued a new release of CICS; we installed it. Our business grew and the old mainframe couldn't process the load; we bought a bigger one. We added employees; we bought more cluster controllers and 3278 terminals.

Life may have been expensive, but it was easy.

Then the kids at Intel, Motorola, Zilog, and a few other companies figured out how to build self-contained computer central processing units (CPUs) using their new integrated circuit technology; companies like Altair, Ohio Scientific, Commodore, Tandy, and Apple built typewriter-sized computers, using the new CPUs, and the world changed.

It changed for two reasons. We were one of them. End-users didn't like us very much in the late 1970s and early 1980s, because we mostly sneered at them and turned down their requests a lot, intent as we were on making sure the company's computing power was used for important things instead.

The other reason was the design of the 3270 interface itself. The 3270 family of mainframe computer terminals let us define entry fields in screen-based forms. Regrettably, the 3270 interface didn't let us force the cursor into those entry fields, and if an end-user naively used the cursor keys to position the cursor[3], (instead of the Tab or Carriage Return keys) and then tried to type, the terminal locked up.

Once end-users got a taste of the personal computer, it was all over—no 3270 interface; no more MIS control. PCs leaked into our companies as if the walls were porous, (IBM PCs as soon as those started to ship) and as soon as they did, end-users wondered why we were so inept that we couldn't hook up their PCs to the mainframe—they were built by the same company, after all, so it should be easy.

Well, it wasn't easy, and IBM spent years failing to integrate the PC into its architecture. Instead, a swarm of entrepreneurs, buoyed by emerging networking standards and the

---

[2]*That leads to an interesting acronym, don't you think?*
[3]*Another example of how stupid end-users are—why would anyone think using cursor keys to position a cursor was the right way to work? (Note for the irony-challenged: This footnote is an example of an ironic comment, not an actual criticism of end-user intelligence.)*

heady sense that they were leading a revolution, gave us a confusing welter of different devices, protocols, and operating systems we could use to hook everything together.

Suddenly, our problem wasn't that we couldn't hook everything up. Our problem was choosing from the wide assortment of options available to us.

Most IS organizations still haven't adapted to this new world of open systems. The mainframe-centric architectures of our past may have been expensive and cumbersome, we may have had a bad attitude about end-users, and the 3270 interface may have been awful, but at least everything was designed to work together, so all we had to do was buy what IBM told us to buy and it would all work.

The proof that we haven't adapted is all around us:

- Many, and probably most client/server application development projects suffer from cost overruns, development delays, and disappointing performance.

- Many of the client/server applications that are successfully installed are perceived as unreliable due to frequent network outages—and what are described as "network outages" aren't network problems at all—they're simply computer crashes except now we call the computer a "server."

- Many of the major IS research companies simultaneously describe the mainframe as "the biggest server on the network" and "less costly than the client/server equivalent" despite the logical contradiction between the two statements[4].

- Distributed computing environments, while technically no more complex than comparable SNA-based mainframe computing environments, are widely perceived to be far more complicated and difficult to manage.

Clearly, something is amiss, and what's amiss is that our distributed processing environments, unlike our mainframe environments, are the result of accumulation rather than design.

The term "architecture" is hard to pin down and is usually defined through metaphor. The architect of a building begins with a sketch—a concept—and adds detail in the form of floor plans, and then precise blueprints, but doesn't dig the foundation or pour the concrete. A technical architect begins with high-level design goals and principles, adds details in the form of specific technical "roles" in the architecture and the standards for

---

[4]*If the mainframe is a server, and costs less than client/server, then it costs less than itself.*

how to fulfill those roles, but doesn't build, install, configure, or maintain the actual technology.

The scope of technical architecture, then, begins with an understanding of business goals and ends with the establishment of specific standards.

Technical architecture has three layers: Platforms, Information, and Applications. Platforms are the stuff on which applications run—host computers, servers, networks, and all of the rest of your computing infrastructure. It's the platform layer of our architectures that's been thrown into disarray with the move to open systems. That's because IBM (or Digital, or, more rarely, some other vendor) designed our architectures for us so that all we had to do was lay out the floor of the data center. Now, nobody designs our architectures for us. It's our job, but few of us devote much time and attention to it.

The results aren't pretty, and have given open systems a reputation for unreliability and poor performance—as always, we've blamed the technology for our own deficiencies.

There's more to managing technical architecture than the platform layer. Since the advent of database management systems, we've understood the need for design at the information layer, and have created a complex discipline around the design and ongoing management of normalized relational data structures. There's more to managing your information architecture than database administration, though—especially since most of the information that needs managing in your company is unstructured and won't fit into the relational paradigm at all. Your buying most of your data designs along with the purchased applications you use doesn't help, either.

Then there's the application layer—the layer that provides the business value of IS. If each application is a tree, then management of the application layer of your architecture is forestry management.[5]

Some items don't classify easily into this scheme.

Electronic mail is a good example, because you could convincingly argue that it's an application—it's a computer program with which end-users directly interact, it runs on other platforms, and processes information.

You could also, however, make a persuasive case that email is a platform, because most email systems make their functionality available to business applications through an application program interface (API) and also provide scripting languages, filtering, and workflow capabilities that let you develop mail-enabled applications.

---

[5]*If applications aren't trees, I guess we're out of luck.*

The solution is fairly straightforward. If a technology is hard to classify, it's because it is composed of more than one element, and each element should be separately classified and analyzed. In the case of email, for example, you probably have an email client (application), software you use to administer the system (application), an email directory (information), and a callable email transport system (platform).

This issue will crop up with increasing frequency, because application vendors have embraced the market's demand that they make application functionality available through a published API. The ERP suites in particular are starting to look a whole lot like platforms on which you build a tailored computing environment for your organization.

Technical architecture design and management is one of the most important leadership responsibilities in IS because you're unambiguously responsible for providing the company with its computing infrastructure, but despite twenty years of personal computing, the discipline of managing technical architecture isn't just immature.

It's nearly nonexistent—IS has substituted the establishment and enforcement of standards for the design and maintenance of a technical architecture, and in the process has chosen bureaucracy over delivery of service. Standards without architecture are nothing more than an arbitrary list of "what we allow."

Architecture-driven standards, on the other hand, define "how we do business in this company." They are rational because the technical architecture creates a conceptual framework that provides context for your standards and a reason for having them.

OPEN, PROPRIETARY, AND OTHER KINDS OF STANDARDS

As an industry, we get very confused over what is open, what is closed, and what is proprietary. It's an old problem. For example, in the early days of local area networks, 3Com built its network operating system on top of MS-DOS, asserting that unlike Novell's proprietary operating system, it (3Com) had used an open standard.

This actually convinced some people, even though MS-DOS and NetWare were both open and both proprietary—open in that the interfaces to both operating systems were available in published documents; proprietary in that the design and evolution of each was under the control of a vendor rather than a standards body.

continues

continued

As with many distinctions that seem like "just semantics," this one is important to you as you analyze, document, and extend your technical architecture because part of how you assess your options will relate to these concepts. So here are some definitions you may find helpful as your organization assesses products and technologies:

A *standard* is anything that has been given a reasonably precise and widely agreed-upon definition—something anyone can use to determine whether a given product either is or is not an example of thing that's been standardized. There are standards for screws, hues, tires, wires, dogs, cogs, LANs, WANs, and oodles of other things, too. Standards are Good Things because with standards you can make things interoperable. Imagine fax machines without standards—there wouldn't even be an industry.

An *industry standard* is a standard lots of people or companies have adopted and put into wide use. There are plenty of standards that aren't industry standards, because while any industry association can create a standard through the expedient of getting a committee of its members to sit down and define one, people have to actually build products based on the standard and then get the marketplace to buy those products before the standard becomes an industry standard.

Open and Closed are opposites. An *open* standard is one with published specifications, and usually those specifications are the interfaces, not the internal construction. *Closed* systems are technologies or standards that don't have published interfaces so you can only use them through the facilities provided by the vendor.

Proprietary and Committee-based are opposites. *Proprietary* standards are defined by private entities—individuals, corporations, or consortia—that maintain control over the design and ongoing evolution of the standard. *Committee-based* standards are, as the name implies, defined by standards committees and aren't under the control of any one company or faction in the industry.

Many people mistake committee-based standards for open standards, but it's a distinction worth preserving. Where closed systems are generally unacceptable in today's business environment, open, proprietary systems are often preferable to committee-based technologies because single companies are more nimble than standards committees.

The term *de facto standard* is often heard as well. A de facto standard is simply an open, proprietary industry standard.

Just thought you'd want to know.

The chapters that follow describe a process for assessing and planning changes to your technical architecture. The process is labor-intensive[6]. Don't undertake it if your plan is to do it once, create a report, and then never revisit the subject again.

The whole point of the process described in this section is to professionally manage your technical architecture. That becomes a manageable task if, after the initial assessment and planning, you institute an ongoing process for planning and tracking changes. Like so many of life's little housekeeping chores, this one doesn't take a lot of effort if you stay on top of things, but once it gets out of hand, you have a mess to contend with.

Oh yeah, just one more thing. All three architectural layers consist of products, whether you've bought them or built them, and for some reason technical professionals form the same attachment to products that Chicago baseball fans have for the Cubs, which is to say it's irrational and intense. Throughout the process of evaluating and managing your architecture you'll have to contend with this tendency.

It takes strong leadership, and not of the bullwhip variety. You need to continually focus and refocus everyone involved on the need to define objective criteria and measures, and to continually challenge themselves as to whether the way they think about a product is a matter of logic or rationalization.

A NOTE ON SCORING

Many of the steps that follow require assignment of a quality score. In all cases, scores will be on a numeric scale ranging from -2 to +2. A score of 0 indicates adequate performance, functionality, or whatever other quality dimension we're evaluating. Negative scores describe technologies that are barriers to progress; positive scores go to technologies that enable or facilitate progress. This means scoring isn't absolute—much depends on the culture and preferences of your organization, which is one reason there aren't any one-size-fits-all answers.

For example, one dimension of evaluation at the platform layer is product maturity, which may be innovative, obsolescent, or at some intermediate state in the market spectrum. Some organizations may prefer taking advantage of new technology early in its life cycle; for these organizations, leading-edge

continues

---

[6]*Consultant-speak for "a lot of work". Hey, I want people to take this book seriously, after all!*

continued

products will receive relatively high scores while commodity products will score more poorly.

Other organizations will be more conservative; they will choose to give leading-edge products lower scores, preferring products with stable sets of features and wide marketplace acceptance—that is, they'll prefer the same commodity products scored low by the first company.

Other scores don't fit the −2 to +2 range. In the applications analysis, for example, several steps require assessment of an application's importance in some context. Usually, a 1 through 5 scoring system works best here.

Which scoring system is appropriate will be left as an exercise for the reader.

PLATFORM LAYER—WHAT YOU HAVE

"There is no course of life so weak and sottish as that which is carried on by rule and discipline."

—Michel de Montaigne

MANAGEMENTSPEAK

The technology is the easy part.

Translation:
I'm not responsible for making the technology work.

The best thing about our product," the sales guy explained to me, "is that it's a complete turnkey solution. Everything is included so you don't need to worry about complicated installation routines, impact on capacity, or incompatibilities with the other applications you're running."

Like so many sales pitches, this one didn't bear up to scrutiny. As a standalone, turnkey solution it would have required a second terminal on every user's desk, and the information in its database was locked there, unavailable for integration with the rest of our corporate data.

Turnkey solutions bring their own platforms with them, and every time you add a new platform unnecessarily you add complexity. We didn't want any more platforms. We wanted to maximize the leverage we received from the platforms we already had.

The most fundamental expression of how well an IS organization does its job isn't anything fancy like "alignment with the company's strategic direction." Sure, strategic alignment is nice. Providing applications that deliver business value is a good idea, too.

Before you get to do the fun stuff, though, you have to get the fundamentals right and in IS, getting the fundamentals right means providing stable, reliable, cost-effective computing platforms[1] with the capabilities and performance needed to maintain the company's databases and run its applications.

ASSESSING THE PLATFORM LAYER

Platforms include computers (mainframe, server, and desktop), operating systems, networks, database management systems, and all the utility software and procedures needed to effectively manage and integrate them. Keeping track of it all may sound like a lot of work, and it is. The good news about this bad news is that, at least from the perspective of technical architecture, you don't need a complete physical inventory[2].

You do, however, need to know the manufacturers, models and releases of each hardware and software platform you have, why you have them, and how good they are at their jobs. Especially, how good they are at their jobs.

---

[1]*The word "robust" probably belongs here too, but because it's awfully over-used, I'm saving it for a special occasion.*
[2]*At least from the perspective of desktop systems, you probably don't need a complete physical inventory ever. Your loyal author presided over two desktop inventories in his career, and in both cases, after we'd finished congratulating ourselves, we never referred to the data we'd collected again.*

Why the Platform Layer Assessment Is Essential

Back in the days of DOS, when we only asked our PC networks to support office automation, I used to tell a joke with no punch line. It went, "How many vendors does it take to print a memo?"

For us, at the time, the answer was 10.

1. *IBM* manufactured the desktop PC.
2. *Microsoft* provided the desktop operating system—DOS.
3. We used *Automenu* as a DOS menuing front-end.
4. *WordPerfect* was our word processor.
5. *SynOptics* (now Bay Networks) was our standard for Ethernet hubs.
6. *Anixter* sold us our Ethernet cable.
7. *Novell* delivered NetWare, our network operating system.
8. We happened to use *Compaq* for our file server hardware.
9. We were a *Hewlett-Packard* shop when it came to laser printers.
10. And back then, we used *Pacific Data* font cartridges to extend our range beyond Times Roman and Helvetica.

"Imagine," I was fond of saying, "how many vendors we'd need to do something complicated."

Now, we're doing complicated things on our networks.

In the era of monolithic systems, troubleshooting was easy. Either the mainframe was up, or it was down. If it was up, you had a few subsystems to check—possibly, you'd need to cycle CICS or VTAM. There just weren't that many different pieces to keep track of, and IBM provided most of them.

The bad news was, if something failed, it affected *everyone*.

With the advent of client/server software architectures layered onto distributed processing systems, there aren't that many more separate components involved in any single application, but they come from lots of different sources, and more significantly, they run on a collection of separate servers. If any of the servers fail, the whole application is unavailable (unless you've built your data center around mirrored servers with automatic fail-over, which is a good idea if you can afford it).

Imagine that you have a mainframe that's up 99% of the time. If you do the math, you'll find you have 99% up-time[3].

Now, imagine each of your servers is nearly as reliable as your mainframe—you get 98% up-time from each of them. Your client/server applications use three separate servers, through—a database server, an application server, and a mainframe gateway. The odds that all the servers are up simultaneously are still pretty good, but nowhere near as good as with a mainframe. With three servers at 98% up-time per server, they'll all be up at once 98%[3] of the time—94% up-time.

On the other hand, even with all three servers down, only a small subset of the company is affected—most use other servers and can keep on working.

With distributed processing, it's essential that you make every component as reliable as you can. That means becoming very good at managing every component you include in your architecture. To become good at managing these components means you need four things:

1. The tools needed to manage them

2. As few separate components as possible while still getting the job done

3. An attitude that says down-time isn't normal

4. A Total Quality Management (TQM) program to relentlessly improve reliability, based on the attitude that down-time isn't normal

You won't get any of these if you don't know what you have, how good it is, and what it's used for. That's what the platform layer assessment will do for you, so without any further ado, here's how to do it:

Step 1: Individual Component Assessment

Begin your look at the platform layer with an assessment of each major technology component. You'll get two important results from this analysis: a better understanding of existing weaknesses, and a framework from which you'll be able to plan extensions to your technical architecture later on.

To assess the state of your platform layer, compare each component you use to commercially available alternatives in terms of its

- *Stability:* How reliably it delivers the services for which it was installed. Stability is measured by the ratio of actual to planned availability.

- *Features:* How well its feature set compares to the alternatives. You can gain this knowledge through first-hand analysis (if you have a lot of time on your hands) or through published product comparisons.

---

[3]*Not all math is hard.*

- *Performance:* How you assess performance depends on the component—it might be standard transactions per second, time to open a file of a standard size, or the duration of a standardized batch process. Once again, you're probably better off relying on published reviews than on in-house analysis. Bring the analysis in-house later on, when and if you seriously evaluate the desirability of platform changes.

- *Manageability:* The extent to which the platform either provides management tools or (better) can be managed through commercial platform management systems. Manageability includes topics such as performance monitoring and tuning, fault detection and automated fault handling, and configuration and change management.

- *Value:* Value is easy to compare with commodity products and gets harder as competitors are differentiated by stability, features, performance, and manageability. One way or another, you need to score the product you use in terms of whether you could get the same characteristics you enjoy now for less money.

- *Maturity:* The product's position in its expected life cycle, which might be[4]

  - Innovative—category-creator, with low market understanding and presence.

  - Leading-edge—characterized by frequent addition of new features, changes in the market's expectations of what features belong in a product of this nature, and growth in the total marketplace for the product.

  - Accepted—well-understood and recognized within the market; the pace of product evolution and new features is predictable and incremental.

  - Commodity—having a stable set of features with little to differentiate it from its competitors, with whom it competes mostly on price and service.

  - Obsolescent—bypassed in the marketplace, possibly unsupported, lacking key features of products viewed as "accepted."

- *Market Position:* The product's marketshare and mindshare[5]. One product can occupy more than one market position—for example, a company can be both a technology leader and a major player—and not all market positions are always filled.

  - Technology Leader—characterized by frequent addition of new features and rapid adoption of its features by competitors.

---

[4]*Note that "state-of-the-art" isn't one of your choices. Cynics might think this is because "state-of-the-art" doesn't mean anything, but they're wrong. It has a precise, well-understood meaning: "Doesn't work right yet."*

[5]*"Mindshare" is the generally held expectation regarding the product's future market share. For example, when Microsoft introduced Windows NT and for several years thereafter, the product had only miniscule marketshare (and poor product quality for that matter). But due to Microsoft's extraordinary marketing ability, Windows NT enjoyed huge mindshare, which led to an inexorable increase in marketshare.*

- Dominator—the marketplace elephant. To qualify as the market dominator, a product must have more than 50% marketshare or mind share (in a contest between the two, mindshare always wins).

- Major Player—a successful product with a large installed base and mindshare, but below the 50% threshold that defines a dominator.

- Entrant—a product that is new to the marketplace but with some characteristic that gives it identifiable mindshare.

- Niche Player—a uniquely positioned product with a relatively small installed base and limited mindshare, but one that, due to its unique characteristics, is unlikely to lose the marketshare and mindshare it owns.

- Fringe Player—a product with a small installed base and no mindshare, unlikely to succeed in the long run.

- Orphan—a product you still use but which no vendor continues to support.

The first five of these criteria don't vary much—no matter who you work for, you'll probably assign each product the same score for stability, features, performance, manageability and value.

Although everyone will also agree on a product's maturity and market position, different companies will have different preferences for these two dimensions, so in addition to categorizing the product, you'll need to determine what score you should assign to each position. A conservative company, for example, might score dominators +2, major players +1, and everyone else –2. More adventurous companies might give dominators, major players and technology leaders all a +2, entrants and niche players +1, and so on.

Different companies will also view the criteria as having different levels of importance, so it's important to assign weighting factors to them. These weighting factors don't have to be uniform across all platform components, either. You might, for example, decide that although you need your DBMS vendor to be a dominator or major player, you're more interested in a technology leader for your intranet servers. Give the matter some careful thought, but don't let any one aspect of the analysis paralyze you either. In the end, no one factor will dominate the analysis anyway.

After you're done, you'll have assigned a Quality Score to every platform component in your current technical architecture.

The results might surprise you.

Step 2: Component/Function Matrix

Your next step is to figure out how you use each component in your platform architecture, and how good a job that component does of its tasks. To perform this analysis, take the components you just evaluated and make them the rows of a large grid. In the columns, list the computing functions you provide and support. In the cells of the grid, place a score wherever a platform provides a "computing function"—a well-defined task such as scheduling, batch computing, or database management.

Each score is your assessment of how satisfactorily a particular platform delivers its computing function. Don't go overboard assessing each platform. Assemble in a room the people who use the platforms, limit discussion of each platform to five minutes or so, then vote.

Some platforms provide computing functions used by other platforms. You might, for example, use Windows NT as the OS platform for your departmental DBMS. Don't get confused by this—the platform layer has sub-layers, but that doesn't change the analysis.

Some platforms provide multiple computing functions. Intranet servers, for example, provide for document management, application development (input forms and database queries), and a variety of other computing functions as well.

List only direct linkages or you'll go nuts trying to sort it all out. Don't, for example, link server hardware to "file and print services." The server hardware is the component that delivers the Network Server Hardware computing function. It's a platform for another component—your Network Operating System (NOS). It's the NOS that delivers file and print services.

Next to the score of how satisfied you are with the component, note the quality score you developed in Step 1. You might find a sizable difference between the two scores, meaning you aren't pushing the envelope very hard with some of your platform components.

Usually, that's simply an interesting fact, to be placed on the shelf next to all the other interesting facts you never use except when playing *Trivial Pursuit*. Sometimes, though, a mismatch between these two scores means your company is missing some significant opportunities.

Think of it this way. If the quality score is higher than the satisfaction score, switching to a competing product would probably improve your computing infrastructure. Although the product you're using is good, it isn't a good match to your requirements. If, on the other hand, your satisfaction exceeds the product's quality, there might be capabilities you could be providing your company but aren't, possibly because your staff lacks the sophistication to envision the potential for this product category.

You can use this grid in several other ways. For example, you can use it to find platform redundancies. When you have more than one platform supporting a single computing function, you probably have a redundancy. This isn't necessarily a bad thing, but it should be a conscious choice, not an accident.

Having two platforms supporting the same computing function also might signal an incompatibility—you installed the second platform because the first didn't support a key application, perhaps. Incompatibilities happen, but you should monitor them because vendors sometimes resolve incompatibilities, providing you with opportunities to simplify your architecture.

You might find the grid useful when managing upgrades, too. Later on you'll see that part of the information and application layer assessments map them to the computing functions they each need. Because this matrix quickly documents which computing functions will be affected by any platform upgrade, you can use it as the starting point for determining what will need testing as part of the upgrade process.

You can also use the Component/Function Matrix as a planning tool. If a business change drives the need for a new computing function, add it to the grid and figure out whether you can (and should) support it with an existing platform, which would be the case with a platform you find highly satisfactory and that has high quality. If, on the other hand, the new computing function would fit on an existing platform but that platform is of low quality or is unsatisfactory, this might be your opportunity to get rid of it.

Most often, of course, new computing functions require new platform components, at which point you'll need to select a product to provide that function and add both the computing function and product to the matrix.

The Component/Function Matrix and Standards

Finally, we're ready to say a word about standards. After you've created the component/function matrix, you're ready to deal with the subject.

You establish a platform standard when, for a particular computing function, you decide it's important to support only one component. Be judicious when deciding to establish standards. Every standard you establish is one you have to maintain (technology doesn't after all, stand still) and it's also one you have to enforce somehow. Both require effort. If you aren't willing to put forth the effort, don't bother establishing the standard.

Step 3: Interface/Integration Assessment

In the old days, network managers figured their job was making sure devices could exchange electrons. So long as the current flowed, they figured, their job was finished.

Then the CIO asked why he couldn't access information from his Novell file servers with his 3278 terminal. The first time someone asked this of me, I thought it was a stupid question. After a fairly strange dialog, I realized the CIO was challenging me to expand my thinking. I learned the difference between an operational network and a useful one that day.

Platform architecture is more than the sum of each component's quality. The components must integrate into a coherent, manageable whole to properly support the company's databases and applications.

One way of performing this assessment uses a matrix, the rows and columns of which are both lists of the components assessed in Step 1. Each cell of the matrix includes a description of the communication path between the components and a score assessing the overall quality of the interface. Only cells above the "main diagonal" have to be filled out because those below it duplicate those above it. Even so, the result will be a large number of individual interfaces to evaluate (if 50 components are included in the analysis, the matrix will include 1,225 cells).

Because this matrix will be so bulky, you should assess each interface quickly and subjectively. Parcel it out to your internal experts and have them scoring the interfaces based on ease of setup, ease of maintenance, performance, and stability.

The toughest part of this assessment is evaluating the "missing interfaces" for components that don't communicate with each other. Although in most cases this will indicate lack of need, in a few cases an interface might provide value if developed.

This matrix will generate two scores for each component: an average of the individual interface scores indicating its overall fit into the processing environment; and an interface tally, which indicates the component's importance to the architecture.

The matrix will also generate an overall average score, which will indicate how satisfactorily overall platform integration has been achieved.

Computing these scores is only useful if you plan to take action on them, so go through the matrix looking for opportunities to improve the score.

Otherwise, don't bother at all.

Schematic Diagrams

Another complementary approach to assessing integration uses diagrams because, well, you know…

The diagrams won't give you a scoring system you can use to find strengths and weaknesses. They will, however, provide convenient ways to plan changes and enhancements to your networks as you're called on to provide new services.

Connectivity Diagram

The first drawing is a physical connectivity map of your enterprise. It doesn't show every device on your network, but does show every class of device that connects through your network.

Your goal in creating this drawing is ensuring more than the flow of electrons between any two devices that need to communicate. You want to know whether or not the connection provides the type of communication you need, too, so next to each connection, list the types of service or session available through it, organized around the standard ISO/OSI seven-layer network reference model.

This list should distinguish between the connectivity services available to client and server processes in each device, especially in devices that act as both clients and servers[6].

For example, you might have a mainframe connection that only supports 3278 terminal sessions (LU2 sessions, to be precise) through the network. That's important to know, because that means your connectivity will have to change when you start using the mainframe in client/server applications, unless you find HLLAPI screen scraping satisfactory. If it supported both LU2 and LU6.2 (peer-to-peer APPC) sessions, on the other hand, you'd be able to support use of the mainframe in this fashion without any changes to your platform layer.

If your mainframe connection supported TCP/IP communication and T3270 sessions, it would also support both 3278 terminal sessions and client/server interactions, although it would do so through a different mechanism.

Table 6.1 shows common entries for each network layer.

---

[6]*As an example, a single Intel-based system that provides intranet services to the organization will run an HTTP host, acting as a server (specifically, a Web server). The same device can run CGI scripts to access a production database on the company mainframe. Even though the end-use of this process is part of the intranet server role this device plays, the CGI script itself acts as a client process to a server process on the mainframe.*

TABLE 6.1 NETWORK LAYERS AND REPRESENTATIVE CONNECTIVITY SERVICE

Layer	*Connectivity Available (Examples)*
Physical and Data Link	Ethernet, Token Ring, ATM
Network/Transport Protocols	TCP/IP, IPX/SPX, SNA
Session/Presentation/Application Services—Server Processes	Telnet, LU2(3270), FTP, HTTP, LU6.2 (APPC), CICS, RPC, CORBA, COM
Session/Presentation/Application Services—Client Processes	Telnet, LU2(3270/ HLLAPI), Web Browser, GUI (calling to LU6.2(APPC), RPC, CORBA, COM)

The connectivity diagram makes it easy to determine which device types can communicate with each other, and in what capacities.

THE ISO/OSI SEVEN-LAYER NETWORK REFERENCE MODEL

Everybody knows there are seven layers involved in networking, but nobody knows what they are and why they're important. In case you're interested, Table 6.2 shows you what they are and why you should care.

TABLE 6.2 ISO/OSI FOR FUN AND PROFIT

Layer	*What It Does*	*What You Care About*
Physical	Defines plugs, wires, voltages, network topology, how bits are represented, and stuff like that.	What kind of LAN you have and your standards for network interface cards (NICs), networking equipment (hubs, switches) and cabling.

continues

TABLE 6.2 CONTINUED

Layer	What It Does	What You Care About
Data Link	Controls access to the network and communication between individual physical devices. Ethernet and Token Ring both are Physical/Data Link layer combinations. In IBM mainframe communications, SDLC (Synchronous Data Link Control) lives in the Data Link layer, too.	•Having the latest soft ware drivers for your NICs. •In a mixed Ethernet/Token Ring LAN, making sure you know which ports are which so you don't plug an Ethernet NIC into a Token Ring port or vice versa. •In SNA networks, assignment of PU (physical unit) addresses. •Monitoring network traffic within single LAN segments to make sure the LAN hasn't become a bottleneck.
Network	Establishes end-to-end communication across the network for physical devices. When communication has multiple "hops" (from a computer, across several routers, to a second computer for example) the data link layer controls each hop; the network layer connects all the hops needed so the two computers can exchange data. IP (Internet Protocol) is the best-known network protocol.	Overall network (LAN and WAN) design; choice of technologies and speeds for WAN, backbones and subnets. Network simulation and monitoring. Virtual Private Networks (VPNs) across the Internet. The Internet itself. IP address administration; BOOTP and DHCP.
Transport	Divides the messages applications need to send into packets and manages their delivery across the network. TCP lives here, along with the less-well-known UDP, which also layers on top of IP.	You don't have much to deal with here—it's largely transparent to you. So long as you've installed the latest patches to whatever TCP/IP software you use, you'll never deal with this layer directly.

Layer	What It Does	What You Care About
Session	Identifies and authenticates processes and connects them to the network resources they need. Security lives in the session layer, which also manages process-to-process (as opposed to device-to-device) communication.	Network administration. Firewalls, assignment of TCP/IP "port numbers" to applications, and other security issues. In SNA networks, assign ment of LU (logical unit) addresses. Determination of the types of session available for each device attached to the network, which determines how client applications can communicate with server processes.
Presentation	Defines character sets and data formatting standards.	Character sets (ASCII and EBCDIC) File formats (HTML, XML, EDI standards, proprietary word process ing and spreadsheet file formats) Font standards and page description languages (True Type, PostScript)
Application	Includes both standard network applications and the application program interfaces (APIs) available for applications you install or develop.	HTTP, FTP, X-Windows HLLAPI (the standard "screen scraping" interface) Remote Procedure Calls (RPCs)

Client/Services Diagrams

The second drawing, really a set of drawings, is a client-centric view of your platform environment. Create a drawing for every device that hosts at least one client process or acts as an end-user workstation. Put that device in the center of the drawing and around the periphery depict the resources—server processes—that device must access.

For each resource, list the client process needed to reach it, where that client process runs, and what protocols and connectivity are required to achieve the connection.

Whereas the connectivity diagram shows all devices as peers, client/services diagrams depict the network from the perspective of each type of device that hosts at least one client process.

Each client/services diagram depicts one of the physical devices that runs client processes in the center, surrounded by the devices that provide services its client processes can access. For example, desktop computers are used to reach a wide variety of resources, using several different access techniques. In a typical example, it would be shown in the center. Around the periphery would be a mainframe computer, the Internet, an intranet server, distributed database server, and whatever other services it has access to.

Where the connectivity diagram lists all connectivity services available in each device, each client/services diagram shows only the connectivity services used within each connection.

Remember that "clients" are software processes (see sidebar).

THE DIFFERENCE BETWEEN CLIENT/SERVER AND DISTRIBUTED PROCESSING

The history of information systems is a history of language abuse. In its history, no term has been more abused than "client/server." In many contexts this is nothing more than linguistic nitpicking. When it comes to managing your technical architecture, however, you either understand what client/server means or you will hopelessly jumble your architecture.

Client/server refers to software, and software only. It's a way of building software that divides an application into multiple programs that communicate with each other to achieve the desired result. Programs are classified as being either "clients"—processes that need something—or "servers"—processes that deliver something to clients.

An application might drive a screen display on an end-user's PC, for example. To populate the screen with data, the application sends a request (making it a client) to a database server, which satisfies the request by returning the requested information.

In a client/server software system, it doesn't matter where each process executes. All the processes might execute on a single computer. It will still be a client/server system as long as the software has been partitioned into multiple, independent executable processes.

Although many clients run on desktop computers, that doesn't make desktop computers clients, and client processes often run on server hardware. A commonplace example: When you fill out an HTML-based form on your browser, the browser isn't the client. The client process runs on the Web server, perhaps in the form of a Perl script. That client process interacts with a host computer in the background, formats the results, and sends them back to your browser.

The term "client/server" is often used in place of "distributed processing"—the term for a hardware architecture composed of multiple communicating physical computers. It's an easy mistake to make because most of the time we implement client/server software with the client running on a desktop PC and the server processes each running on a dedicated computer. In fact, we usually call those dedicated computers "servers" for convenience. "This is one of our NetWare file servers," we might say. In reality, the server is the software running on that computer—execute a different piece of software and the same hardware is transformed into a desktop system instead.

Which brings us to the term "thin client," a term so often misused that it's lost all meaning, other than "good."[7] Good software design separates applications into multiple layers in order to handle, for example, database management, legacy system integration, security, and computations. One of those layers handles the user interface when there is one. That's the only work it does, driving all the screen objects, sequencing of events, and validation of input. Because the other layers do most of the work, they contain most of the code, which is why the client is "thin."

More often than not, though, you'll find the term "thin client" used to mean "thin desktop," pretending that wasting the processing power on the desktop is good design. There are times when a thin-desktop hardware architecture makes sense and times when it doesn't. Just don't confuse it with a thin-client architecture.

Keeping client/server and distributed processing straight is important because your organization needs to do both well: client/server in order to design good software, and distributed processing for efficient, reliable networks.

---

[7]*I'm guessing that if we lived in the time of painter Paul Rubens, when plumpness was sexy, fat clients would be good and thin clients would be bad. For that matter, if the kids in software marketing had used terms like "anorexic" and "muscular" to describe the various options for client software, we'd think about software design very differently.*

Whether you use the matrix, drawings, or both, simplification is your goal. The more commonality between different connections, the simpler and easier it is to manage your architecture. The fewer components involved in any single computing task, the more reliable you can make it.

Keeping your architecture clean and simple is good. The simpler it is, the more easily you can predict its behavior, tune its performance, and troubleshoot problems.

Keeping it simple isn't, however, your top priority. When simplifying your architecture reduces the level of functionality you provide, be careful. You might, for example, find the idea of using a browser as a universal "client" attractive. It might be attractive to you, but a browser interface is second-rate compared to a full-featured GUI. It has to be because too much has to wait while a message crosses the network to a server, which wakes up, handles the work, and then sends a return message back to the browser to be displayed. When you substitute your convenience for what's best for the business, you've misunderstood your responsibilities.

WHAT'S IT MEAN?

There's lots to know about your computing platforms. From the perspective of assessing your technical architecture, your main focus should be on detecting weaknesses. Individual platform components are weak when they're unstable, when they perform poorly, when they integrate poorly, and when they're at risk in the marketplace.

Your platform layer is weak when it has weak components. It's also weak when integration is poor and when complexity is high.

Use the techniques described in this section (or some other, more informal and less labor-intensive methods if you prefer) to detect weaknesses in your current platform architecture so you can develop plans for addressing those that most need to be fixed.

INFORMATION LAYER—
WHAT YOU KNOW

"We've heard that a million monkeys at a million keyboards could produce the complete works of Shakespeare; now, thanks to the Internet, we know this is not true."

—Robert Wilensky, University of California

MANAGEMENTSPEAK

In a perfect world...

Translation:
We don't try for perfection. We don't even try for quality. Just get something done we can put into production.

For some reason, we never manage to simply introduce a new technology into our bag 'o tricks. That would be too easy. No, every time we introduce a new technology, we add a new methodology as well.

Not that this is automatically a bad thing. "Methodology" is simply the five-syllable word we use for "process" within IS[1], and because new technologies mean new capabilities, we should redesign our processes to maximize the value of those capabilities.

We always seem to do it backward, though.

The history of successful technological innovation is that early implementations look a lot like the technology being replaced. The first automobiles, for example, looked a lot like horse-drawn carriages. Automobile buyers and manufacturers jointly and gradually eased into the possibilities offered by the new technology, learning incrementally what automobiles should look like.

Technologies we ignored until after they'd succeeded evolved this way. LANs spring to mind—they began by emulating local hard drives and printers, so end-users immediately understood them.

We, being smarter than this, try to create our new methodologies in mature form, much as Athena sprang full-grown from the head of Zeus[2].

We half succeed. Our new methodologies aren't mature, but they are big. Maturity is a consequence of experience; obesity happens at all ages. Our new methodologies are easy to spot—they're bloated, overweight, and impractical, and their authors uniformly claim that the proper exercise of the methodology generates value beyond, and sometimes exceeding, the creation of working business applications.

So it was that when database management systems emerged from the primordial ooze of sequential, and then indexed file systems, we immediately went nuts. What we needed was a methodology for designing optimal databases. What we got was Enterprise Data Modeling.

---

[1] *Just as writers charge by the word (although my publishers disagree with such authorities as Groucho Marx and myself when we claim "ha ha ha" is three words), IS charges by the syllable. That's why I personally don't use "methodologies." I prefer "lightweight methodological frameworks" which, at nine syllables, represents an 80% increase in billability.*
[2] *It's scholarly-sounding allusions like this that give this book its patina of authority, don't you think?*

"What will we do with the Enterprise Data Model after we've created it?" I asked our DBA innocently[3]. I don't recall the specifics of his answer, but the gist of it was that we had to make sure every database we implemented would fit into the grand plan.

Enterprise Data Modeling eventually collapsed under its own weight. It required definition of the numerical relationship (one-to-one, one-to-many, or many-to-many) between every pair of data elements included in the model, including the pairing of each data element with itself. Even a small, simple company has more than 5,000 data elements in its existing and planned databases, so even a small Enterprise Data Model requires definition of 12,502,500 relationships[4]. Do the math and you'll find that if you are able to define each relationship in one second, and can work a full eight-hour day every business day until we you're done, you will spend close to two years just defining the data relationships. And that's just one step in creating an Enterprise Data Model.

The early methodologies for developing database designs for business applications were just as unwieldy, but simply smaller in scope. Fortunately, we've since discovered some shortcuts so we don't have to inspect every single data relationship to design a database anymore. As the methodology matured, it slimmed down into a useful participant in the process of designing and building applications.

Instead of learning from this mistake, we went on to create Enterprise Business Models (with the introduction of Computer Aided Software Engineering, or CASE) and, now, Enterprise Object Models (with Object-Oriented Design). CASE simply failed. Object modeling is starting to show some promise. In the meantime, when we next start thinking of another form of "Enterprise Modeling" we should all just go to the local toy store and buy a kit we can assemble into a plastic model of an aircraft carrier, or maybe a Nebula-class starship. Then we'd have an Enterprise model and we could quit[5].

INFORMATION—THE POINT OF IT ALL?

At least since the success of database management technology fifteen years ago, we've been claiming information is the point of what we do. It isn't, of course. Information is a useful byproduct of process automation—our main job—much as the hooves and horns of cattle, which are used to make gelatin, are a byproduct of the beef creation process.

---

[3]*As with most of the dialogues in this book, I was nowhere near as smart in the actual discussion, nor was my interlocutor as obtuse. Don't think of this process as self-aggrandizement. Think of it the way you think of vectorizing a photograph—I'm simply picking out the key features to increase clarity.*
[4]*The formula is that for the number of cells including and above the main diagonal of a matrix with n rows and columns, which is $n \times (n+1)/2$.*
[5]*If you didn't see that coming two sentences before, you weren't paying attention.*

This doesn't reduce the importance of information. It simply places it in context. Most of the processes we automate depend on the availability of high-quality information because most of the processes we automate consist of a sequence of decisions, with each decision depending on the information made available to it.

DATABASES—THE POINT OF IT ALL?

According to a statistic I've bumped into a half-dozen times[6], 80% of the information in a typical organization is "unstructured." Unstructured means it can't be broken down into tables, records and fields, the stuff of relational databases. Unstructured information is what we deal with in memos and letters, pictures, live telephone conversations and voice mail messages, meeting notes—stuff like that.

Proof That the Author Is Telepathic

Right now you're probably thinking, "What's he talking about? I can store text in memo fields, voice and images in BLOB[7] fields, and use the rest of the relational record to classify and index the information."

Sure, you can store it, index it, and find it again. But you can't *process* it in any meaningful way. Imagine you are CIO of an advertising agency specializing in print media. The head of creative services wants you to create a database of all print ads. His biggest problem is copycat advertising (clichés), and he wants to use this database to avoid them. So, for example, when an artist sends him a graphic of two hands shaking, he wants to query the database for all ads with this image[8].

A human could satisfy this request easily, although it would take time. No computer in existence knows how to recognize when a picture contains two shaking hands, unless someone manually coded the image when it was scanned.

And few companies have even taken this step.

Most companies haven't yet converted all their legacy systems to database technology, but your future makes the move from sequential files to database look easy. Here's your future in microcosm: You'll digitally record all conversations in your call center. Here's how you'll process them:

---

[6]*Equivalent phrases: "It is commonly known that," "It's widely believed that," "I've lost track of the original reference."*
[7]*Binary Large OBject.*
[8]*As of this writing, the query would return 57,862 separate advertisements representing 1,983,209 insertion orders. Two hands shaking has not been under-used.*

1. Create an initial index that attaches them to the customer record with a data/time stamp.

2. Apply speech recognition to them to turn them into text.

3. Run them through a full-text indexing system to make them searchable.

4. Run them through a parser capable of identifying the subjects being discussed.

Or maybe you'll do something even wilder than this. The point is, IS has largely ignored 80% of the information our companies process because we don't know how to deal with it. We limit our involvement with unstructured data to providing telephone systems and voice mail and making sure PCs get installed and put on the LAN. Oh, and we'll grudgingly upgrade them to the latest version of whatever office suite we use while complaining that "nobody uses 90% of the features." (This is an idiotic thing to say, by the way, when firstly, throughout the entire corporation we probably do use 90% of the features; and secondly, the main reason end-users don't use more features is our ineffectual end-user training programs.)

END OF RANTING AND RAVING—ON WITH THE SHOW

The scope of the information layer encompasses all the information managed or processed with technology, and that includes the messy stuff. In other words, it includes all company databases, file stores, and other repositories of structured and free-form information used and managed by computer technology within the organization, including your telephone and voice mail system.

Many of these repositories will be closely linked to the applications evaluated in the next chapter. That might be true, but to the extent it's true it's a weakness. In your analysis, you need to treat applications and the information they use separately.

Very Important Clarification

Database management systems (and the sequential and indexed file systems that preceded them) are part of the Platform Layer, not part of the Information Layer. If you didn't assess them when you performed your Platform Layer Assessment, go back and do that.

Document management systems, COLD systems, and other file-oriented data management technologies, along with the basic network file systems that manage most file-based information, are both platforms and applications. They provide an end-user interface—that makes them an application. They also manage information; that makes them platforms. If you haven't already assessed them as platforms, do that too.

Information repositories are no better than the platforms that manage them, so you'll need those assessments in the process that follows.

Now, here's how to go about assessing the information layer of your company's technical architecture.

Step 1: Repository Assessment

The first thing you want is a basic understanding of how good your information repositories are. Their assessment involves quite a few factors that range from the reliability of the information they store to their underlying structure and the technology used to manage them.

Rate each information repository according to the following criteria. Right now the gap between structured and unstructured information is pretty wide, so the criteria you'll use are different (although there are lots of parallels).

Criteria	Structured Information	Unstructured
Organization: The more your systems "understand" information, as opposed to simply storing and retrieving it, the higher the score.	•*Best:* Organization into normalized tables •*Middle:* Non-normalized indexed files •*Worst:* Un-indexed sequential data files.	•*Best:* Management through an object database, document management, or library system •*Middle:* Management through a well-structured directory tree •*Worst:* Flat, unstructured list of files.
Data Access: Ease of access is good, as is ease of managing access. Uncontrolled access is bad, and lack of access is horrible.	•*Best:* Databases accessible via standard access syntax such as SQL or ODBC. •*Middle:* Databases using well-defined non-standard access methods supported by a wide variety of third-party software. •*Worst:* Proprietary access methods and storage formats accessible only through prepackaged applications.	•*Best:* Document management functionality with librarian-style check-out and check-in functions, version management, and the ability to keep track of changes and comments. •*Middle:* Information managed through a publishing model with version and update control limited to a small number of administrators or Webmasters. •*Worst:* A bunch of folders on local hard drives.

Criteria	Structured Information	Unstructured
Data Format: "Smart" formats that facilitate calculations and data manipulation are good. Formats that don't preserve any intelligence are bad.	•*Best:* Field types that provide maximum utility. For example, for date fields, values based on serial numbers receive the highest score. •*Middle:* Field types that are usable but sub-optimal. For date fields, for example, Julian dates receive a middle score (they are usable but more cumbersome in calculations than serial numbers). •*Worst:* Field types that lack intelligence or make computation cumbersome. For example, non-Year-2000-compliant date fields gain very low scores; storing dates as text strings would score even lower. (If, as you're performing your Information Layer assessment, you find a lot of non-Year-2000-compliant data fields, stop everything else and fix that problem—otherwise you're out of business and the rest of your technical architecture won't matter.)	•*Best:* Open and widely-supported file formats that provide rich functionality and preserve document intelligence. IGES is an example (for CAD files), XML is emerging as a promising candidate for a wide variety of documents. • *Middle:* Proprietary formats presented through well-defined interfaces; widely-used open formats that provide a reasonable level of functionality. JPEG and GIF are examples for graphics, J (they preserve little intelligence about the image but are compact and widely recognized); .rtf and the MS-Word file format are examples for documents (.rtf has limited functionality but is open; MS Word is widely accepted and has rich functionality but is closed). •*Worst:* File types only readable through prepackaged applications receive low scores.

continues

continued

Criteria	Structured Information	Unstructured
Data Quality: Information you can rely on is good. Information you can't rely on isn't information at all—it's just bits.	•*Best:* Sources of data have been reviewed for reliability; all updates handled by a transaction management system that enforces all-or-none updating; perishable data includes a data/time stamp or is refreshed on a defined schedule; access is controlled according to a defined and approved security policy; recovery is possible to the last transaction through regular backups plus transaction journaling. •*Middle:* All input data edited and scrubbed to ensure it can be processed; access is controlled through logins and passwords; recovery is possible to time of nightly backup. •*Worst:* All you know is that the system didn't choke on it.	•*Best:* Sources of information have been reviewed for reliability; information changes in draft or "living" documents tracked through redlining, annotation, document "check-out/check-in"; documents with "published" status frozen with document version controls to track additional changes; access is controlled according to a defined and approved security policy; documents protected through nightly backups. •*Middle:* Document repositories administered according to well-defined editing/publishing processes; access is controlled through logins and passwords; documents protected through nightly backups. •*Worst:* A bunch of unprotected files on personal hard-drives or unmanaged network folders.
Data Utility: Does the repository store what the business needs?	•Best: Yes—it stores everything business users want, and also stores information that may prove useful in the future[9]. •Middle: Yes—the repository meets all of the requirements that	•Best: Yes—it stores everything business users want, and also stores information that may prove useful in the future. •Middle: Yes—the repository meets all of the requirements that have been articulated by business users.

Criteria	Structured Information	Unstructured
	have been articulated by business users. •Worst: "Oh, we just ignore that database and use this spreadsheet Fred created for us."	•Worst: "We bought a scanner down at CompUSA and use the software that came with it. It's pretty cool. We just wish more than one person at a time could use it. And also … "
Data Management Platform: Platforms that do a lot of the work for you are good. Platforms that push a lot of the effort onto application developers are bad.	Identify the technology used for each repository (sequential or indexed file system, database management system, post-relational data store). Apply the rating established for this technology in the Platform assessment section.	Identify the technology used for each repository (network file system, document management system, COLD system). Apply the rating established for this technology in the Platform assessment section.

Establish appropriate weights for each criteria and tabulate the score for each information repository.

Step 2: Enterprise Information Model

You need an Enterprise Information Model. No, not an encyclopedic, field-level Enterprise Data Model. Not only is that too much like work, but maintaining it is a Herculean effort you almost certainly can't afford.

You do need one, though. You simply need one you can create and manage without having to mount an overwhelming effort for its construction or create a bureaucracy for its management.

---

[9]*Two philosophies of data design compete for your affections. One is minimalist, telling you to throw away any information you don't have a use for. The other is "maximalist," telling you that if you captured the information, there's some chance you might want it later on, so you should stash it away somewhere. Because a megabyte of storage currently costs about a dime, I side with the maximalists. Especially when the information is about customers, keep it—customer knowledge is an increasingly valuable commodity.*

Why do you need one? It will be valuable in assessing the quality of your information architecture (you'll use it in the next step—be patient). It also will be invaluable in planning changes to your information architecture. And if you end up building any kind of integration technology such as a data warehouse or Enterprise Application Integration engine, you'll need an Enterprise Information Model (or perhaps an Enterprise Object Model) as an early step in its creation.

For structured information, an Enterprise Information Model should identify repositories, major data tables, primary keys, and a few important, representative data fields. Use whichever of the popular and well-known formats for documenting data designs you're most comfortable with.

For unstructured information, identify the major repositories and for each one list the document types it manages (examples: word processing files, hypertext, scanned images, CAD files, help text), and the search information (folder hierarchies, naming conventions, keyword indexes, full-text indexes) available for each data type.

Step 3: Information/Repository Matrix

Think of your Enterprise Information Model as the ideal state for your information layer architecture and the repositories you have as the current state. By creating a cross-reference between the two you accomplish two tasks: You perform a gap analysis, and you create an easily navigated map of the information you currently manage.

The cross-reference is another large matrix, similar in both form and purpose to the component/function matrix you created as part of your platform-layer assessment. To be consistent with that matrix, make the information categories defined in the Enterprise Information Model the columns and your existing repositories the rows.

Score each item in the data model to reflect the quality of that item as assessed in Step 1. The result will be a map to all data used throughout the enterprise, along with a picture of the quality of the company's information resources.

You can use this matrix to identify redundant or overlapping data stores. When you do, add a code to each cell indicating whether the data store in question is the master data store (the one you update and manage), a slave data store (one updated from the master), or one of several kept synchronized through a managed update mechanism.

When you discover overlapping data stores, it's worth your while to analyze redundant data fields with more precision. When identical fields occur in more than one place, you don't have much of a problem to deal with. Yes, you need to make sure you establish a synchronization mechanism, but data synchronization is easy these days.

Life gets more interesting when the redundant data fields don't line up exactly. Sometimes the difference is merely an issue of data formats. One system might store logical data as 1 or 0; another as "Y" or "N". Formatting differences are also easy to deal with because you can handle them algorithmically; they're still worth documenting in your matrix[10].

Address information is even more interesting. Some systems store address information in conformance to standards established by the USPS, others do not. The technical terms for these two kinds of systems are "Good" and "Bad." The whole subject of address management is amazingly complicated to anyone who hasn't studied it. My suggestion: Check with your DBAs. They either understand the issue and will explain to you, in detail, exactly what kind of shape your data are in, or they don't. If they do, ask them to put a plan together. If they don't, send them to a seminar on the subject and then ask them to put a plan together.

Semantic Problems

And now we come to the really fun problem: Semantics. Redundant data fields often will have definitions that are similar but not identical.

Performance measures are especially prone to this issue. Take manufacturing time, for example. It's common to have more than one system keeping track of different parts of a manufacturing plant, although the advent of MRP, MRP2, and ERP systems has alleviated this situation. If you do have different systems, though, you'll probably find at least these definitions:

- The time between receiving an order and shipping the product
- The time between the factory receiving the order and sending a finished item to the shipping department
- The time between the factory starting work on an item and the time that the item leaves the factory[11]
- And others as well

Manufacturing management can usually keep track of the differences. If you're in IS, though, you're at risk of creating misinformation when you try to integrate different systems to create a consolidated report of some kind, so you'd better keep track of this stuff.

---

[10]*Perhaps as a footnote.*

[11]*The difference between this measure and the previous one is that most factories predict order volume, so the items needed to fulfill an order are usually already in production.*

Reconciling semantic distinctions among your data remains one of the most complicated problems in IS. There's no magic bullet for this problem—you'll have to solve it on a case-by-case basis.

Metadata

As of this writing, the major database vendors have started to develop a technology called "metadata." If metadata lives up to its promise, it will provide both the mechanism and a methodology for creating the Enterprise Information Model and mapping it to real information repositories.

Monitor the evolution of this subject carefully. Given our industry's history with methodologies, being an early adopter is probably a bad idea. In the long run, though, some form of metadata is in your future.

Step 4: Data Management Process Inventory

It isn't enough to understand what information you manage. You also need to understand how you manage it. It's important because as you plan changes to your architecture, you also need to plan changes to the processes through which you manage the information. Failing to do so is equivalent to building a warehouse with a process for locating its contents, but not for stocking inventory or retrieving and shipping it.

You manage some data through business transactions. That's the beginning and end of the problem—you're done.

You have other data, particularly customer data, that changes without your involvement. Customers move. They marry, changing names and addresses. They divorce, changing names and addresses again. They die, greatly reducing their buying power.

And so on.

When you manage data that changes without your involvement, the business users of that data need to decide what to do about it. In the case of customer data, for example, you can wait until customers let you know about the change; periodically survey customers to verify the information you have; or buy list information from commercial sources and merge/purge it with your customer database.

From the perspective of technical architecture management, you should create a two-column chart showing the major information repositories and the process(es) used to maintain the data in them.

> **A WORD ABOUT DATA WAREHOUSES**
>
> DANGER!!!
>
> Which do you prefer: Being ignorant about a subject, or knowing something about it that is wrong?
>
> Data warehouses bring together data from multiple systems not designed to work together. Through a sophisticated set of data scrubbing and transformation mechanisms, everything is made to fit together so the company's business analysts can analyze[12] the data looking for trends and correlations.
>
> It's a great thing to do. Here's the problem: Statisticians have known for centuries that when you use data for purposes other than what it was collected for, you can easily reach erroneous conclusions.
>
> Your loyal author made this mistake early in his career, leading to a skin shade that would have turned a lobster green with envy[13], analyzing production data to prove our best piece of equipment was actually our worst. When I proudly showed this striking "discovery" to the plant manager, he took me aside and gently informed me that they always ran the tough jobs on that piece of equipment. It performed badly because it ran the hardest jobs, not because it ran the worst.

So here's the advice: Always include a professional statistician on your data warehouse design team to make sure data are properly merged and defined.

WHAT'S IT MEAN?

Of all the components of technical architecture, information management is the best-developed. Your DBAs have already documented most of what you need to know and keep it in good shape. That's what they're there for.

They've probably ignored unstructured data, though, so you'll find this to be new territory. You might also find a cultural issue to deal with: Administration mutates into bureaucracy very easily, and DBAs are prone to a police mentality that turns them into bottlenecks rather than facilitators.

And although the information layer isn't the point of it all, despite our having named ourselves "Information Systems," it is the core of our designs. Weaknesses in the information layer manifest themselves in too-costly application maintenance, inability to automate important processes, and insufficient ability to provide answers to important business questions.

---

[12]*What else would an analyst do?*

[13]*And when the lobster turned from red to green it would have been even more envious—assuming lobsters are capable of envy. If you've ever dissected one you'd be doubtful.*

APPLICATION LAYER—WHAT YOU DO

"If we knew what it was we were doing, it would not be called research, would it?"

—Albert Einstein

MANAGEMENTSPEAK

The system has to be flexible.

Translation:
We don't have any idea of what we want.

When I first started in this business, I learned to use computers, and in doing so I became a programmer. Programmers were people who wrote computer programs, which were the things that made computers perform useful tasks.

We don't do any of that stuff anymore. Now, we learn to use information technology, and in doing so we become developers who create business applications, which are the things that make computers perform useful tasks. If someone asks us to write a program, we instantly recognize their naiveté and double our estimates.

I'm just as much in favor of being cool and using the latest slang as anyone else[1], and the change in jargon actually does have some utility. Business applications are one of several kinds of computer programs, after all, so in addition to sounding more significant, calling something an "application" clarifies which kind of program we're talking about.

The assessment of our technical architecture began with the platform and information layers. These are the shared resources on which we build our applications, and we can't properly evaluate our applications without understanding their underpinnings.

It's the collection of business applications we make available to the organization that creates value, though. Although it's impossible to provide applications that generate a lot of value when they are build on shaky platforms and unreliable information, with the best platforms and information we can still succeed in providing no business value if we don't deliver high-quality applications that are highly relevant to the work people need to perform.

The application layer is the junction of business and technology, so its assessment is the means by which you determine how well you're supporting the business.

Let's get started.

ASSESSING THE APPLICATION LAYER

Step 1: Applications Assessment

The first step in assessing the application layer of your architecture is figuring out just how good each application is.

---

[1] *So long as nobody asks me to use "architect" as a verb, at least...*

The applications assessment evaluates each application from the following perspectives. (If this looks a lot like the platform-layer assessment, it isn't a coincidence. The issues are similar, since applications are a platform on which the business builds its processes just as you build your applications on your computing platforms.):

- *Platform Quality:* List every platform component (computer, operating system, utility package, network, or other hardware or operating software component) necessary to the successful operation of the application. Average the quality scores you assigned to them in the platform assessment section.

- *Information Quality:* List every information repository used by the application and average the quality scores you assigned them in the information assessment section.

- *Stability:* Applications crash. Sometimes, when they appear to crash the problem is really in the platform layer, but applications do crash—far too often. Measure the stability of multiuser applications by the ratio of actual to planned availability. Measure the stability of single-user applications by the number of crashes per day per user. Because end-users don't call the help desk every time their word processor crashes, you'll have to make a special effort to collect this data, much like "sweeps week" for the TV networks.

- *Functionality:* The most important functions provided by the application, and the most important functions absent from the application that would be desirable, given its organizational role. Absent functionality includes every activity requiring either manual intervention or concurrent use of other applications to get a job done.

- *User Interface:* Quality of the user interface as assessed by the length of time needed to become productive, length of time needed to become proficient, wasted steps imposed by the interface on proficient users (an indicator that the application has traded off ease of use for ease of learning), and end-user comments regarding the application's overall aesthetics and visual appeal.

- *Performance:* How you assess performance depends on the application and is complicated by dependence on the underlying platforms for measurement. Because you can usually compensate for poor application performance by buying bigger hardware, you might choose to ignore this factor. If you do assess it, do so by identifying comparable applications and determining the hardware they would need to achieve a comparable level of performance, measured either by transactions per second or response time.

- *Manageability:* With applications, manageability covers a variety of topics such as ease of installation, tools for performance tuning, integration with standard security and administration facilities, and the process through which problems are diagnosed and corrected.

- *Value:* Value is easy to compare with commodity applications like word processors and gets harder as competitors are differentiated by stability, features, performance, and manageability. One way or another you need to score the applications you use in terms of whether you could get the same characteristics you enjoy now for less money.

- *Maturity:* You'll have to make some decisions on how to assess applications created in-house—being objective about them will be difficult because the people who create and maintain them will have a strong emotional attachment to them. Regardless, score the application's position in its expected life cycle as:

  - Innovative—category-creator, with low market understanding and presence.

  - Leading-edge—characterized by frequent addition of new features, changes in the market's expectations of what features belong in a product of this nature, and growth in the total marketplace for the product.

  - Accepted—well-understood and recognized within the market; the pace of product evolution and new features is predictable and incremental.

  - Commodity—having a stable set of features with little to differentiate it from its competitors, with whom it competes mostly on price and service.

  - Obsolescent—bypassed in the marketplace, possibly unsupported, lacking key features of products viewed as "accepted."

- *Market Position:* The product's marketshare and mindshare. One product can occupy more than one market position—for example, a company can be both a technology leader and a major player—and not all market positions are always filled. Ignore this factor when evaluating applications developed in-house.

  - Technology Leader—characterized by frequent addition of new features and rapid adoption of its features by competitors.

  - Dominator—the marketplace elephant. To qualify as the market dominator, a product must have more than 50% marketshare or mindshare (in a contest between the two, mindshare always wins).

  - Major Player—a successful product with a large installed base and mindshare, but below the 50% threshold that defines a dominator.

  - Entrant—a product that is new to the marketplace but with some characteristic that gives it identifiable mindshare.

- Niche Player—a uniquely positioned product with a relatively small installed base and limited mindshare, but one that is unlikely to lose the marketshare and mindshare it owns due to its unique characteristics.

- Fringe Player—a product with a small installed base and no mindshare, unlikely to succeed in the long run.

- Orphan—a product you still use but which no vendor continues to support.

As you'd expect, you need to assign weightings to each of these factors tailored to your particular situation. With those weightings, assign each application an overall suitability score.

Step 2: Function/Application Matrix

The next step in analyzing the application layer is documenting your company's uses of each application. Your goal in this analysis is to discover where you're providing insufficient support, either by not providing enough information systems or not providing them in the right way.

To perform this analysis, create another matrix[2]. The columns are your company's major business functions. The rows are a list of all applications you support, plus two additional rows. The first is a row for manual processing—tasks unsupported by technology. The second is a row for *ad hoc* or departmental systems—those created by end-users without your involvement or support.

Rate each application (including manual processing and *ad hoc* systems) in terms of its importance to that function, with applications built into core processes rated most important, and those incidental to the core processes rated least important. For the purpose of this analysis, it doesn't matter whether members of a business function interact directly with the application or whether it's hidden from view. Here, we only care how important it is.

Total the rows of the matrix. The row totals will let you rank your applications in terms of overall impact on the organization. Not importance—that's subjective and not worth worrying about. Impact measures the extent to which the organization is built around the application, something very much worth knowing.

Total the columns of the matrix, too. The interpretation of this total is abstruse, but quite significant. It's a measure, although an imprecise one, of IT complexity for the support of each business function.

---

[2]*By the time you're done with this section you'll be known as the Grand Poobah of Matrices.*

MEASURING COMPLEXITY

Different businesses have different appetites for complex math. If you have the appetite for it, you can make use of information theory to calculate sophisticated complexity measures that behave more reliably than simple sums and percentages. Here's how:

We'll use the function/application matrix as an example. Total the rows, columns, and create a matrix total, too. The total complexity of the company's applications environment is equivalent to what information theory would describe as the uncertainty about which application and business function a randomly chosen task is involved in. In other words, imagine somebody told you they'd just observed a randomly chosen employee at a randomly chosen moment, and asked you what business function that employee was working on and what application that employee was using.

What are the odds of guessing right? That's your uncertainty, and the total uncertainty is the total information in the matrix.

Information theory defines total uncertainty as "entropy," but we'll call it complexity instead because that's how we're using the measure. Regardless, you calculate it using the formula

$$\text{Complexity} = -\sum_{i=1}^{n} P_i \log_2 P_i$$

where i is the particular cell (assuming you've numbered all the cells); n is the total number of cells in the matrix, and p_i is the probability of cell i—that is, the ratio of the cell score to the matrix total.

Summing from 1 to n gives you a measure of complexity for the whole company. Summing only the elements of a single row gives you a refined measure of the impact of a single application on the company; summing the elements of a single column tells you how complex that business function is.

The reason this measure is superior to simple totals and percentages is that it behaves properly. Intuitively, a computing environment involving more applications is more complex than one involving fewer; this measure goes up as the number of applications goes up. So, of course, do simple totals.

Intuitively, a computing environment is less complex if one or a few applications dominate and the others are used incidentally; it is more complex the more applications are used in important ways. This measure also goes up as applications are given more equal importance where simple totals ignore the relative importance of different applications.

On the other hand, explaining this measure to the innumerate won't be easy. You can, of course, look haughtily at whoever doesn't get it and ask, in an exasperated tone, "Isn't it obvious?!?!"

But that won't make you any friends, and probably won't convince anyone either.

BUSINESS FUNCTIONS

Business function is the highest level grouping of activities in an organization. Examples include new business acquisition (sales, marketing, and advertising); manufacturing; distribution; human resource management; and financial management. Some business functions might match up with business units or divisions within your company, others will be distributed across the organization. As a general rule, whenever you're involved in an analysis of the business you're better off working with logical functions than existing organizations because although the business might reorganize, the functions will remain.

Step 3: Work Environment/Application Matrix

The function/application matrix documents the significance of each application to the organization when you view things from a functional perspective. You also need to look at the organization in terms of how people get their work done. To do so, you need to relate applications to the groups of people who use them.

Make a list of the large workgroups that perform well-defined processes. They might work a core process like order entry, or a supporting process like accounts payable—the qualifier is whether the group is large enough to worry about from an architectural perspective, and whether the group supports a well-defined process rather than being composed of individual problem-solvers. Turn this list into the columns of a matrix and your business applications into the rows. As with the previous analysis, include rows for manual processing and *ad hoc* systems.

For this analysis, only include applications with which workgroup members directly interact. You're measuring the complexity of the work environment, so when you hide 37 separate applications behind a single integrated GUI, you've simplified the work environment and ought to get credit for it.

In each cell, score each application by how much complexity it adds to the work environment. This assessment will be somewhat subjective, and will depend both on how important the application is for the workgroup and on how complicated it is for members of the workgroup to use.

What matters is how things look from the perspective of each workgroup in the performance of its work. For example, the company's payroll system gets a maximum rating for the company's payroll clerks, but isn't even on the radar screen for the product design engineers. Similarly, your standard word processor might be an awfully complicated piece of software, but its complexity rating will vary by workgroup. The Graphics Design department will totally depend on it and use a lot of its features (when creating brochures for example), whereas manufacturing supervisors will probably restrict themselves to simple formatting options and handwrite notes whenever possible. As a result, the former will rate the application as much more complicated (in terms of how they make use of it, that is, not in how much anxiety it engenders) than the latter.

WHAT'S IT MEAN?

The goal of the analysis phase is to identify specific issues with the current architecture that should be addressed to improve the company's computing environment regardless of any business changes that might drive a need for new or different applications. The preceding process will provide strong indicators regarding weaknesses in the existing architecture that need to be addressed.

Weaknesses come in the form of applications whose quality assessments are low, and in particular whose assessments drop below the zero line (that is, they're an impediment to progress).

Weaknesses also come in the form of excessive complexity, either from a business function or workgroup perspective. From a business function perspective, whenever lots of applications are needed, it's almost certain the processes that rely on them are disjointed or poorly integrated. And from a workgroup perspective, excessive complexity translates to long training cycles, re-keying of data from one application to another, and difficulty in adding any additional technology (no matter how easy to use a new application is, it still adds additional complexity to an already-too-cluttered computer screen).

Then there's an obvious indicator—lots of entries in the "manual processing" row. Not everything has to be automated, of course, but the odds that an important business function or workgroup task is best handled without the support of automation are increasingly low. High "manual processing" scores should lead to scrutiny and lots of questions.

When *ad hoc* systems are important, you have a different problem to deal with. *Ad hoc* systems aren't a bad thing, nor are they an indicator that you aren't doing your job. Often, the opposite is true because the company's use of information technology shouldn't be limited by the resources IS can bring to bear.

Ad hoc systems are often more fragile and unsupported than those managed by IS, though, so you should have a plan for either bringing these into the fold, or for helping department heads review their own processes for managing them.

The scores are only indicators, though, and should be used as discussion topics to build consensus around which applications need to be modified, replaced, or eliminated. Good enough might be the enemy of better, but so far all we've talked about is polishing and repairing what you already have in place.

You need to do this, of course, but you also need to look to the future.

PLANNING ARCHITECTURAL CHANGE

"How evolved can a man be who drives a Dodge Dart?"

—Agent Fox Mulder, The X
Files

MANAGEMENTSPEAK

We can't release any development tools for use until we develop and fully document a robust, secure platform.

Translation:
We're going to committee this thing to death, keep doing things the way we've always done them and hope the delay makes you go away.

When I was a kid, most of the great television shows—except for the comedies—were about doctors, lawyers, and the police. We had *Ben Casey* and *Doctor Kildare* as role models for curing the sick. *Perry Mason* and *The Defenders* (two shows, not one rock group) got people off the hook. But the greatest were *Highway Patrol*, *Dragnet*, and of course, *Car 54, Where Are You?* to show us how to handle bad guys.

As IS professionals we've carried some of all three of these genres into our profession. Wearing our doctor's masks we diagnose sick computers (some even have deadly viruses) and cure them. Wearing our lawyer suits we look for loopholes in our system designs to get the business off the hook when it wants to do something unanticipated[1].

Unfortunately, when we pin badges to our chests and shrug on our shoulder holsters, we take on the worst aspects of law enforcement, searching high and low for end-users who have strayed from the straight and narrow.

That's right...we become the Standards Police.

Whenever the subject of technical architecture management comes up, the question of enforcement follows close behind. The motivation behind the question is a good one: What's the point of documenting your current architecture, determining future needs, and planning a path to the future, if the rest of the organization does whatever it feels like in happy ignorance of your carefully crafted architectural plans?

Good question.

It's important to ensure conformance to the architecture (although "conformance" does include allowance for variances when the situation calls for them). If you make enforcement the centerpiece of your strategy, though, you've taken hold of the wrong end of the horse.

The wrong way to ensure people adhere to the architecture is to force them to through fear of consequences. The right way is to create an architecture-driven IS culture, in which everyone understands that by adhering to the architecture their work will get done faster, better, and with less effort than by every team making *ad hoc* decisions about platforms, data design, and application partitioning.

The first step in creating this architecture-driven IS culture is to make sure your architectural plans will achieve these three goals. Otherwise, what's the point?

So far, all we've done is to document what we have. There's value in that—you need to take stock for two reasons. The first is your need to determine how well IS is doing the

---

[1] *Okay, it's a stretch. Go with it.*

job it already has. The second is to provide a baseline against which you can plan for change. Take the two together and you're successfully managing your technical architecture.

IT'S TIME FOR A METAPHOR

Technical architecture management has many parallels with home design, redecorating, remodeling, and ownership[2]. For example:

- Homes and technical architectures both serve a lot of different purposes. Just as different companies need different kinds of business applications, so different families have different needs for their homes—some families do a lot of entertaining; some need a place for Joe's rock band to practice; some need a place for toddlers to bounce off the walls without hurting themselves; some need facilities for gourmet cooking[3].

- Translating how families will use their homes into a design and floor plan isn't like creating a shopping list. ("Let's see, that's four bedrooms, a rec room, big kitchen, and patio. Okay, we're done!") The process of translating family needs to home design requires insight and creativity. So does the process of translating business needs to technical architecture.

- When designing a home, esthetics matter. Two designs might satisfy a family's needs equally on paper, but an intangible quality of livability makes some homes more enjoyable to live in than others. Two technical architectures might satisfy a company's needs equally on paper too, but that doesn't mean they're equally good. Some designs, for intangible, esthetic reasons, are just better than others.

- The process of home design begins by translating use to floor plans and room layouts. Floor plans drive design of the underlying systems—the foundation itself, plus the plumbing, electrical, heating and air-conditioning. There are clear parallels between this process of home-building and the process of designing a technical architecture. The big difference is that with information systems we begin by designing business processes and the business applications they will need, and use those to drive specification of the underlying information and platforms.

9

PLANNING ARCHITECTURAL CHANGE

---

[2]*Usually, the architecture crowd talks about building subdivisions, rather than single homes. If you like this metaphor, go with it. It makes me nervous because it usually leads to discussions of building permits and things like that. Having grown up in Chicago, I hear "building permit" and I think "grease someone's palm." The metaphor doesn't work for me.*

[3]*Which your author defines as anything more sophisticated than using a microwave oven.*

- Few of us ever get to design our dream homes. Instead, we drive around looking for a house—new or "pre-owned"—that comes close to fitting our needs. Before we buy, we review the underlying electrical, plumbing, heating, and air conditioning systems. Sound familiar?

- Whether we've just bought a house that doesn't fully satisfy our needs, or because our needs have changed, we sometimes find ourselves redecorating, remodeling, renovating, and building additions to our homes. These activities all have parallels in technical architecture as well: Although redecorating (systems maintenance) and remodeling (system upgrades) rarely have architectural impact, renovating and building an addition (replacing or adding major technologies) require the services of a professional architect. It's the architect's job to make sure our planned changes fit with the existing architecture or extend it in a logical and aesthetically pleasing way. It's the technical architect who makes sure the new stuff integrates into and makes optimal use of platforms and information repositories already in place, who plans any architectural enhancements needed by the new systems.

TECHNICAL ARCHITECTURE MANAGEMENT PROCESS

Metaphors are fun. Metaphors are fine. As any debating coach will tell you, though, arguing by analogy loses you points, so let's move onto the real work. Our task is to create a process for managing technical architecture. To manage technical architecture you need:

1. Change drivers.
2. Design goals.
3. Architectural design principles.
4. Technical standards based on the design principles.
5. Process for defining and reviewing architectural requirements and impact.
6. Process for planning and implementing architectural changes.
7. Assignment of responsibilities.

Identifying Change Drivers and Translating Them to Design Goals

Good architecture is a matter of design, not assembly. Design quality has two meanings, and both are important. First, there's the matter of elegance, a measure of the design's internal characteristics. Second, there's the pragmatic question of how well the design accomplishes its goals. Another way of looking at the matter: Good architecture means something is built well and is well-suited to the task.

Because form follows function, "built well" has no meaning outside the context of what something is for, so figuring out "what it's for" is the first step in managing technical architecture.

The process of translating the business strategic, tactical, and infrastructural goals established in the first section of this book into design goals is simultaneously one of the easiest and least time-consuming aspects of technical architecture management, and one of the most difficult and frustrating.

Why is it both easy and hard? Because it isn't a connect-the-dots analytical process—you can't develop a successful architecture through a paint-by-numbers exercise.

What you have to do is to distill key themes from the company's business goals and determine which of them will have a significant impact on the company's information systems. These themes will drive change to your architecture because if you can't establish a cause-and-effect relationship between business goals and architectural change, you have the dreaded "technology for technology's sake," disease, or even worse, the evil "change for the sake of change."

Next you need to integrate the architectural impacts you just identified—which are statements of how the existing environment needs to evolve—into a single, simply stated core design goal or small set of complementary design goals.

As long as you're planning architectural changes, you might as well address those current-state deficiencies you identified in the last three chapters. In some cases the design goals will make the current-state deficiency irrelevant because the design goal includes retiring the components that led to the deficiency. In other cases, you'd better make addressing your current deficiencies a high priority because otherwise you'll never achieve the larger design goals.

Let's try a couple of examples.

Example 1: Mass Customization and Personalized Customer Relations

Let's imagine your company has decided its future rests in mass customization in its manufacturing operations[4] The company decides it will need to develop capabilities in computer integrated manufacturing (CIM) and manufacturing resource planning (MRP2).

[4]*If you're unfamiliar with the term, "mass customization" means building items to order in an efficient, high-volume, factory. It combines the mass production of a traditional factory with the customized products of a low-volume craft shop.*

Because yours is a forward-thinking company, part of your strategy for mass customization includes a marketing strategy that involves an increase in the amount of customer knowledge available for marketing and service operations so the company can personalize marketing and service as well as its products.

These strategic needs are your change drivers.

In reviewing the existing architecture, you note that current applications have been purchased as separate modules, and that IS has developed batch interfaces between them that successfully avoid most re-keying of information.

Two of the most important applications will severely limit the company's ability to achieve its strategic goals. The inventory control system provides automated ordering based on reorder points and restocking quantities rather than using a more sophisticated system based on projected use. And the factory's process control system has two major deficiencies. It makes no provision for serialized items, handling production of batches of identical items only, nor does it provide for sophisticated management of work-in-process inventory.

The current architecture's limitations aren't limited to the individual applications, either. The delays introduced by batch integration add a full day to the time needed to process any order—unacceptable given the company's delivery goals.

You distill these insights, and your knowledge of the technology marketplace, into a single architectural goal: The company should replace its current suite of independently developed and acquired applications with an Enterprise Resource Planning (ERP) suite.

Example 2: Product/Service Diversification

Imagine you work for a company that delivers a single product or family of products. Many very big companies are in this position: Long-distance providers, newspapers, insurance companies, banks, advertising agencies, and printers are examples. Your business strategy is built around product line diversification, product line integration, electronic customer self-service, and the integration of marketing and service using extensive knowledge of your customers[5]. These new capabilities are your change drivers—it's the need to provide technology that will enable the company to achieve its strategy that drives changes to your technical architecture.

---

[5]*There aren't many businesses that aren't building strategies around improved customer care, and most of them give at least lip-service to increasing their customer knowledge. It's a hot trend (as opposed to all those cold trends you want to avoid), so be ready for it.*

Your company's products are complex, so many of your core applications are product administration systems tailored for managing them. Your review of these applications shows that most of them are adequate—not outstanding, but adequate—for the existing product lines. Here's what makes the situation really ugly: Although the remaining applications are inadequate, no better alternatives can be found in the marketplace, nor does developing replacements internally makes any sense—the cost and time that would be needed makes this option unworkable, too.

The current product administration systems won't be able to handle the new product lines envisioned in the strategy, so you'll need to add new product administration systems. You also know part of the plan is the formation of alliances with other companies to provide some of your new service offerings, relying on your partners' business processes and information systems to administer them.

Now it's time to worry about product line integration. Looking at what you've already done, you find you've adequately integrated your systems at an information level through the creation of a data warehouse, but not at a transaction level. The data warehouse will provide for one goal of product line integration—creation of consolidated monthly statements—but even a basic transactional goal like applying one payment to the various items that appear on the consolidated statement is cumbersome enough to create serious operational problems.

The need for product line integration also points out the need for both integration and new interfaces at the user interface level. Each product administration system provides its own user interface. Each is different, many are based on "green-screen" 3x78 terminal emulation, and some require excessive training before employees can be productive interacting with customers.

Worse, because each interface is tied to a single product administration system, there is no logical place to introduce capabilities for defining transactions that cross multiple systems. And finally, as product lines diversify and the company adds new product administration systems, the desktop will inevitably become overly crowded, with overlapping windows representing the different systems turning into a confusing mess instead of exploiting the ease of use intrinsic in a graphical user interface (GUI).

Because ERP suites are fashionable, you do some investigating, but a quick trip around the Web convinces you nobody is close to delivering what you need.

You conclude that the right answer is to create an integrated GUI that both simplifies and integrates all the company's product administration systems. It must also provide facilities for integrating, in real time, information received from your company's business partners.

9

PLANNING ARCHITECTURAL CHANGE

And although it isn't a startling conclusion, you also figure you'll want to make many of the services built into the GUI available to your customers through the World Wide Web and through an interactive voice response system so they can get service on the phone.

Pulling all this information together, you decide the right answer—the overall design goal—is an architecture that facilitates not only information integration, but also transaction and user-interface integration as well.

Establishing Design Issues and Principles

Architecture is a matter of design. You could achieve a consistent, coherent, stable, aesthetically pleasing design instinctively, if you're really good, and if you made all decisions yourself.

Okay, you're good. You're very good. Unless you want to be the architecture police, that isn't good enough. One of the best techniques you have for making technical architecture management a facilitating discipline instead of a bureaucracy is to communicate it as widely as possible. Not just any communication will do, either. You need to communicate it in a way that helps people make architecturally consistent decisions.

One tool for achieving this goal is to define design issues and design principles. Because form follows function, the design of a technical architecture begins with an understanding of the functions the architecture needs to accomplish or the problems needing resolution—issues, to choose a word—and then resolves those issues. These resolutions—design principles—serve as touchstones against which you can measure specific product, service, and process decisions. Design principles establish the parameters within which all product and service decisions will be made.

Therefore, the logical first step in the process of establishing design principles is to create a list of key design issues. This list should be categorized into platform, information, application, and global issues.

Determining the Central Design Issue and Principle

The central design issue is the starting point for all architectural decisions. It establishes not only the top priority, but a measure with which all other design decisions must be consistent.

It sounds like a tricky thing to define. Luckily, you've already defined it. Your change drivers are your central design issue, and your design goal is your central design principle. Every other design principle has to support it.

For the manufacturing example, the stated goal was: "The company will need to completely replace its current suite of independently developed and acquired applications with an ERP suite." That's your central design principle.

The other example is just as straightforward. "An architecture that facilitates integration of information, transactions, and the user interface," is a central design principle everyone can understand.

Defining Design Issues

The process of establishing design principles begins with a list of design issues—architectural decisions that must be made prior to designing the architecture itself.

Design issues are generally grouped around the major architectural layers, so there are application-layer design issues, information-layer design issues and platform-layer design issues. In most cases, a design issue for one layer has mirror issues in other layers, so identifying the equivalent "global" design issue can help achieve consistency of practice across layers, when consistency is a valuable goal. Table 9.1 provides examples of global design issues and their expression in the different architectural layers.

An important part of developing the list of design issues is understanding their interdependencies. Decisions regarding one design issue will, in many cases, determine the design principle established for another one or will determine the significance of another design issue. For this reason it is important to determine the order in which design issues will be resolved.

In our second example—the company that had established a product diversification and service integration strategy—the architecture planners recognized "build versus buy" as an important design issue, and chose "Buy best-of-class when you can; build when you have to," as the design principle. The architecture planners in the first example didn't recognize "build versus buy" as an important design issue because they had already decided to buy everything they needed from a single source—their ERP vendor.

TABLE 9.1   EXAMPLES OF DESIGN ISSUES

Global	*Application Layer*	*Information Layer*	*Platform Layer*
Integration Strategy	Integration Technique	Integration Technique	Integration Technique
Strategy for Leveraging Investments	Code Reuse Techniques	Management of Redundancy	Definition of Standards

continues

9

TABLE 9.1 CONTINUED

Global	Application Layer	Information Layer	Platform Layer
Design Strategy	Partitioning Strategy Interface Strategy Product Selection Strategy Product Customization Strategy	Information Modeling Strategy Object Modeling Strategy	Network Design and Simulation Strategy Product Selection Strategy
Tools	Development	DBMS	Network Management Environment Administration Strategy
Toolkit	Performance		Monitoring Strategy

Selecting Design Principles

For each design issue, list the possible ways you can deal with it—your candidate design principles. Figure out how you're dealing with the issue now (it might not be formally documented, but there's usually some design principle that's understood within the IS culture). Assess that design principle based on your central design principle, other design principles you've already decided on, and on your expectations for the evolution of the technology marketplace.

SAMPLE DESIGN ISSUE: DATA REDUNDANCY

As one example of a design issue, most companies understand the need for a strategy regarding management of data redundancy. Candidate architectural design principles are

- Eliminate all redundancy other than data backups[6].
- Eliminate all redundancy other than data backups and summary information fields.

---

[6]Although not generally acknowledged, tape libraries and mirrored disks contain data that is redundant with what is stored online.

- Eliminate all redundancy other than data backups, summary information fields, and data warehouses.
- Eliminate redundancy (other than the standard exceptions) where practical; automate synchronization of redundant data where necessary.
- Establish an information architecture with three tiers—legacy, central operational database, and data warehouse. Eliminate data redundancy within the central operational database and within the data warehouse, and manage legacy and inter-tier redundancy through managed synchronization.
- Eliminate redundancy (other than the standard exceptions) only in systems developed in-house; automatically synchronize redundant data in all purchased systems.

You begin with a previously decided design principle. You had already identified customization of purchased applications as a design issue and decided that the right design principle was to avoid customization as much as possible. This decision eliminates all but the final two options.

Weighing them, you decide you prefer to create an integration engine that goes live against the legacy databases rather than creating a three-tier information architecture.

SAMPLE DESIGN ISSUE: APPLICATION PARTITIONING STRATEGY

Lazy and sloppy thinking is a luxury you don't get when designing and managing technical architecture, any more than the architect of a building gets to think sloppily. Just as every room needs a door, and the difference between doors and windows is important when designing a building, so seemingly fine distinctions matter when designing technical architecture as well.

Lots of companies have established a pseudo-design principle of preferring thin clients. As was mentioned in the introduction to this section, half the time "thin client" really means "thin desktop." What matters is that applications are managed and executed on a server instead of a desktop computer[7].

continues

---

[7]*Thin desktops rarely lead to thin clients. All that happens is that monolithic applications execute on the server and are displayed on a browser that runs on the desktop. And because browsers have blown up to be as big as word processors and spreadsheets, the desktop doesn't end up that thin either.*

continued

> From an architectural perspective, the design issue you should deal with isn't how thin your clients are—it's the larger issue of how to partition applications.
>
> Modern application design divides processing into multiple, independent, communicating layers. We often read about "3-tier" architectures. They're referring to application layering, except that three is generally the wrong number—software engineers generally talk about "n-tier" architectures to reflect the number of different functional tasks that ought to be segregated into distinct processes.
>
> A typical application architecture divides applications into at least these functional layers:
>
> - Presentation Layer: Controls the user experience. The presentation layer manages the logical flow of events, and performs data validation[8]. It also handles user interaction in ways that are highly dependent on the computing medium: In a graphical user interface (GUI), the presentation layer displays all screen objects and accepts keystrokes; in an interactive voice response system, it speaks prompts and either listens to caller responses or accepts DTMF[9] inputs; in a batch report, it includes the interface needed to accept input parameters and the formatted report itself. A module that includes only the presentation layer is equivalent to the legendary "thin client."
>
> - *Business Logic Layer*: Handles computations and makes decisions based on defined business rules. It's business logic if it manages neither data nor the user experience.
>
> - *Integration Layer:* A layer that acts as an intermediary between specific services and clients that need them, providing a consistent, abstract, vendor-neutral interface. For example, when the presentation layer needs data, it will request that data from the interface layer. It's the integration layer that knows where to find the data and, later on, all the places that data must be updated so as to keep all redundant data synchronized. The integration layer also can be used to manage resources like document
>
> *continues*

---

[8]*Data validation is a murky subject in that some validation is clearly part of the presentation layer—enforcement of data types, for example—and some, for example, comparison to a value that's the result of a complex calculation that's performed in a legacy system, clearly is not. Most data validation, like table lookups, is somewhere in the middle. Choose an answer with which you're comfortable and move on—this is a case where pragmatism, not ideology, should rule the day.*

[9]*Dual Tone Multi-Frequency—the technical term for "touch-tone." Use it three times and it will become part of your vocabulary, much to the annoyance of your spouse and anyone else in the immediate vicinity. Trust me on this.*

management systems or directory services where you might not be able to have just one, but you want your architecture to act as if you did.

- *Information Layer:* Databases, document repositories, and all the other information stores you take care of. This layer consists of the information itself and, depending on your point of view, the interface provided by the database management system or document management system that manages it (the other way of looking at the situation is that the DBMS or document management system is a computing platform, not a software layer).

- *Legacy Wrapper Layer:* A "wrapper" is code you use that lets legacy systems not designed to be externally callable act as servers. The wrappers interact with the integration layer to expose the legacy systems to the remaining application layers without having to write a lot of custom code every time. Wrappers make both legacy data and legacy logic available to the remaining layers.

    The two most common wrappering techniques are screen-scraping and the creation of CICS transactions, although there are others. Wrappering is a great example of the "great theory, but..." syndrome—wrappering is a great theory, but not all legacy logic can be wrappered because a lot of it hides deep in the depths of batch programs. To wrapper it, you first have to rewrite the batch program.

Notice that with the exception of the presentation layer and the database management layer, every layer is both a client and a server, so don't get all twisted around with those terms. They're clients because they request services from other layers and they're servers because they provide services to other layers. Don't worry about it—what matters is the layering, not what's a client and what's a server.

In a great architecture, all layers are entirely portable across all computing platforms. That lets you swap out hardware and operating systems without changing the application. In an ideal architecture, the layers aren't just portable but automatically load-balance at run-time. That way, if the servers are bogged down, an object will execute on the desktop; but if the server is lightly loaded, objects execute there to take advantage of the additional horsepower the server brings to bear.

Right now your opportunities to create great architectures are limited and involve risky trade-offs; the opportunity to create an ideal architecture is slideware.

continues

9

PLANNING ARCHITECTURAL CHANGE

continued

In the meantime, you can still gain real-world benefits by establishing a specific application layering strategy as one of your design principles. It positions you for the future, maximizes your opportunities to reuse code, helps you divide up programming tasks to multiple developers, helps you performance-tune applications when you put them into production and, most important of all, it saves everyone else from having to cook up application partitioning strategies every time they face a new programming problem.

Sample Design Issue: Development Environment

Here's a story problem for you. Back when COBOL and the 3278 were the king and queen of computing, an average business application development project involved a project team of about 25 people and took about two years to complete—about 50 programmer-years. We now have "fourth-generation languages[10]" (4GLs) that make programmers easily a hundred times more productive than they were using mainframe COBOL compilers.

Dividing 50 programmer-years by 100, we find the same project should now take one programmer six months to complete.

What's that you say? Your projects still involve 25 people for two years? That can't be! You can't argue with math!

Part of the problem, as already noted, comes from methodology bloat. Another problem is the increasing scope of IS systems.

And then there's the risk you face when you adopt one of the ultra-high productivity fourth-generation languages as your development standard—that the language, being both proprietary and nonstandard, could go away, leaving you stranded.

Several design issues are involved in establishing your development environment. The most important are:

- **Proprietary versus non-proprietary and standard versus non-standard technology.**

  Most IS organizations are comfortable making use of proprietary technology so long as it's an industry standard[11]—SNA and Windows come to

---

[10]*The first generation was machine code—pure ones and zeros. The second, assembly language, added a layer of abstraction to machine code. The third language generation, which created FORTRAN, COBOL and BASIC, changed programming from specifying which internal operations to perform to a procedural description of how the computer should solve a problem. Fourth generation languages, also called "nonprocedural languages" operate at an even higher level of abstraction, letting programmers describe what the computer should do ("Sort"), rather than how to do it.*

mind. Languages present a special category of risk compared to other platforms, though. If you build an application for one operating system or database management system and have to move it to another, you face a conversion, which is a big pain in the neck. If your development language goes away, though, you don't just have to convert the application. You have to redevelop it.

- **One Development Language, One Language for Each Application Layer, a Different Design Principle for Each Layer, or...**

How many languages will you support? You have lots of candidate design principles to choose from (their enumeration is left as an exercise for the reader). A reasonable approach is to settle on one standard language for each layer, plus special-purpose languages for each platform to handle situations (report-writers, for example) for which the standard language isn't suited.

For the mainframe, COBOL is a given and you might also allow a 4GL. For the server layers (as of this writing), "Java when you can, C++ when you have to, and PERL on Web servers too because it's handy for lots of stuff," is a popular design principle.

For the presentation layer, most shops select different languages for different media, but try to establish a single standard for each.

As an alternative, some shops go for maximum productivity by selecting a single development environment built to support all application partitions. Unfortunately, because all the ones currently available are proprietary, this strategy contains a great deal of risk to go along with its high rewards.

- **What You Should Do**

There is no single solution that fits every IS organization. The key to your decision is recognizing that deciding to develop applications in a proprietary development environment means you might need to redevelop the applications in a different development environment if the one you choose goes extinct.

That isn't as bad as it sounds, though. Redeveloping an application isn't all that bad, if all you do is port it to the new language. Redevelopment gets out of hand because business units see it as an opportunity to throw all kinds of new features into the application and developers see it as an opportunity to fix all the shortcuts they took the last time (not a bad

continues

9

Planning Architectural Change

---

[11]*Because an industry standard is something used by a lot of IS organizations, this is hardly a startling insight, of course.*

continued

thing except that it leads to overruns that result in a whole new set of shortcuts).

- **The Columbo Effect**

  Oh yeah, just one more thing. Most development methodologies are built on the assumption that up-front analysis is cheaper than redevelopment later on, and an unstated assumption that it's possible to understand business requirements through up-front analysis.

  Anyone who's ever built a real-world application knows that up-front analysis never gets everything on the table because it isn't until business users have the application in front of them that they know what the application really should do.

  The other assumption also gets shaky with high-productivity development environments. You're sometimes far better off building the wrong application as fast as you can, letting business users pick it apart until you understand how to build the right application.

  If you aren't willing to adopt a methodology that takes advantage of high-language productivity, don't adopt a proprietary high-productivity language.

- **The Columbo Effect, Part 2**

  Just one more thing—I promise.

  Choose your strategy based on the programming tasks you'll really be taking on. As has been noted before, few IS organizations do much new development work. Most of the job is systems integration, and perhaps creating new user interfaces for the commercial applications you buy.

Establish your design principles accordingly.

SAMPLE DESIGN ISSUE: PRODUCTION READINESS

Back in the old days, one of the things we did very well was put programs into production. Production control defined what it meant for an application to be production-grade and any application that didn't pass the test didn't go into production.

End of story.

It ain't magic and it ain't hard, but it's something a lot of IS organizations have forgotten as they've moved off the mainframe into the wild and woolly world of distributed processing and client/server application architectures.

It's time to remember what we've always known.

There isn't a whole lot that's more annoying than putting an application into production only to find you don't know when it's crashed, it has major security holes (or even worse it has a separate logon and authentication process) or otherwise causes production problems. It's easy to avoid the aggravation.

As part of your technical architecture definition, define what it means for an application to be production-ready. Your production control department should be eager to take this on, so assign the task and move on.

Establishing Strategic Product Standards

Many design principles, particularly platform-layer design principles, lead directly to a need to establish strategic product standards[12]. As an obvious example, every IS organization needs to determine how it will store and organize its structured data. A typical design principle might be:

- The preferred method for storing production data will be a standard RDBMS and all IS-developed applications will use that product.
- Whenever possible, purchased applications will be installed using the preferred RDBMS, but use of a competing RDBMS will not disqualify an application's vendor from consideration when evaluating its products.
- Production data will be organized within applications or application suites.
- A data warehouse will be used to provide an enterprise view of corporate information, implemented on a separate platform chosen for that purpose.

The preceding design principle calls for two separate strategic product standards—an enterprise RDBMS and a data warehousing platform.

Design principles in the other layers also can lead to definition of IS standards. For example, the design principle, "Eliminate redundancy (other than the standard exceptions) only in systems developed in-house; automatically synchronize redundant data in all purchased systems," leads directly to establishment of one standard, and indirectly to another.

The former is making synchronization with pre-existing information part of the standard process of integrating all new purchased applications.

The second is establishing a new platform component—a standard data replication tool.

Product selection is a core process within IS, and doing it well requires design principles to guide it. You can either use design principles as screening tools to eliminate candidate products prior to in-depth analysis, or you can make them high-weight evaluation criteria in your decision matrix.

---

[12]*It's a strategic product standard if it's required by a design principle. Otherwise it's just a standard, and possibly a standard you don't need to establish.*

Either way you need to select your strategic product standards—those on which you build your architecture—with care. Take care to select sturdy[13] products from stable companies you expect to be around for awhile to provide support.

Even more important, make sure you really need to define a standard. Unless an architectural design principle or unfilled computing function calls for it, standardization might not be the right answer.

Defining the Target Technical Architecture

Chances are that if you're putting yourself through a technical architecture analysis it's because you recognize the need to change what's currently in place. Your current architecture might be unsatisfactory for some reason: It's unreliable, performs poorly, or simply costs more than you think it should. You might need capabilities your current architecture can't provide, so you need to extend it. You might be facing both issues at the same time.

Regardless, you need a way to define a target technical architecture. To do this you have to combine information from several sources and synthesize it into a target technical architecture. To do so, you create an architectural description using the same tools you used to document your existing architecture. Your most important sources of information are

- Component/Function Matrix.
- Enterprise Information Model.
- Information/Repository Matrix.
- Function/Application Matrix.
- New functional requirements as established through your involvement in planning the business's strategic, tactical, and infrastructural goals.
- Core design goal(s) and architectural design principles.

Fixing What's Broken

Start with areas in which your current architecture is unsatisfactory and flag them in the documents just listed. Be careful of one thing as you do this: What appears to be an architectural defect—having the wrong product as a standard, for example—often turns out to be a matter of managing the resource you have poorly. If your network is unreliable, the answer might be adding better network management tools and practices, not replacing your routers and servers.

---

[13]*I figured you were tired of "robust," so here's an alternative.*

When you're done, make a list of the architectural changes you need just to shore up what's already in place. In the process that follows, you'll be making decisions about what to enhance and what to replace. Use your fix-list to help make those decisions—when something is working well, enhancing it is usually a good idea, whereas when something is broken you're usually better off using this process as your vehicle for replacing it.

Application Layer Changes

Now, factor in the new business functions you've defined through the business planning process. Add them to the function/application matrix and see what happens—you'll need to either enhance existing applications with new capabilities, replace existing applications with more capable ones, add new applications to the suite already in production, or some combination thereof.

WHAT ABOUT DATA WAREHOUSES?

Most businesses are at least worrying about whether to implement a data warehouse. If you are, you might wonder how you'll get there when this methodology drives all change from the application layer.

The answer is simple: A data warehouse is just a field of dreams if you don't start with the application—you hope that if you build it, someone will magically show up and generate enough business value to make the whole effort worthwhile.

Good luck.

The application-based approach starts with a business need for ad hoc analysis of gobs of data about something or other. Start by understanding that business need (and, probably, by helping the business folks understand the dimensions and limitations of any data warehouse so they know what they're getting into). Next, select the analytical tools (the category, not the actual products—yet) that will satisfy the business need. Analytical tools are applications, and it makes sense to start with them because there are several types of data warehousing platforms and each is optimized for a different kind of analysis.

Wait! You aren't done yet. Spread the word among the company's top executives that you'll be adding this capability to your repertoire and find out who else has been thinking along these lines. You'll almost certainly find a need to support more than one analytical tool, so you're better off figuring that out before you decide on the right data warehousing technology.

Now you're off and running, and the architectural analysis for your data warehouse fits nicely into the overall framework for planning architectural change.

Now that you've added new application functionality, go back to the Applications Assessment. If you're adding a new application, create a skeleton entry for it. If you're enhancing an existing one, determine how the assessment will change as a result of the changes you've planned. Particularly in this skeleton entry, list the kinds of information the application is likely to need, using the same information categories you defined in your Enterprise Information Model.

Information Layer Changes

Now, you're ready to decide whether the various application changes you've planned will call for new information repositories or changes to existing ones. Start with the Information/Repository Matrix and modify it so it demonstrates where the new information categories will go. Next modify the Enterprise Information Model so it includes the new information categories.

Platform Layer Changes

The application and information layer changes you've listed might call for computing functions you don't currently support. Add them to the component/function matrix, then decide whether an existing platform can support the new computing function or if you need to add new platforms.

If you have to add new platforms, add place-holders for them in the matrix.

Revisit the Fix List

Go back through your list of what needs fixing. Scratch out any items that are irrelevant now because you're replacing the technology that's caused the problem. Highlight the ones that will cause problems given the changes you have planned. You need to do something about these.

An Example

Imagine you have an order-entry call center but want to let customers place orders electronically as well, both through an interactive voice response system and through the World Wide Web[14]. And oh, by the way, the call center system does not have a reputation for reliability—it frequently loses its connection to the mainframe because the mainframe gateway has a glitch you've been unable to track down.

---

[14]*This won't stretch your imagination very far, I'd guess—the stretch would be if your business didn't want to do this.*

With this information in hand you're ready to plan architectural changes. They start with:

- *Application-layer enhancements*
  - Enhance your Web site with e-commerce capabilities (secure transactions, credit card verification, ability to validate orders and post them to your legacy order processing system).
  - Modify your IVR application so it can verify credit card information, validate orders as they're entered, and post them to your legacy order processing system. You'd also prefer to add a speech recognition interface to the IVR system if at all possible.
  - A bit of investigation shows that your call center application was built using a two-tier client/server architecture that doesn't conform to the application partitioning standards you established as your design principles, so the credit card verification logic, order validation logic, and legacy order processing system integration logic isn't available for use with your Web and IVR applications. You decide to restructure this application rather recreate the functionality.

These enhancements lead to

- *Information-layer enhancements*—The planned Web site enhancements call for display of product images and you have a large catalog. You need to create an information repository that can manage digitized photographic images.

The application-layer and information-layer enhancements lead to the need for

- *Platform-layer enhancements*
  - Replace your current Web server platform with one that supports secure transactions.
  - Purchase enhancements to your standard RDBMS to add object/relational capabilities that will let it handle digitized photographs.
  - Add an application server platform on which to run the middle layers of the restructured call center application.
  - Add a standalone speech-recognition server platform with which your existing IVR can communicate. A bit of investigation reveals that your IVR has the flexibility to work in this fashion so you don't need to replace the IVR platform.
  - Replace the mainframe gateway, which provides a screen-scraping interface to the legacy order-processing systems, with something sturdier and callable from the integration layer processes that will reside on your new application server.

That wasn't so bad, was it? Now, you're ready to create a migration plan.

9

PLANNING ARCHITECTURAL CHANGE

Creating the Technical Architecture Migration Plan

Very few businesses will let you just fix architecture. For the most part, you have to embed architectural changes in business initiatives to create a migration plan. The migration plan includes three categories of effort: Key business initiatives, core technology projects, and (sometimes) implementation of new IS management practices.

Life gets interesting right about now because this isn't an IS initiative any more. You're about to plan a Big Program. That's the subject of a later chapter, so hang on until we get there. Right now you have to plan the core technology projects and new IS management practices you'll need so the Big Program can happen. You need those in your pocket when program planning begins.

The basic rule is: Make your architectural changes early enough that developers have a stable, well-managed environment in which to create new applications or integrate purchased ones. Make them late enough that business benefits come as soon after you make the technology investments as possible.

Implementation of New IS Management Practices

The one thing you don't have to wait for is making changes to your own organization. If, for example, you discovered that a lot of the unreliability in your networks is the result of their not being managed as production, mission-critical platforms, it's time to fix that.

If you defined new application partitioning standards, you probably need to educate your developers in how to use them, and to create processes and organizational structures to manage reusable objects. Don't wait—do that now, too.

Most architectural changes call for new or different processes within IS to make them work properly. If you don't properly implement those processes, which often lead to organizational changes as well, the new technologies you're bringing in have no chance of succeeding.

Don't do that.

TECHNICAL ARCHITECTURE MANAGEMENT

A technical architecture study is a poor investment for any company not planning to implement technical architecture management as an ongoing process within IS. The process of technical architecture management isn't all that complicated after you've gone through the effort described in this section. To succeed, you should create a *small* Technical Architecture Management Office to administer the process.

Staff it with your best people. To avoid creating a bureaucracy, your technical architects must understand strategic design, not just programming. They also must have a track record of delivering working systems. Otherwise, you've put theoreticians in charge. This discipline is theoretical enough without that—you need pragmatists running it.

The Technical Architecture Management Office's responsibilities are to

- Make sure everyone in IS understands the architecture and design principles, and the logic behind the various decisions that went into its definition.
- Participate in program and project planning so as to anticipate the need for major architectural changes.
- Participate in vendor and product selections to ensure all new products either adhere to the architecture or lead to planned, well-understood changes to it or variances from it.
- Participate in system design efforts to ensure application designs make the best possible use of existing platforms, information repositories, and reusable application code, and also to make sure system designs adhere to application partitioning and production standards.
- Maintain all technical architecture documentation so it remains current as products change and the architecture evolves.

A responsibility you don't want to assign to the Technical Architecture Management Office is policing the architecture. If it lives up to its responsibilities, there will be no need for a policing function. There will, however, be a need for an escalation process if the technical architects and development teams reach an impasse on an issue that requires the balancing of architectural integrity and business requirements.

Make sure you've defined this as part of the process. Otherwise the first dispute will lead to unproductive arguments, sniping, and a retreat of the Technical Architecture Management Office from being a productive part of IS to being a bunch of officious bureaucrats.

Don't do that.

PROCESSES

The military, I'm told, is an organization designed by geniuses to be run by idiots. I have no idea if any genius was ever involved in its design. Having met quite a few officers and former officers in the course of my career, I can state unequivocally that the military is run by the same mix of competent and incompetent, dedicated and politically motivated, wise and foolish leaders as any publicly held corporation.

I worked for a year on a military contract, which exposed[1] me to the Federal Information Processing Standards (FIPS) and Federal Acquisition Requirements Standards (FARS). FIPS and FARS, which between them define the process military organizations must go through to buy information technology, fill a small library. Designed by the genius lawyers we elect to Congress, only lawyers and lawyer wannabes have any hope of understanding them, so military personnel put themselves through serious contortions to avoid having to buy stuff.

Between fighting an enemy of the United States of America and fighting FIPS and FARS, most military officers would much prefer dealing with the enemy.

---

[1]*In the same sense that one is exposed to chicken pox or the flu.*

Now don't get too uppity there, buddy. When it comes to how work gets done there are only a few kinds of organization. Employees either:

1. Improvise constantly because there are no well-defined processes.
2. Slavishly follow poorly designed processes that led to mediocre results.
3. Fight with poorly designed processes that interfere with achieving results.
4. Improvise constantly, ignoring the well-designed processes that would facilitate the creation of high-quality results.
5. Follow well-designed processes to create high-quality results.

Chances are pretty good you don't run a Type 5 organization. If the odds were better, IS would do better than our miserable 30% success rate on system development projects.

THE PROCESSES OF INFORMATION SYSTEMS

Process redesign weenies like to talk about "core processes." In process redesign jargon, a core process is directly involved in the delivery of an organization's products and services, where a supporting process—well, supports the core processes.

The first stage of process redesign is determining your core processes. We've already agreed that our mission is the automation of company processes, and that we deliver value through business applications[2]. Our core processes, then, are the creation or selection of business applications, and the processes of implementing, operating, and supporting their use. More formally, the core processes are

- Vendor and Product Selection
- Systems Development[3]
- Systems Installation and Integration
- Data Center Operations
- Systems Maintenance
- End-user Support

To make us effective in our execution of these core processes, we need a handful of key supporting processes as well. In addition to the processes dealt with in the first two

---

[2]*"We agreed" means your loyal author has asserted this, and it's hard to argue with an inanimate object like a book.*

[3]*Well of course this comes below Vendor and Product selection. You do have a design principle that says, "Buy when we can and build when we have to," don't you? If you meant that when you said it, which is more important?*

sections of this book, we need to be good at decision-making, project management, data modeling,[4] and data management, systems library management, and training.

We're not going to go through the whole list in this book. We're going to focus on the biggest problem area in IS today—the "big project" processes of building or buying, and then installing and integrating new business applications. The others usually aren't broken, with one exception, which is this:

Many organizations don't run their distributed systems with the same level of professionalism they apply to their mainframe operations. This happened because distributed systems usually grew out of office LANs which arrived on the scene in spite of IS rather than because of it.

The solution is simple: Implement the same kind of system monitoring tools, backup and recovery practices and so on, for your distributed systems as you have for your mainframe. It's a matter of will, not difficulty—the combination of frame relay, Ethernet, and TCP/IP is remarkably easy to set up and manage when compared to the nasty days when everything was SNA and you had to take down the mainframe every time you wanted to add a terminal to your network.

If you want to put a shine on your data center operations, implement a program of Total Quality Management (TQM). TQM was created to handle factories—situations where you do the same thing repeatedly. That's exactly what you do in your data center, and companies—very large, very successful companies—have enjoyed terrific results through the application of TQM to the management of their computer and network operations.

(TQM has since been misapplied to all sorts of disciplines where you don't do the same thing repeatedly, like systems development. Don't make this mistake. Systems development is custom work, and TQM doesn't apply to custom work.)

We're not going to deal with the data center in any more detail in this book. We're going to focus our attention on the processes you need to excel at in order to implement major new systems. We'll begin with decision-making because in my experience there is no source of project delay quite so excruciating as an inability to make decisions and have them stay made.

Then we'll deal with project management. Bad project management is rampant in IS. With bad project management you'll never finish anything substantial; with good project management you'll always have something to show for your investments in technology.

---

[4] *If you've decided to adopt object-oriented technologies, add object modeling to this bullet.*

Finally, we'll look at the build/buy alternatives: systems selection and systems development, along with the process of systems installation and integration. If you're good at these processes, you're in great shape.

You're also in the minority.

MAKING DECISIONS

"If you board the wrong train, it's no use running along the corridor in the other direction."

—Dietrich Bonhoeffer

MANAGEMENTSPEAK

It's a no-brainer.

Translation:
I don't have a brain.

Good leaders can make decisions. Great leaders make the right decision at least half the time.

How about you?

Organizations face nothing as paralyzing as decision-drift. The symptoms are obvious: Nobody can figure out who owns a decision, the paperwork is lost, or we revisit a decision we made last week because someone missed the meeting.

At one time, organizations were very good at making decisions—the boss decided, and that was that. The good news was that decisions got made. The bad news is, the boss wasn't always in a very good position to make the decision, and often made some very bad ones.

Most organizations recognize five basic ways to make decisions: Command, consultation, delegation, consensus, and voting. Each has its place. What follows is guidance on what kind of circumstances call for each of them.

Even more important than using the right decision style, though, is making it clear to everyone involved in a decision which decision style you're going to use. It's even a good idea to establish a fall-back style if the preferred style doesn't work. For example, you might tell everyone you're planning to use a consultative style for a decision, but if it turns out to be so complicated you don't feel comfortable with it, you might decide to delegate it to a team member who has demonstrated a better grasp of the situation.

Through the simple expedient of setting everyone's expectations up front, you'll defuse a lot of the tension that often accompanies a difficult decision.

COMMAND DECISIONS

Command decisions are those made by the boss and only by the boss. Reserve these for emergencies, when you don't have time to do anything but make the call and move on.

Command decision-making has fallen out of favor as organizations started to recognize the value of employee empowerment. For the most part, an excessive reliance on command decision-making is a symptom of poor leadership, because command decisions only recognize and make use of the expertise of the decision-maker.

We lost something when command decision-making fell out of favor though. Command decision-making requires courage. The others don't, and whether there's a causal relationship or not, the rise of "getting along" as a core executive competency seems to have coincided with the decline of command decision-making.

Strength: Fastest decision style.

Limitations: Unreliable quality, no staff growth.

CONSULTATIVE DECISIONS

You make a consultative decision every time you gather facts, ideas, and opinions from lots of different people, but make the actual decision yourself.

Effective leaders make extensive use of consultative decision-making. It has the advantage of visibly involving a large number of people in a decision, without leading to the excessive delays associated with consensus decision-making.

Consultative decision-making has two limitations, though. First, it's still heavily reliant on the expertise of the decision-maker. The process of involving lots of people improves the ability of an unqualified decision-maker to make the right decision, but that's still less desirable than having the best person or group make the call.

The second limitation is that consultative decision-making doesn't lead to staff development. When you make a decision, nobody else takes any risks or does any growing.

Strength: Excellent balance of involvement, efficiency, and quality.

Limitations: No staff growth; quality limited by judgment of decision-owner.

DELEGATED DECISIONS

Delegation is one of the most important techniques available to a leader. It's too bad so many leaders are so bad at it, and so many employees don't understand it. Empowerment, by the way, is nothing more than institutionalized delegation, although you'd never know it from all the fuss that's been made about it.

When you delegate a decision you assign authority, responsibility, and credit for good results to someone who works for you, while retaining accountability. Retention of accountability is one reason some leaders avoid delegation, in fact. Many reasonably figure that if they're going to be held accountable for something, they should do it themselves[1].

The second reason many leaders avoid delegation is that they want credit for everything. That's human nature, and you probably aren't immune to the feeling.

---

[1] *The risk factor isn't all one way, though. Every time you make a decision yourself, you bear the risk that someone who works for you might understand the subject better than you do and could make a better decision.*

Here's some encouragement: You'll only be noticed for two kinds of decision anyway: The important ones, and the bad ones. No matter how well you do a small job yourself, nobody except the people who work for you will notice, and they probably won't be impressed that you're doing work at their level. You might as well delegate them.

The third reason leaders don't delegate is that it takes work (see the section entitled, "Effective Delegation."

One important fact to understand about delegation is that the first thing your delegatee must do is decide which of the remaining four decision styles to use—pushing a decision down a level doesn't change how decisions must be made.

The second important fact to consider is that when you delegate, you have structure the assignment so the delegatee can fail, because when someone can't fail, they can't succeed, either.

Strength: Excellent balance of involvement, efficiency, and staff development.

Limitations: Adds risk of reduced quality.

EFFECTIVE DELEGATION

Effective delegation isn't all that complicated, but it isn't just a matter of handing a piece of work to someone and walking away, either. There's work involved on your part. Here's a step-by-step approach to delegation that will maximize the benefits while keeping your risks and workload reasonable.

1. Decide if this is a decision that should be delegated at all. This is a judgment call. Delegate when it's a decision you shouldn't be making, or whose risk of failure isn't large enough to be worrisome. Don't delegate just because your workload is too high. You're better off working with your own manager to adjust your priorities than to take on the excessive risk you and the company would experience from delegating important decisions to people unqualified to make them.

2. Assign the decision to someone who is likely to succeed at making it. You aren't doing anyone a favor by assigning them a task just because it's his or her turn.

   Don't, however, fall into the trap of always delegating to the same one or two departmental "stars." There's always work worth doing that you can assign to your average performers. And they might surprise you—some average performers are average because you expect them to perform at only an average level. Many employees are quite adept at living down to your expectations.

3. Make sure the employee understands the decision. More than any other single factor, failure to clarify causes employees to fail.

   Don't assume the employee understands what you're looking for, just because you don't hear any questions. Many employees don't feel comfortable asking clarifying questions. They think that if they ask a lot of questions about an assignment, you'll think they're not bright enough to handle it.

   When you delegate, ask for a brief written description of the decision, its overall purpose, why it's important, what form it will take, and the employee's strategy for making it. Don't just tell an employee how to do make a particular decision, unless there's a standard procedure for this kind of decision that everyone is supposed to follow. On the other hand, don't make this a case of teaching the class to swim by tossing everyone into the deep end of the pool either. Help your employee develop a good plan—help, but don't make the plan yourself. This is, after all, an exercise in delegation.

   This step will tell you early if there are any fundamental problems with the assignment.

4. Schedule regular follow-up meetings to check status and determine whether you need to get more involved to help your employee through any rough spots or remove any barriers. In the first review meeting, go over the memo described in the previous step. In the rest, get to specifics. Review the week's progress, plans for the upcoming week, and whether the initial plan still holds up.

   It isn't true that you should never "undelegate" something. That's tantamount to saying you have to live with a mistake forever. Taking back a decision you've delegated is serious business, though, so don't do it often. Any decision you have to take back represents a failure for both the delegatee and you.

   As you gain more knowledge of what each employee is and isn't capable of, you'll be able to take shortcuts with the more independent ones. Even with them, make sure you've agreed to a completion date and a description of what they're supposed to accomplish.

CONSENSUS DECISIONS

The nature of consensus is widely misunderstood to mean "what most of us think after we've finished flogging the dead horse." The second most popular wrong definition of consensus is "suboptimal compromise."

The process of arriving at consensus can feel like dead-horse flogging, and the results can sometimes be a suboptimal compromise, at least from the perspective of those on the team who have strongly held views that aren't fully realized in the decision. That isn't however, what consensus is.

A consensus is a decision that every member of the team agrees to support. Not everyone has to agree *with* it. They all must, however, agree *to* it—voluntarily, not just because you or peer pressure makes continued disagreement embarrassing.

If one or more team members can't agree to support a decision, the whole team is better off falling back to a different decision style than to pretend to a consensus that doesn't exist.

Consensus came into vogue as the use of teams gained in popularity several years ago. Consensus, many of us were taught, was the *sin qua non* of an empowered, self-managed team because it was the mechanism through which the whole team would buy into a decision.

As with so many one-sided declarations of this nature, the proponents of this perspective failed to look at its logical consequences. People who were being organized into teams didn't hear that consensus is a good way to achieve buy-in. They heard that unless a decision had been made by consensus, they had no obligation to accept it.

Oops.

Consensus decision-making is time-consuming, expensive, and difficult. Not only are consensus decisions difficult to achieve, they're difficult to maintain as well, because when a team has made a decision, it has to enforce that decision when individual team members forget or ignore it. Because the team makes consensus decisions, the team has to own them, and that means it can't delegate enforcement to you.

The process of arriving at a consensus varies from circumstance to circumstance and from team to team. In the end, it invariably comes down to hashing out the advantages and disadvantages of various options in a team meeting.

It's especially important, especially with new teams, to determine what your fall-back will be if the team can't reach consensus on an issue. Sometimes, teams can't get there—hung juries happen, for example—and somehow you still need to move on. Usually, you'll want to make consultative decision-making your fall-back; sometimes you might just want to let the team vote on it.

However you and your teams deal with consensus decisions, always make a consensus check your final step. This is nothing more than writing the decision on a white board or flipchart, and then asking each team member, in turn, whether he or she will support it.

Read expressions and body language along with the spoken reply, and don't hesitate to probe if a "yes" sounds reluctant.

If consensus-checking isn't part of your routine, you might be surprised at the results.

Strength: Maximizes team buy-in and commitment.

Limitations: Time-consuming and expensive; not ensured to reach any decision.

HOW TO AVOID BRAINSTORMING

If consensus is a salad, brainstorming is a dressing that's been in the sun too long and has started to turn.

Teams brainstorm the way high school kids in old Mickey Rooney movies said, "I know! Let's put on a show!" Brainstorming has become a feel-good reflex for involving the team in a subject.

Way back when I was taking Psych 101 in college, though, researchers had already proved that **brainstorming doesn't work**, and I haven't run across anything in the intervening years that suggests it does.

The idea of brainstorming is that one person's wild idea will trigger thoughts in other team members, creating group energy that eventually results in better and more creative thoughts than any one team member could achieve in isolation.

How are we taught to brainstorm by the self-proclaimed experts who teach these things? We're taught to plod around the room in a clockwise direction, with each of us respectfully listening to each other's ideas until it's our turn. Critiquing an idea is forbidden—critiquing will interfere with the creative process!

This is simple nonsense. If the idea of brainstorming is to create group energy that enhances creativity, team members have to feel free to break in out of turn, critique, offer alternatives and modifications, and otherwise have an actual conversation. When we follow the official rules of brainstorming, if by some chance someone else's idea does trigger a new thought, we have to wait our turn to present it. By then, even if we remember our new idea and present it, the team will have lost all continuity and the idea will probably die of malnutrition.

Save yourself a meeting. Ask everyone to forward their ideas on the subject to you via email. Sort through them, consolidate them, organize them, and send

continues

continued

> them back to the team before your meeting so everyone can review each other's thoughts on the subject.
>
> Spend your meeting time reviewing the ideas, collecting any new thoughts that have occurred to team members in the interim, and reaching a consensus.
>
> If you must hold a brainstorming session, make sure no more than seven people are in the room (three to five is optimal). Then, make it a real brainstorming session—a free-for-all where every participant is allowed to speak freely, without worrying about sounding dumb, inadvertently hurting feelings, or ticking off the boss.
>
> But brainstorming by taking turns and holding all comments until after the idea-generation phase is done? Be honest with yourself—have you ever seen this approach trigger any useful thoughts?
>
> If you aren't sure, gather a group together and brainstorm the possible benefits of structured brainstorming. Just remember to take turns.

VOTING

A group of kindergartners found a stray cat and brought it into class. Their teacher, new to the profession and not yet wise enough to simply call the Humane Society, asked its name.

The whole class talked at once, of course, shouting out possible names to each other with exuberant vitality, but no cohesion. Finally, the teacher quieted down the class and, having ascertained that the feline lacked a known name, asked the class how it would go about choosing a name. Unanimously, the answer came back, "Let's vote on it!"

The class voted, and the results came in—"Benjamin" won by a nose, so Ben it was.

Two weeks later, Ben gave birth to a litter of kittens.

Voting is an awful way to make a decision. When a large group of equals must decide between options, there's sometimes no alternative, so sometimes (as when choosing public officials) we have no choice. But even in governance, our founders wisely chose to form a democratic republic, not a pure democracy.

In other words, as citizens we delegate our decisions to representatives. We vote to choose those representatives because every other means for selecting them would be either impossible, awful, or both. Except for the occasional referendum, though, we don't directly vote on the issues that affect us, and we shouldn't. When our system works well, it's because our representatives have the time to learn more about the issues than we do and try to choose the best course of action based on their knowledge and judgment, which usually exceeds our own.

Even with the institutionalized bribery we call "fund raising" distorting the system, using our votes to elect representatives probably works better for most issues than decision by referendum, though.

Take this lesson into your teams. If you must vote on an issue, handle it the way it's handled in government—write down the alternatives, allow an extended discussion so everyone gains sophistication in the implications of each available option, and make sure that even though you aren't trying to form a consensus, every team member will still support the results of the vote.

Now change your mind. If the group is small enough, make it a consensus decision after all, with the team's understanding that if it can't reach consensus, you'll make a consultative decision instead.

If the group is too big, divide it into no more than seven subgroups and have each one select (by voting if necessary) a delegate empowered to represent it. Form the delegates into a task force and charge the task force with reaching a decision through consensus.

Voting is an acceptable way to choose leaders or representatives. That's about all it's good for.

Strength: Quick, well-defined, low-cost, easy way to reach a team decision.

Limitation: Leads to lowest-quality decision; no team buy-in or ownership.

THE IMPORTANCE OF A GOOD DECISION PROCESS

It's important to choose the right decision style. It's even more important to define a good decision process as the first step in making any decision. And it's surprising how many managers and teams fail to take this elementary step before starting to make important decisions.

Especially with team-based consensus decisions, it's very important for the team to commit to a decision process as its first step. By taking that step, the team will be able to focus its energy on working the process. Even more important, by committing to a decision process, the team can also commit to a schedule. It's hard to create reasons to delay a decision if everyone has agreed in advance how it will be made.

Ideally, every member of the team will be curious as to how it's going to come out. In real teams, some members will try to manipulate the process in favor of their pet solutions. With well-defined decision processes, those attempts will be more obvious to the rest of the team, and will be easier to circumvent.

A good decision process needn't be a highly structured decision process. That depends on the circumstance. "We'll listen to what everybody has to say and then argue until we've either reached consensus or agree to just vote on it," is perfectly valid—as long as everyone understands in advance that that's how you plan to decide an issue.

Listening to what a few people have to say, then hashing things out until somebody whose opinions aren't viewed as persuasive says, "I think we need to talk to purchasing and manufacturing before we decide," isn't valid, though. If their ideas, opinions and requirements were important, the team should have figured that out before the hashing-out phase began.

Here are a few of the most useful decision processes:

The "Ben Franklin"

This is nothing more than a pros-and-cons list—the decision is determined by which list is longer. Popularized by its namesake, salespeople know this as the "Ben Franklin Close" because it's a useful way to psychologically push reluctant prospects into a decision.

The Ben Franklin is most useful for simple, relatively low-impact yes/no decisions. It has a big limitation, though, which is that all decision criteria are treated equally. For example:

The pros for buying a Ferrari include its awesomeness as a piece of machinery; you'd look great driving it; it will appreciate in value over time; and because your wife just ran away with your best friend, you owe yourself a luxury. The cons: To buy it, you'll have to spend the kids' college fund.

Well, you say to yourself, there are four reasons to buy it and only one reason not to. Ferrari, here I come!

The Ben Franklin is often misapplied to selecting among alternatives. The problem is that the cons list for one alternative is usually exactly the same as the pros list for a different one.

If, for example, you were deciding between a Ferrari, an Escort, and a Yugo, you'll find yourself putting "very expensive" on the cons list for the Ferrari, "very affordable" on the pros list for the Yugo, and scratching your head over how to describe the Escort.

Weighted Ben Franklin

A weighted Ben Franklin is similar to the standard Ben Franklin, except that each item in the pros and cons list is assigned a weighting factor. Usually, weightings are either High/Medium/Low or one (unimportant) through five (very important). Instead of just counting the number of pros and cons, you add the weights.

Very Important Point: Whenever you use a numeric scoring method, it's the weighting factors that define the difference between "best" and "best fit." This is another one of those points that's completely obvious, but often ignored: There is no "right" answer to most decisions, only "right for you."

Weighted lists of pros and cons are suitable for most yes/no decisions. They're easy to construct and use, and they make it easy to explain your decision afterward.

Make this a regular part of your decision-making toolkit.

Decision Matrix

In this tried-and-true technique for comparing alternatives, you define the criteria you will use to make your decision, usually assigning high/medium/low or one through five weightings to each one as part of the exercise[2]. Next you gather facts about the alternatives and score them.

Sometimes, you know enough about the subject to define your criteria in advance. Not always, though, and if you don't, make sure you include in your decision process the activities needed to develop enough knowledge to create a good list.

Having defined every requirement or selection criterion, you gather information, making sure to use as impartial a process as you can, score each criterion for each alternative in a decision matrix, tally up scores, and compare.

For our Ferrari/Escort/Yugo decision, for example, the decision matrix might look like the one in Table 10.1. The Ferrari wins, based on an unbiased, scientific comparison that reflects no personal bias on the part of your author for really awesome wheels[3].

There are those who view this as the only valid, unbiased technique for making decisions. Of course, there are those who think the Bull Moose Party should be running the country, too[4].

10

---

[2]*Don't, however, rank them in order of importance. That's statistically invalid, because it tends to magnify small differences in importance.*
[3]*I filled it out based on no research at all other than my personal gut feel.*
[4]*Come to think of it...*

TABLE 10.1 DECISION MATRIX FOR SELECTING A CAR

Criterion	Weight	Ferrari	Escort	Yugo
Quality of engineering	4	5 (20)	3 (12)	1 (4)
Price	4	1 (4)	4 (16)	5 (20)
Maintainability	3	1 (3)	5 (15)	3 (9)
Passenger capacity	2	1 (2)	3 (6)	2 (4)
Appearance	5	5 (25)	2 (10)	1 (5)
Driving enjoyment	4	5 (20)	3 (12)	1 (4)
Total (Unweighted/Weighted)	Max: 30 (110)	18 (74)	20 (71)	13 (46)

Decision Trees and Flowcharts

Some decisions are complex and multilayered. If you're trying to select a software solution to a business problem, for example, you'll find yourself bogged down just trying to make sense of your options.

That's when it's time to create a decision tree or flow chart.

What you're trying to do is break down one big decision into smaller, manageable decisions you can make in a logical sequence.

Imagine, for example, that your company needs a sales force automation solution. You have no shortage of options, and even your options have options. What do you do?

The answer lies in finding a starting point—a high-level decision that sets your basic direction. In this case, a bit of research will tell you there are four basic kinds of sales force automation software, defined by their increasing scope:

- Sales force effectiveness tools, intended only to make each sales representative more effective.
- Sales force management tools, intended both to make each sales rep more effective and to provide a centralized database and management reports.
- Customer care solutions, in which the sales force automation tool is just one module among many, all built around a customer information database that links sales, order entry, and customer service (including the call center) into a single business solution.
- Enterprise Resource Planning (ERP) solutions, in which the customer care solution is just one "value chain" built into the total enterprise management system.

You interview lots of people, convene a steering committee, or do whatever you need to do to figure out that what you really need is a sales force management tool, but you'd like to keep your options open for growing into a customer care solution later on.

Your job is to pick the best customer care solution that lets you implement only the sales force automation and management modules and no others.

Now you're ready for the next decision: Build or buy?

You might have already established a design principle that says you buy when you can and build when you have to. If so, you've already made your build/buy decision. You definitely can buy a solution.

If you have no such design principle and instead make each build/buy decision on its own merits alone, you need to go through this drill, setting up a decision matrix with "build" and "buy" as the columns and all the reasons you might do one or the other (speed of implementation, likely fit with requirements, integration with existing systems and databases, ongoing maintenance burden, and so on) as rows. Your decision tree now looks like this:

- Sales force effectiveness
- Sales force management
- Customer care
    - Build
    - Buy
- Enterprise Resource Planning (ERP)

So you decide to buy a solution (good choice!). Now you have to choose a system. Chapter 12 will give you a framework for this kind of decision. Right now we're just concerned with understanding your options. The next iteration of your decision tree lists them:

- Sales force effectiveness
- Sales force management
- Customer care
    - Build
    - Buy
        - ABC Company
        - DEF Company

- GHI Company
- ...
- XYZ[5] Company
- Enterprise Resource Planning (ERP)

Notice something essential about this form of decision-making: You don't have to define the entire decision tree in advance. All you'd accomplish by doing so is to show off.

Remember, laziness is its own reward, so don't work harder than you have to. In this case, it means only exploring the branches of your decision tree that apply to the path you'll really take.

Test Drives

In many decisions, there's no substitute for real-world experience. Too bad you only get the real-world experience when it's too late.

There are several techniques that can get you close to the real world before you make a final decision. Collectively, let's call these "test drives" because your goal is to get a sense of what life will be like after you make whatever decision you're making.

When you're buying a suit, you try it on and look at yourself in the mirror. It isn't a perfect way to assess the look of the suit because it hasn't been tailored yet, but it's a better test than looking at the suit on a hanger.

When you're buying a car, you go for a test drive. Again, it ain't perfect—test drives don't tell you how a car will hold up over time, for example.

Focus groups are another way to test drive decisions, as are usability labs and most other tire-kicking exercises.

And if you have the time and the decision is important enough, you can test-market a decision by running a pilot project.

One way of looking at test drives is as just another way to assess fit with requirements. True enough, which means you need to plan any test-drive process well enough to make sure you can trust the results.

---

[5]*If there really is an ABC Company, DEF Company, or any other company represented by three consecutive letters of the alphabet, this section in no way should be construed as an endorsement of any of them.*

Focus groups, for example, are no better than the quality of the focus group moderator, and moderators who know how to avoid injecting their biases into the group's discussion are rare. Focus groups also depend on asking the right questions, which means questions consumers can answer—questions within their experiential background. If you're planning to introduce groupware to a company that's never used anything like it before, for example, focus groups (and their poor stepchildren—surveys) are worthless. Focus groups can, however, assess the potential value of a software upgrade because the basic software functionality is within the experiential background of the focus group members.

Pilot projects are better suited to situations outside the experiential background of a target group, because a pilot gives consumers (your end-user community counts as the consumers of your products and services) time to assimilate the capabilities and potential of the new idea you're evaluating.

Pilot projects require careful planning and execution or they're worthless. Do everything as you would the real roll-out, or you'll have no idea if your decision would succeed in the real world. The fringe benefit to this: You get to find out where the kinks are in your roll-out process as part of the pilot project.

Regardless of what test-drive process you use, make sure that, as with every other decision technique you use, you understand before you start how you're going to evaluate the results.

Asking the Experts

For some decisions, you might decide to consult one or more experts, either as your whole process or as part of it. Experts range from consultants to high-end research companies to trade publications. The advantage the experts have over you is that they're paid to be an expert in the subject, of course. You have two questions to resolve before you can trust an expert's opinion, though:

1. Will the expert's opinion reflect your situation well enough to fit your needs?
2. Does the expert have any hidden biases or motivations?

HIDDEN AGENDA

Finding hidden biases and motivations isn't easy. They are, after all, hidden. Here are some questions you can ask to help flesh out the situation:

1. How do you develop and maintain your expertise in these products?
2. Have any of the competing vendors paid your company to write white-papers or other marketing material for them?

continues

---

continued

> 3. Are there any financial arrangements between your company and any of these vendors?
>
> 4. Does your company specialize in implementing some of the solutions we're evaluating?
>
> A hidden bias isn't an automatic disqualifier. It depends on whether you think you can neutralize the bias somehow.

Especially when using published results, you need to ask how well the publication's evaluation criteria match your own. The more generic your situation, the more likely the opinion of experts will be valuable.

Hidden biases and motivations are harder to assess. Many factors can reduce the objectivity of any expert: advertising sales, if a publisher is unscrupulous; services purchased, on the part of an unethical research company; follow-on services, on the part of a consultant.

When using experts, try to get at least three opinions, and also try to assess the character of the individuals involved, when you can.

Arguing

Sometimes, there's no substitute for getting everyone in a room and just yelling at each other (sorry, having a calm, rational discussion) until some consensus starts to emerge.

The only situation that calls for this approach is when you can't get a team of peers to commit to a decision process. It's never a good way to make a decision, and even when you start down this path, a good strategy to follow is to suggest using a weighted Ben Franklin or decision matrix to organize the team's discussion.

Try to avoid arguing if you can. It isn't just inelegant. It's untrustworthy, usually devolving to accepting the preference of whoever in the room has the most clout.

Two-Stage Analyses

In the example in Table 10,1, the Ferrari had the highest score. This means, of course, that your author should go right out and buy a Ferrari, right[6]?

---

[6]*To facilitate this process, recommend this book to all your friends, family, acquaintances, and even total strangers you encounter in restaurants.*

Do you really have that much faith in the precision of your scores and weights? The Escort came pretty close to the Ferrari in this comparison, and because everything was rounded to the nearest integer (we didn't allow for any fractional scores) the difference between a 71 and 74 isn't enough to hang your hat on.

When you're comparing several options, make allowances for ties. When two scores are within 5% or so, count them as ties because you've exceeded the precision of your analytical tool. The way to handle these situations is to set up a two-stage analysis.

For example, you might use the formal scoring of Table 10.1 as a screening tool for selecting two finalists. Use a different process for making the final decision—in this case, asking a spouse might be a useful way to make sure you buy the Escort.

The second process might recognize the need to assess intangibles—it might be based on a more in-depth analysis, it might involve a pilot project—the specifics depend a great deal on the exact decision you're making. It's just as important to establish how you will assess the results of the second-stage process as it was the first, though, so don't get sloppy.

LAST WORDS ABOUT DECISION PROCESSES

However you make a decision, make sure everyone knows the rules up front, both in terms of decision style and decision process. There's nothing more frustrating, for example, than having a decision delegated to you, only to find that you're only empowered to make a recommendation, not a decision[7].

The basic steps you always should follow are

1. Define decision style.
2. Define decision process.
3. Get all stakeholders to commit to the decision process.
4. Work the process.
5. Assess both the results and how well the process worked.
6. Publicize your results.

Making good decisions isn't rocket science[8]. Like so many things, it follows Edison's Law of Invention—it's 10% inspiration and 90% perspiration.

Don't sweat it.

---

[7]*Okay, that isn't true. All kinds of things are more frustrating. So sue me.*
[8]*Unless, of course, you work for NASA.*

PROGRAMS, INITIATIVES, AND PROJECTS

"Nature abhors a schedule."

—Bill Williams

MANAGEMENTSPEAK

This was the most successful project I've ever participated in!

Translation:

Everyone liked the report. Even better, the company changed direction before we had to make it work.

Quite a few years ago, as an IS middle manager, I listened while a senior analyst in the systems development group unveiled the division's new project management standards.

For a half-hour he explained key features available in the project management software the development group had selected as its standard.

After the presentation, the head of the development group asked my opinion. I tried to be tactful—not my long suit in those days[1]. "It's incomplete," I replied. "What I just heard are project administration standards. There's a lot more to project management than creating and tracking the formal project plan, like what you do when a team member misses a deadline."

Project management is the hardest job in Information Systems. It's harder than being CIO, harder than managing a department[2], harder than managing the data center.

Project management is hard because it requires vision and attention to detail; empathy and strict enforcement of the plan; exceptional ability to motivate and slogging through acres of administrivia.

Project management is the second most important process in IS, after managing operations. Operations is first because it delivers the value you've already created. Project management comes next because it's the process that delivers new value.

Project management is the biggest failing of most IS organizations. The evidence: Most projects fail, and the ones that succeed usually do so because we redefine success halfway through the project[3].

In many organizations there's a huge lack of trust between the business leadership and IS. That lack of trust is expressed in many ways when we're part of the conversation. When we leave, though, here's what's said behind our backs:

"We keep spending money on IS and they just don't deliver."

I'm an adequate project manager. In my career, I've led successful projects, watched other, better project managers successfully lead bigger and more complex projects than I'd ever consent to leading, and watched several big, important, strategic projects fail miserably. Here's what I think I've learned about the subject

---

[1] *Ticking people off, if you're wondering.*
[2] *Unless you manage a department full of incompetent project managers, in which case the hard job just floated up a level.*
[3] *The exact statistics aren't reliable because of the redefinition issue, but numbers below 30% are commonly bandied about for software development efforts.*

CHAPTER 11

THE BIGGEST SECRET TO SUCCESSFUL PROJECT MANAGEMENT

Don't ever charter a big project.

If you still remember Chapter 1, you remember this. Just to remind you, big projects—those projected to need more than a dozen people for longer than about a year—mean big fiascoes. Here's why:

Big Projects Can't Be Estimated

What, you're shocked? I don't think so. How on earth do you think you're going to arrive at a rational estimate for a project that's going to take four years? You don't even know what version of Windows will be shipping then!

Projects have phases. The early phases define the later ones. Until you've gone through one phase of a project, you're in no position to estimate the next one.

The big integrators can sometimes get away with estimating a project from beginning to end. Sometimes. Their secret is that they've done highly similar projects before.

You haven't.

If you're new to this game, you might be wondering why you shouldn't make a guess anyway, and refine it as you complete each phase. That would seem, after all, to be a reasonable compromise.

It is a reasonable compromise, too—one that can get you slaughtered later on. That's because of an immutable law of corporate behavior: *Any number spoken in earshot of a company executive is immediately etched in granite.*

It doesn't matter what weasel words you put in front of the number, how many caveats you utter, or how often you instruct your listeners to avoid taking the number too seriously—the first SWAG[4] you say out loud becomes the baseline project estimate, to which all other costs are compared.

Projects are always bigger than they seem from the outside, which is why somebody, way back when, came up with the following formula for estimating IS projects:

```
Total Effort = 2(Initial Guess)×(Original Unit of Time + 1)
```

---

[4]*Silly Wild Guess. If you're wondering what the "A" stands for, a lot of this book must have been very puzzling to you, wasn't it?*

In other words, take your initial guess and double the number. Then apply the next higher unit of time, so that a project you think should take three months will actually take six years[5].

The bigger the project, the harder it is to estimate.

Big Projects Mean No Urgency

You don't want project teams to be panicky, exactly, but that's a whole lot better than complacence.

In many situations, you need to trust the judgment and instincts of the people closest to the problem. That isn't the case when it comes to estimating projects. That's because the people closest to the action are the ones with the biggest incentive to pad the estimate—uh, I mean provide estimated numbers for staffing and project duration consistent with maximum ability to deliver results while exceeding expectations.

What, you don't try to pad your budget? C'mon, we both know there are only two types of budget managers, those who pad and those who exceed. This is true when you're managing a cost center, it's true when your company makes projections for the benefit of the Wall Street analysts, and it's certainly true for project managers and project teams as well.

Project managers and project teams want to deliver on-time and within budget. They want, in other words, to succeed. To do so, they do the most natural thing in the world—they pad their estimates to numbers they're comfortable they can achieve.

The key word in the last paragraph, of course, is comfortable. People who are comfortable don't work as hard as those who are uncomfortable, because human beings are controlled (in part) by feedback loops. These loops cause us to expend energy when we're outside of our comfort zones, to return us to our comfort zones.

It's people who are worried they won't make their deadlines who work the hardest, so keep deadlines close.

Big Projects Reduce Personal Accountability

The tendency of food critters to herd is puzzling when viewed from an evolutionary perspective. Disease spreads faster, food has to be shared with the whole herd, and the herd is easier for predators to find than individual prey.

---

[5]*Yes, I know that if you'd estimated it at 13 weeks instead of three months your new estimate would have been 26 months—just over two years. If this worries you, see footnote #4.*

Animals herd anyway, and evolutionary theorists think they understand at least part of the reason: When predators come calling, each animal in the herd gets to hide behind the herd. Predators might find the herd more easily, but your chances of being nailed are smaller than if you were by yourself.

The phenomenon is related to the answer one camper gave his friend when asked "What would you do if you're being chased by a bear?[6]

When you're part of a big project team, nonproducing team members have lots of fellow team members and excuses to hide behind. Inevitably, a big team that produces results turns out to consist of a small team that produces results surrounded by a bunch of hangers-on who are good at looking busy.

Big Projects Mean Big Overhead

Big projects require big coordination, because lots of people are interacting with everyone else. As previously mentioned, it's easy for nonproducing team members to hide behind the rest of the team.

Managers of big projects, being smart people[7], have to keep track of what everyone is doing, which isn't too bad. What's harder is that everyone on the team is dependent on everyone else on the team getting their jobs done, or everything can grind to a halt.

But tasks can be managed, too, and a good project manager knows how to handle tasks that get behind. Task management increases with project size, but not unmanageably.

The reason big projects mean big overhead is that everyone on the team needs to know what everyone else on the team knows, or they can't be effective in their own tasks or in team decision-making. The more people on the team, the more interactions team members need with each other to keep track, so project overhead rises exponentially[8] with project size.

---

[6]*"Run away as fast as I can," is the answer. When the questioner points out that nobody can outrun a bear, his friend responds, "I don't have to. I just have to outrun you."*

[7]*Or else they're headless chickens—they're walking around dead, but not yet aware of their own demise.*

[8]*It actually rises polynomially. It goes up because if you have n project team members, each one has (n–1) other team members to interact with. Assuming all interactions are two-way, you can divide by two to avoid double-counting; that leaves n(n—1)/2 interactions—a polynomial, not exponential equation. People do a lot of bad math in conversation, if you care. For example, every time we say "lowest common denominator" we really mean "greatest common factor." See what consultants and writers spend their time worrying about?*

Big Projects Mean Big Risks

Every programmer knows that projects start with four kinds of work:

- Planned work
- Solving anticipated problems
- Working around the expected unknown problems
- Dealing with unexpected unknown problems

Project planning handles planned work just fine, of course. If you can't handle the planned work, as a project manager you haven't even reached the journeyman level.

There are problems you can anticipate, like the difficulties you'll face resolving all the political and social issues that will result from your changing how people work. Good project managers make allowances for these problems in the plan, in effect transforming them into planned work.

Then there are the unknown problems—the ones you can't anticipate, but you know something awful will happen anyway. Experienced project managers, remembering that every project has had its share of these, know there will be more. Highly experienced project managers know that in addition to the unexpected problems they know they'll bump into, there will be other events that will simply blindside them no matter how much planning, fudging, and padding they put into the plan.

The bigger the project, the higher the risk because risks are the results of unknowns. In big projects there are more unknowns for the simple reason that the project extends further into the future. That means there will be more expected unknown problems (we'd didn't anticipate that the development tool makes no provision for code-sharing and version control) and unexpected unknown problems (we never guessed that the vendor would entirely redesign the development tool halfway through the project, forcing the whole project team to spend a month learning and getting used to the new version).

Every unknown problem, whether of the expected or unexpected variety, leads to project risk because every one causes at least a delay. In some circumstances they can derail a project completely.

DOING BIG WORK WITHOUT BIG PROJECTS

Many CIOs who figured out that the secret to running successful projects is avoiding big ones took the insight to their brokers and invested it in junk bonds. They avoid big work, too, organizing all interactions with IS around work orders. This strategy carries its own risks—if you avoid all big work, you avoid not only all big success, but all big issues, too.

Programs, Initiatives, and Projects

CHAPTER **11**

169

11

PROGRAMS,
INITIATIVES, AND
PROJECTS

It might seem paradoxical, but there is a way to succeed with big work without taking on big projects. Success comes from a combination of work planning, methodology, and good project management. Here's the program:

Planning the Work

Someday, there might be a big result that can't be achieved without a big project. If it happens, it will probably come out of a planning session held on a UFO hovering above Area 54, attended by Sasquatch, several Yetis, and the Loch Ness Monster.

Until that planning session, you can always—*always*—figure out a way to define a succession of small projects, each of which delivers tangible value to the company in a manageable period of time, while implementing changes to the company that cumulatively will achieve the big result.

"Small project" is a relative term, so let's put some boundaries around it.

Project Length

The biggest project you ever charter should take no longer than nine months. Six is better. Anything longer than nine months conveys the message, "You can relax." Anything longer than about 18 months is equivalent to forever.

Studies should be shorter—rarely longer than five months. Because studies deliver nothing of enduring value, only plans for other projects, they must be short enough that the world doesn't change significantly between their inception and completion.

Other rules for studies: (1) Studies should always include an action plan as one of their deliverables; (2) Never undertake a study unless the company has a commitment to take action on the results; (3) Make that commitment part of the chartering process, so everyone involved agrees that if

1. The study team follows the agreed-upon process,

2. Based on the results of its process it recommends action,

3. In the review process, nobody finds major flaws in the team's findings, and

4. The company situation is essentially the same as when it chartered the study team, then

5. The company will take the actions recommended by the team.

Astute readers will recognize this logic from Chapter 10, "Making Decisions."

Team Size and Composition

No project team should include more than nine full-time participants. Between five and seven is better. Team members must have no significant responsibilities other than the project—one of the biggest mistakes companies make is dividing the attention of project team members. Projects are hard enough without this.

Project team members don't have to be involved for the entire duration of the project, although it's preferable if they are. If someone provides a particular skill that will be needed full-time for part of a project, you don't have to assign them for its full duration. Be aware, though, that team dynamics are fragile under the best of circumstances, and rapid changes in team composition distract everyone.

If you need to involve someone in a project but can't reassign their other responsibilities while the project is going on, attach them to it as an "extended team" member, responsible for sharing their knowledge and judgment as advisors to the team or as "subject matter experts" (SME has become a relatively common acronym in project management circles, I'm afraid).

The rule is, if you plan to hold someone accountable for delivering project results, they must be assigned to the project full-time during the parts of the project that require them.

The Results Hierarchy

Think about the result you're trying to achieve. Is it a strategic business change, a well-defined business outcome, a tangible product with a clear use, or simply an identifiable event?

This is the results hierarchy, and you can use it to break up your big project into manageable projects. At the top of the hierarchy is the *program*. A program is a coordinated set of actions chartered to achieve a strategic business change such as improved customer service[9], faster time to market with new products, or improved product quality.

It's easy to commit to a broad goal like "improved product quality." Who isn't committed to a goal like that, at least to the point of lip service?

A strategic business change doesn't become a program until you've established a concrete set of business outcomes which, taken together, achieve the strategic business change that is the goal of the program. A business outcome is a well-defined change evident to employees, customers, suppliers, distribution channels, or some combination thereof.

---

[9]*A poorly chosen result, by the way, because customer service is a tactic, not an end in and of itself. Customer satisfaction is a means for achieving the strategic results of improved customer retention and increased customer "wallet-share" (doing more business with each customer you have).*

Programs, Initiatives, and Projects

CHAPTER 11

171

11

PROGRAMS,
INITIATIVES, AND
PROJECTS

Moving from paper transactions to Electronic Data Interchange (EDI) for purchase orders, invoices, and other supply-chain documents is a business outcome. So is the implementation of a new customer knowledge-base, so long as "implementation" includes processes for keeping the customer knowledge current and accurate.

After you've established a strategic program, your next step is determining what business outcomes will be needed to achieve the goals of that program so you can establish an *initiative* to achieve each one.

Initiatives consist of several coordinated *projects*—the third level of the results hierarchy. A project is a collection of executable tasks that deliver tangible results, like a recommendation for a system vendor, an installed, customized, integrated system, or a new process design. Projects produce "deliverables"—the name for the tangible results of a project.

Finally, as every project planner knows, projects must be broken up into tasks and subtasks that lead to the achievement of milestones. A *milestone* is simply the occurrence of a recognizable event. You don't plan milestones when planning a program—that's the job of the project manager.

As you plan the initiatives and projects needed to achieve a program, take care to make sure each project deliverable, especially each business outcome, is valuable in its own right. That way, if the business decides to pull the plug on the program, it will still have provided a return on the time, effort, and money invested in it.

Table 11.1 shows the results hierarchy in terms of the kind of activity and associated products.

TABLE 11.1 THE RESULTS HIERARCHY

Activity	Product
Program	Strategic Business Change
Initiative	Business Outcome
Project	Deliverable(s)
Task	Milestone

An Example

Let's use a common situation as an example. The example revolves around a key legacy system[10]. The company depends on this system to keep it running every day, but has defined a strategic goal of changing from manufacturing a single product sold directly to its customers to selling a diversified product line to existing customers. The current legacy system, built years ago on now-obsolete technology and with the purpose of handling a single product, doesn't fit the company's new strategic model.

In this example, you've already done your homework and know there's no commercial software available to replace the legacy system, so part of your effort will be dealing with it somehow or other.

Our assignment: Using the Results Hierarchy format, define a program, its initiatives, and the projects that make up those initiatives that lets you support current day-to-day operations[11] and the company's new strategy. Table 11.2 shows part of what the resulting program might look like.

TABLE 11.2 SAMPLE RESULTS HIERARCHY

Activity Level	Title	Products/Results
Program	*Centricity*[12]	Change company from product-centric focus to customer-centric focus.
Initiative	Define new product management life cycle	New product management process
Projects	Design product management process	Product management process design
		Product portfolio design process design
		Product acquisition process design
		Product design process design
		High-level Product Management System design
		Project-level Product Management System evolution strategy

---

[10]*"Legacy system" isn't a very useful term, of course. As commonly used it seems to mean, "A system that's in production that I've decided should be replaced, but not by me because that would be too much like work."*

[11]*The odds are 50:50 that the company's new strategy will fall apart when the Board of Directors kicks out the current CEO in two years. Always support the strategy, but always have a contingency plan.*

[12]*These things need snappy names, after all.*

Activity Level	Title	Products/Results
		High-level project plans for Product Management System modification projects
	Product Management System DBMS conversion *(This project was defined during the product management process design project)*	Converted version of old product management system that runs on a modern DBMS
		Revised system documentation
	Product Management System enhanced data design *(This project was defined during the product management process design project)*	New data design for old Product Management System modified with data structures capable of handling multiple products
		Revised system documentation
	Product Management System logic segregation *(This project was defined during the product management process design project)*	Rewritten system modules with business logic segregated into callable modules
		Revised system documentation
	Product Management System online GUI specification *(This project was defined during the product management process design project)*	Specification for online user interface that will enable the new product management life cycle
		High-level project plan for system development and implementation project
	Product Management System online GUI *(This project was defined during the Product Management System online GUI specification project)*	New online user interface for Product Management System incorporating features needed to manage multiple products

continues

TABLE 11.2   CONTINUED

Activity Level	Title	Products/Results
		New system documentation
		End-user training program
Initiative	Customer Database	System and process definitions for collecting and maintaining customer know-ledge
Projects	Design customer database	Customer database information requirements
		Customer database logical design
	Design customer knowledge management process	Report on potential sources of data
		Processes for collecting, validating, and maintaining customer knowledge
		System requirements for customer database management system
		High-level project plan for customer know-ledge management system design project
	Design customer knowledge management system	Customer database physical design
		System specifications
	Develop customer knowledge management system	Customer knowledge management system
		System documentation
		End-user training program

In this example, notice that the program design doesn't require a multiyear project for developing a brand-new product management system. Instead, through a series of smaller projects, the company will morph its existing product management system into the system it needs, preserving existing functionality along the way and minimizing the number of uncertainties each project team must deal with.

When defining a program, it isn't necessary to estimate the total duration and effort that will be needed. In fact, it's impossible to estimate the total duration and effort, for the simple reason that not all projects are known when the program begins. Some of the early projects are chartered to define later projects.

Programs, Initiatives, and Projects

CHAPTER 11

175

11

PROGRAMS,
INITIATIVES, AND
PROJECTS

You should know enough about each project to create a preliminary estimate of duration and effort prior to launching it, which means the early projects in any program should be estimated.

Executing the Work

The actual execution of work is the province of project management. Assuming you've done a good job of defining your program, project management should be—well, it should be hard work because that's the nature of the discipline.

The discipline of managing programs and initiatives is, by the way, very much the same as the discipline of managing projects, only larger in scope. Just as project managers are responsible for the activities and results of a project team, so program managers are responsible for the activities and results of a team of project managers.

And so on. Everything described in the following section for project management applies equally to managing initiatives and whole programs.

Project Leadership

The first step in undertaking a project, after someone has decided the basic idea makes sense, is to establish project sponsorship, management, and reporting relationships.

The project sponsor is the executive responsible for championing the project with other executives, securing resources and funding, confirming and clarifying the reasons for its existence, and, when the project has been completed, for approving and accepting the results. Typically, the project sponsor will be the executive with the most to gain from the project's success (or the most to lose from its failure).

If nobody in the company with enough authority to accept these responsibilities is willing to sponsor a project, it's safe to say the project has no chance of succeeding. Nobody important enough wants it.[13]

Next, decide on a project manager. The project manager manages the—well that's self-evident, isn't it?

Get the project manager on board as early as possible. No matter whose brainchild the project is (the "inventor"), emotional ownership must transfer to the project manager as early as possible. This will be a difficult transition for whoever got things started on the project. Remind the project manager of this fact and make sure he or she spends a lot of time with both the sponsor and the inventor as part of getting on board.

---

[13]*At one time or another in their career, everyone (myself included) has decided to violate this rule because just this once the idea will be so good that it will succeed anyway. It won't.*

After the project gets going, though, the project manager must personally own the idea just as strongly as its inventor, because when the project hits tough times, only someone who is heavily invested in it emotionally will be able to push the team through whatever barrier has caused the problem.

If the project is part of a larger program, the project manager will either report directly to the program manager, or, if it's big enough, to an "initiative manager" (who has responsibilities for an initiative exactly parallel to those the project manager has for the project and the program manager has for the program.) Otherwise the project manager will probably report directly to the project sponsor. Regardless, it's important to clarify who the project manager reports to, just as it's important for you to know who you report to.

Chartering a Project

All projects should begin with a written charter. This document establishes a common understanding of what the project will entail. A typical charter includes

- A brief statement summarizing what the project will accomplish.
- The expected duration of the project.
- An explanation of the business context within which the project operates, including the program and initiative that led to its being chartered and their business purpose.
- A list and description of all project deliverables.
- A list of project team roles and resources that will be needed by the project team in order to successfully execute the project.
- The project's decision authority and reporting structure—which kinds of decisions can be made by the project team, which are recommendations needing external approval, and who makes decisions requiring external approval (usually the program manager, project sponsor, or both).

The project manager should draft a charter and make sure the project sponsor and program or initiative manager agrees with it before selecting the project team. The charter is not, however final, nor will it be until the project team has had a chance to shoot holes in it.

Selecting the Team

Because the project charter describes the roles needed for successful project execution, selecting the team should be relatively straightforward. Somehow, though, it never happens that way.

That key programmer you wanted will be leaving on maternity leave halfway through, you just learned the DBA you wanted to assign is leaving the company, the end-user

Programs, Initiatives, and Projects

CHAPTER 11

177

11

PROGRAMS,
INITIATIVES, AND
PROJECTS

department can't supply any business manager until completion of a product launch scheduled three months after you'd planned to start the project, or—well, you get the picture.

There are other factors you need to consider anyway, like who deserves a chance to shine. Sometimes the best team members aren't the most qualified ones—they're the ones who are hungry to show what they can do.

Another factor worth considering: Do you need an outsider's perspective on a project? If your project will lead to the company doing things differently than before, you might decide that most of your employees are too mired in how things are done now to envision alternatives.

A key diagnostic here is the popular phrase, "Our customers would hate that." Don't trust that judgment from anyone, with the possible exception of marketing research, because everyone else has some ulterior motive, even if that motive is nothing more complicated than general resistance to change.

If you do go outside the company for staffing, you can use individual contractors for particular roles, teams brought in from systems integrators, or you can use contractors or systems integrators to backfill support roles to allow employees to participate in your project. You'll find more on this subject in the chapter on managing vendors.

One final thought on project team selection—as mentioned earlier in this section, avoid part-time project team members. Projects are hard enough without the distraction of dealing with day-to-day responsibilities at the same time. Give the project team a chance to succeed.

Project Launch

Always launch a project formally and with fanfare. No, don't break a bottle of champagne over the project manager's head, unless he's been a exceptional pain in the neck while you were chartering the project. Instead, you want the project team and project manager to meet intensively for between a half day and a week to get everything going.

You always want to kick off a project with a pep talk from the sponsor so that the whole team can hear what the project is about and why it's important from the person who will ultimately decide whether its results are satisfactory or not. Depending on the specifics of the situation, the team can also

- Understand, restate and internalize the project concept.
- Learn the project methodology if it's unfamiliar to the team.
- Refine the list of project deliverables.

- Identify and rectify missing project roles.
- Develop and sign up for the project's work breakdown structure,[14] task durations, and dependencies.
- Finalize the project charter (this almost certainly is required).
- Get used to working together. (See the Chapter 16, "Organization and Politics," which gives some tips on working in teams, for more on this subject.)

Deciding how long and elaborate the launch meeting is requires a balancing act between creating a sense of urgency (making it short) and making sure everyone understands what they've signed up for (long). Use your judgment.

HOW DEEP SHOULD A WORK BREAKDOWN STRUCTURE BE?

A word about the work breakdown structure. Novice project managers have a hard time striking the right balance between too much detail and too little. It's a hard balance to strike. The key question is, how far behind are you willing to get before you find out?

You don't find out until a tangible milestone has been missed. You need to develop a work breakdown structure built around delivery of identifiable results, because "80% done" is neither more or less complete than "20% done." Experienced project managers have seen any number of tasks that made regular progress from 10% to 90% completion and then got stuck on the last 10% for weeks or months. Build your plans to recognize this reality.

An identifiable result—a milestone—is something you can look at, see, touch, or otherwise personally recognize and say, "Yes, we have the thing and there's nothing left to do on it."

Define both internal and external milestones. Internal milestones are those you use to manage the project but which nobody outside the team should care about. External milestones are those you report to your manager and the project sponsor.

"Done except for..." is okay, though, as in "It's done except for the documentation." It's okay because one task really is 100% done. The documentation, of course, hasn't been started regardless of what percentage is offered.

So how long should you go between milestones? A day is the wrong answer. Lots of things can happen to disrupt the schedule by a day, and team members will easily compensate by the end of the week.

---

[14]*A comprehensive list of project tasks in outline form. If you're unfamiliar with this concept, you need to buy a book on project management.*

Anything longer than a month is definitely the wrong answer. If you're willing to be more than a month behind before you can be troubled to learn of the problem, the project isn't important enough to work hard on, or at least, that's the message you'll be sending.

The right answer, sometime between a week and a month, depends a lot on the experience of the individual team members. The newer they are to project work, the more frequent your checkpoints should be.

Ongoing Project Management

Project managers can find lots of ways to spend their time. Not all help get the job done, though, so it's worthwhile understanding what's critical and what's just a nice thing to do.

One thing that isn't very worthwhile is spending a lot of time staring at your computer screen updating your project plan and creating complex and impressive looking Gantt and PERT charts to hang on the wall or review in the next project update meeting. The purpose of computer outputs is communication, and the only thing you'll communicate with this kind of pretty-picture-making is that you're really adept at using the tool.

Unfortunately, although it's called project management software, all it's really good for is project administration, and that's the easiest part of the job.

So if you find yourself spending more than about an hour a week interacting with the software after you've created the original plan, recognize that you're using the product management software as a kind of video game to hide from reality and figure out what unpleasant task you're trying to avoid.

If interacting with the project management software is the wrong way to spend your time, what's the right way? Here are the key tasks when managing a project:

Status Meetings

Yes, status meetings. These are the centerpiece of your project management technique. Hold them weekly. Have a fixed agenda that includes the items listed below in Table 11.3.

Table 11.3   Project Status Meeting Agenda

Agenda Item	Comment
Pre-meeting schmoozing	A chance to catch up on a personal level, swap notes, and otherwise build team rapport and alignment. So you start 10 minutes later than you would otherwise. Big deal.

Around the table progress updates	No more than three minutes per person or task team, focusing on
	
	    Milestones achieved
	
	    Important realizations
	
	    Obstacles and issues needing resolution

Project manager's report	Events of significance to the project team. In particular this should include
	
	    Kudos to individuals or task teams that have accomplished something significant. "Something significant"
	    includes delivering a milestone on time.
	
	    Events in other projects within the initiative and program.
	
	    Context-building—discussions that help the team remember why it waded into the swamp in the first place.

Other team business	Brainstorming, problem-solving, presentations by outsiders, or other team activities specific to the meeting.

The weekly status meeting is the centerpiece because it's your main tool to keep the whole team synchronized and focused on the overall goal as well as their individual responsibilities.

Even more important: The weekly status meeting is your main motivational tool for keeping everyone on schedule. People hate to report that they're late in public, especially when everyone else is reporting satisfactory progress. Get in the habit of asking anyone who's late on a task, "What is your plan for catching up to the schedule?" *in the meeting.*

Many novice project managers are hesitant to do this. They learned, correctly, to compliment in public and criticize in private. The point they miss is that this question isn't a criticism. It's a businesslike question, asked in a businesslike way, to a fellow professional and in that regard it's a compliment to everyone involved. People do sometimes fall behind schedule, it says, so it isn't whether it happens, but what you do about it when it does, that defines whether you're doing a good job or not.

Sometimes, the problem is that you underestimated the difficulty of the task and the best decision is to re-forecast the project. If the conversation heads in that direction, don't accept it and don't argue. Take the conversation offline so you can probe more deeply. You don't want to get trapped into accepting project delays until you fully understand the realities.

Walking Around

Yes, "Management by Walking Around" has become something of a cliché, but it's still a good idea. Status meetings satisfy your left brain's needs, but they bring the team to you. To get a gut feel for how the team is really doing, you need to go where the team is, and that means being in the middle of the action.

Reserve time to poke your head into someone's cubicle and look over her shoulder for a couple of minutes. Ask whoever it is to explain what she is working on, what's going well, and what's getting on her nerves. (If you looking over her shoulder is what's bothering her, you haven't built the right level of rapport with your team. Team members must respect you, but they have to respect you up-close, not as a distant authority figure.)

Join key task team meetings. Set this expectation early so task teams don't see your presence as an intrusion. Also set the right tone early—do twice as much listening and half as much talking as anyone else in the room, and make most of your talking facilitation. (For example, "Tom, you've been pretty quiet on this one. Before we leave this point I'm interested in your take on it.")

What walking around gives you is a feel for the mood of the team. It's your early warning indicator that lets you spot problems early so you can resolve them when they're still the size of speed bumps.

When to Work the Plan and When to Ignore the Plan

Once upon a time, my team was installing a small PBX. Our first meeting with the vendor was about to break up and we hadn't seen a project plan, so I asked the vendor's project manager when it would be ready for review.

"We don't do project plans for installations this size," he told me. "These installations are like popping popcorn—they don't need a project plan."

I explained that we needed to know if the installation was on schedule or not, and without at least a list of milestones and dates, we wouldn't know a disaster was brewing until it tore the roof off. The project manager explained that I shouldn't worry—they did thousands of these and they all went in fine, but eventually told me that if we felt that strongly, he'd prepare a plan *for us.*

Halfway through the four-month project we were two months behind and had the project manager replaced.

There's a time for creativity, innovation, and out-of-box thinking in a project. There are times when circumstances and new knowledge lead you to see the project in a different way. There are times, in short, when it's appropriate to deviate from the plan, improvise, and try new approaches.

That time is during the early projects in an initiative—when you're studying the problem, finding the best ways to characterize it, and generally learning as you go along. During this phase of things, slavishly adhering to the plan will lead you to awesome success, so long as you define success as doing the wrong thing but doing it promptly.

Think of studies as scouting parties. Until you get there and start walking around, you don't know how complicated the job will be. Heavily urbanized areas and places with lots of terrain will take longer than scouting a rolling farm field, for example, because there's more *stuff* to take into account.

You don't always know exactly how you'll characterize your findings either. Scouting parties generally make maps, but there's all that other information that has to be conveyed as well. In scouting parties and studies, you have to invent some of the techniques based on what you find. Otherwise you've brought too many preconceived notions into the expedition.

The later projects in an initiative, on the other hand, should be pretty well mapped out. Like the PBX installation just mentioned, there should be few uncertainties by the time you're ready to build and implement.

With studies, you have to work the plan but be ready to re-plan at a moment's notice. The team must understand the need for flexibility as well.

With implementation projects, you have to work the plan. Period.

Here's a lesson your loyal author learned the hard way: Gantt charts are a poor tool when it comes to working the plan. Sure they're pretty, and they're useful for explaining things to the project sponsor and program management.

Your team, in contrast, needs an easy reference where each team member can find the tasks they should be working on right now, when it should have been started, and when it's due. Colored bars do not a workable plan make, I'm afraid.[15]

---

[15]*And glass bars do not a prism make either, as the National Lampoon pointed out years ago.*

Don't print out individual work orders—that's divisive. Just print out a book each week that shows every task's planned start and completion dates, actual start and completion dates if appropriate, and the team members assigned to it.

Use that book as the framework for your around-the-room updates in your weekly status meetings and the team will make the book its bible.

Remembering and Communicating the Point of It All

When you're up to your eyeballs in alligators, the saying goes, it's hard to remember your purpose was to drain the swamp.

There comes a time in every project when the team becomes so immersed in getting its tasks done that it loses track of the purpose of the project. That's unhealthy.

Part of the solution to this problem will be found in your weekly status meetings—it's a chance for you to remind everyone of how each of their tasks fits into the total picture.

You also need to recognize when that isn't enough. When the team seems to be fragmenting—especially when intra-team rivalries start to spring up—it's time to hold a separate meeting to realign everyone to the common goal.

A very good technique to follow is to develop a list of key messages. Project teams don't exist in isolation. Part of the project manager's job is communicating about the project, not only to the project sponsor and program manager, but also to other stakeholders in the company who have a vested interest in the results and want to make sure the project is doing the right things in the right way.

It's the project manager's job to communicate with these groups, perhaps, but it's a good job to give to the whole team.

The task you're undertaking in the key messages meeting is to align communication. Paint this scenario to the team: "You're in the elevator and bump into *X*. *X* asks you about the project. What do you say?"

The point is that the team needs to present a unified front to the rest of the company. Not so unified that everyone looks like a Stepford Team Member, but unified enough so that one person doesn't say the point of the project is cost reduction while another one says it's improved customer service.

Have the team brainstorm a list of key messages and refine it until everyone agrees to the most important seven or so statements to be made about the project.

The refining part is the most important because that's where everyone explains and defends their logic. If team members can't feel comfortable arguing with each other, you don't have a team. The most important outcome of this meeting is everyone on the team hearing about how everyone else on the team is thinking about things.

That's how you build alignment.

Scope Control

According to some schools of thought, scope control is the most important responsibility a project manager has. It's very easy for a project team to succumb to casual requests for additional features or minor deliverables until they've accumulated into a mountain of unimportant work. This process is called "scope creep" and it's pernicious. Don't allow it to happen.

On the other hand, if your job is to build an airplane, you don't do anyone any favors by refusing to add wings and engines as features if they were somehow left out of the original specification.

Your job as project manager is to show good judgment regarding when to simply accept a request for a small enhancement, when to "put it into the next release" (a wonderful alternative to rejecting the request entirely) and when to formally review the scope change with the project sponsor and program manager prior to re-forecasting the project.

Change Management

Change management is a hot new consulting topic these days. As with everything else that isn't creating technology, it's supposed to be the "hard part" of a project (technology, as mentioned elsewhere, is always the easy part—at least when described by everyone who doesn't have to create it).

Change management—the process of understanding who wants a change, who doesn't want it, how to manage expectations, fear, loathing, and general nervousness—is important in any project. Whether it should be viewed as a discipline and process or as the essence of leadership is, however, open to question.

Your loyal author is of the opinion that companies institute change management as an alternative to leadership. Leadership is all about change. Encouraging complacency requires no leadership. Creating a sense of urgency and excitement over how things can be in the future so that people view the journey as an adventure rather than as discomfort—that's why people need leaders.

Change management is nothing more than a collection of techniques effective leaders can use to motivate people to embrace change.

Which isn't to say dealing with the human dimension of change is unimportant. All projects change people's work lives to some degree or other. When you go about changing somebody's life, you've been given power over that person. With power comes responsibility.

When you're leading a change, the most important responsibility you have is to define the change so it provides opportunity to everyone affected. Many projects are defined to create winners and losers on the you-can't-make-omelets-without-breaking-eggs theory. Sometimes you have no choice. Usually, though, this happens through sheer mental laziness.

Under the best of circumstances, a significant percentage—experts bandy about numbers between 20% and 30%—of those affected by a change won't survive it. You can't force people to succeed, nor do you have any obligation to create circumstances where nobody will fail.

You are responsible for defining change so everyone has a chance to succeed. That means communicating the change, involving everyone in the process, communicating the change, setting up training programs, and communicating the change.[16] You're replacing the omelet theory with the horse theory (you can drive a horse to water but you can't make it drink).[17]

Getting Product Out the Door

In Rick Cook's hilarious *Wizard's Bane* series (about a programmer who becomes a mighty wizard by adapting the FORTH programming language to the practice of magic), the hero says, "There comes a time in the course of any project to shoot the engineers and put the damn thing into production."

The ancient Greek philosopher Zeno, through his eponymous paradox, accidentally explained why many projects stall. You can't go anywhere, he claimed, because in order to get there you first must get halfway there. After you get halfway there you must first get half of the rest of the way there, and so on.

The invention of calculus resolved Zeno's paradox, but it didn't fix what can happen toward the end of a project, when you start to feel like you're wading through molasses. Project team members can develop an awesome and infinite list of new things to do before putting something into production. That's because there's no risk until people start using the product—that's when you find out whether you were right or wrong, whether you forgot something, whether people love you or hate you. In other words, you can stay in rehearsal forever because it's safe.

It's your job to fight that tendency. Instill a bias toward getting product out the door, or the play in front of an audience, if that's what you do. When you get near the end of a project, don't let the team construct reason after reason to delay implementation.

---

[16]*Also, it's important to communicate the change. This isn't just explaining what's going to happen. It's the full story: Who, what, when, where, and most importantly, why?*
[17]*More accurately, a horse can find water by itself, but a pencil has to be lead.*

Which isn't to say you should be reckless. Be methodical. Builders create "punch lists" when they've nearly completed a project, and you should too. A punch list, if you're unfamiliar with the term, is simply a to-do list under a different name. It's a bunch of small tasks you have to complete before you're done.

Creating a punch list is exhilarating. You set 'em up and knock 'em down, and when the last item on the punch list is done, so are you.

Throw the team a big party, buy them t-shirts or coffee mugs, give them some time off, and play a round of golf on company time.

You've all earned it.

BUSINESS APPLICATIONS

"Lots of folks confuse bad management with destiny."

—Kin Hubbard

MANAGEMENTSPEAK

The project team has been working diligently and has made significant progress.

Translation:
The project is behind schedule.

Insanity, we're frequently told, is doing the same thing over and over again expecting different results[1]. Because every time we realize we don't deliver working business applications to our companies with any reliability, our response is to add yet more up-front planning to our methodologies, and every time we do, our success rate drops a bit more, what does that say about us?

We developed most of our legacy systems in the late 1960s and early 1970s. Unencumbered by today's visual development tools, ample RAM, cheap storage, and sophisticated methodologies, we were able to develop working code that ran our businesses.

After we put the code into production, we had to maintain it. When you maintain something, everything you encounter is something you didn't anticipate. Sometimes, the maintenance is easy anyway—the new report requested by the head of manufacturing is easy to program; the additional data needed by marketing is easy to add to the system.

Other times, though, the features we were asked to add didn't easily fit into the application and we were faced with either kludging together a quick fix or investing in major rework.

Usually, we kludged, which made the next modification harder.

That's when we made our fatal mistake. We decided the problem was that we didn't spend enough time planning before building the system. If we were to spend more time planning before we started to build, we proclaimed, the investment would pay for itself through reduced maintenance costs.

Our problem is that we've spent too much time with the finance and accounting crowd, and not enough time with marketing[2]. In finance and accounting, the future looks very much like the past because the basic principles of accounting haven't changed all that much since Luca Pacioli published them in Venice more than 500 years ago.

In marketing, the future is pretty murky. Because it's marketing, not finance and accounting, that drives business changes, our excessive faith in the value of planning is misplaced. It's surely true that we shouldn't write code before we understand the problem we're trying to solve and how we're going to solve it. We need to recognize two countervailing factors as we decide how to implement business solutions: Business change and the limitations of design.

---

[1] *Of course we've all used either Microsoft Windows or the Mac OS, so we're used to doing something, watching our system crash, rebooting, doing the same thing, and having it work. We do the same thing more than once and do get different results, so I guess it's true that using PCs will drive us all nuts.*

[2] *Fringe benefit: Marketing throws much better parties. Trust me on this.*

THE IMPACT OF BUSINESS CHANGE

The longer we spend planning, the more the business changes before we implement. In large development efforts, there comes a time when we have to freeze the design so we can get on with creating the solution. The design we can freeze. The business we can't. Short design/implementation cycles solve this problem.

If you take a long time to solve a business problem, your solution, no matter how fabulous, will be irrelevant.

THE LIMITATIONS OF ANALYSIS AND DESIGN

No initial analysis or design is ever perfect. No matter how good something looks on paper, you never know how good it really is until it's in use. Whether you spend three months or three years designing a system, you'll still have to make changes when end-users put it to real-world use.

A desire for perfection will kill every project. Usually, it's an excuse for cowardice—an unwillingness to put a design to the test of real-world use. Whether you build a solution or buy one, situations will arise that you didn't anticipate. Expect that, make sure your end-users expect it too, and deal with the situations as they come up. Nobody yet has created a utopia on any scale, so you shouldn't be surprised when your new system isn't utopian either.

Your goals shouldn't be to achieve perfection. They should be to create as small a system as you can that works usefully and is built to be extensible.

Someone once pointed out that every big system that works started out as a small system that worked. The bad news about our legacy systems is that they're the result of incremental accumulation of features so they don't conform to a clean design.

The good news about our legacy systems is that they exist and they work—something that isn't true of most big design efforts.

THE ROLLING RELEASE OPTION

Sometimes, in order to get an application into production within the nine month limit advocated in this book, you'll have to eliminate everything but vanilla—the hot fudge sauce, chocolate sprinkles, almonds, and cherry can't be included.

This will make everyone who wanted the full hot fudge sundae very sad, which translates to ongoing discontent throughout the life of the program.

continues

---

continued

> In the art of negotiation, saying no is usually a bad tactic. The alternative is the rolling release option.
>
> Build your program around the principle of having two teams working on the application. Each works on a nine month schedule: Three months to create a specification, and six months to build it. As each team completes its release, the other team should be halfway through the process of creating the next one.
>
> This takes the pain out of having a needed feature rejected because it's out of scope. It can always be put into the next release, which on the average only delays its availability by four and a half months.

CHOICES FOR IMPLEMENTING BUSINESS APPLICATIONS

You have two alternatives when the time comes to implement a business application. You can build a solution yourself, or you can buy one. If you decide to buy, you have two sub-alternatives: You can buy a focused, best-of-breed application, or you can implement the relevant modules of an Enterprise Resource Planning (ERP) suite. Each of these alternatives has advantages[3]. Let's look at each in turn. Table 12.1, a decision matrix for the build/buy options, summarizes the analysis. You can use it as a starting point to make your decision.

Build It Yourself

The advantages of building the solution yourself are fairly obvious: You get exactly what your business needs, not what some hypothetical "average" business in your industry needs; and your new application will integrate perfectly with all the other applications you've built yourself.

Building it yourself has more subtle advantages as well: You upgrade your system on your own schedule based on your own business needs. You avoid the pitfall of needing to stay current with a vendor's next release in order to have a supported application that will run on current platforms.

When you build a system yourself, you've reduced your vulnerability to marketplace changes as well. You're still at risk if one of the platforms you've selected vanishes or loses market momentum (and consequently fails to keep pace with competitors). But you aren't at risk of finding yourself with an unsupported application as long as you're smart enough to maintain a big enough maintenance team that knows the application.

---

[3]*No, not advantages and disadvantages. Go back to the chapter on decision-making. Listing advantages and disadvantages would be using a "Ben Franklin" to choose among alternatives.*

Buy It

Buying a solution has two advantages: speed and reduced risk. Because you're buying working code, you get to skip most of the development process, meaning you're up and running faster. Also, the chance of waking up in a few years with software that doesn't work is minimal.

In tax-sensitive applications, including many accounting functions, you gain the third advantage of having someone else take responsibility for keeping the application in sync with tax law changes. That can be a huge advantage.

Vanilla or Chocolate Sprinkles?

A question every business must answer when installing a package is whether to customize the package to the business's needs or whether to install the package "plain vanilla" and adapt the business's practices to the software's design. Here are the major trade-offs:

1. If you decide to customize a purchased solution to your particular needs, new releases of the software will sometimes create maintenance nightmares when you have to upgrade your customizations to fit the new release.

2. If you customize, you might contort the software into unnatural acts—that is, you might end up forcing it to do things its designers never intended it to do. The result of this level of customization almost always is to create exactly the same maintenance monster we've grown accustomed to in our patchwork legacy systems.

3. If you don't customize, you usually have to change your business processes and practices to fit the ones designed into the application you're purchasing. This is good if (a) your current processes are cumbersome and need redesigning anyway; and (b) you like the design that comes with the application. Otherwise, you're letting your choice of technology dictate how you run your business. Bad idea.

Best-of-Breed Solutions

Best-of-breed solutions are tightly focused on specific business problems. Depending on your knowledge of the problem, they might even fit your needs better than a solution you'd build yourself because the application designer has the benefit of having solved the business problem for multiple companies, some of which might be more sophisticated than yours.

Even if a best-of-breed solution is a poorer fit than a custom-built one, it still has all the benefits of any purchased application.

ERP Modules

ERP suites are a big deal. For many industries, you can buy a complete solution for every aspect of your business from a single vendor.

The big advantage you get from an ERP suite is integration. Everything works together automatically because it's designed to work together. Compared to the other alternatives, though, the quality of each particular solution generally suffers.

Also, it almost never makes sense to install just a couple of ERP modules[4]. Enterprise Resource Planning is more than a software category. It's a philosophy of management that tightly integrates the entire business. If your organization doesn't buy into the philosophy, you probably shouldn't buy into the software.

Keep in mind that although "integration" is as worthy a goal as saluting the flag and baking an excellent apple pie, it has a dark side many businesses have experienced to the ongoing frustration of their business unit managers: a loss of flexibility. Tight business integration is to microeconomics what centrally planned economies are to macroeconomics. There's a point where diseconomies of scale favor improved flexibility over maximum efficiency.

TABLE 12.1 DECISION MATRIX FOR BUILD, BEST-OF-BREED, AND ERP ALTERNATIVES TO SOLVING BUSINESS PROBLEMS

Trade-Off	*Build*	*Buy Best-of-Breed*	*Buy ERP Modules*
Fit with requirements	High	High	Medium
Likelihood of success	Lower	High	High
Speed of implementation	Low	High	Medium/Variable[5]

---

[4]*The exception: In some cases, an ERP vendor is noted for a particular specialty—manufacturing, HR/payroll, or accounting, for example—in which case those modules are both best of breed and positioning you to move into an ERP direction later on if you so choose.*

[5]*There are a variety of methodologies used to implement ERP suites. Some are intended for rapid implementation (relatively speaking); others are geared to massive process re-engineering and take longer.*

6*As noted in the sections on technical architecture, this can be mitigated through the use of various integration technologies.*

7*Depending on the vendor—many will provide whatever you need if you're willing to pay for it; also, you always have the option of buying another package if you need specific functionality.*

Trade-Off	Build	Buy Best-of-Breed	Buy ERP Modules
Technical Integration	High	Low[6]	High
Business Integration	As needed	Low[6]	High
Resistance to upgrade problems	High	Low	Low
Flexibility	Medium	High[7]	Low
Protection from tax and regulatory changes	Low	High	High
Insulation from changes to the software marketplace	High	Medium	Low

MAKING THE BUILD/BUY DECISION

You can, if you like, make a separate build/buy decision for every project you undertake. There's an easier, better way, already mentioned in the previous section: Treat this subject as a design issue within the application layer of your technical architecture.

It's easier because you only have to make the basic decision once. It's better because your decisions will be in a consistent style, which means you get to become competent at whichever approach you settle on. Here's a list of candidate design principles:

- *ERP all the way:* The ERP business philosophy fits where your business is going, so you're going to sweep through your applications suite and replace everything you can with modules from your ERP vendor. You'll buy best-of-breed or custom-develop a solution only if you need something your ERP vendor doesn't and has no plans to ship.

- *ERP most of the way:* The ERP business philosophy fits where your business is going, but in specific cases you might opt for a best-of-breed or custom solution if the ERP module is simply inferior.

- *Best-of-breed when you can, build when you have to:* If you can find one or more packages that are close to matching your requirements you'll buy the one that fits your needs the best; otherwise you'll build a custom solution.

- *Best-of-breed only when it fits well, build otherwise:* If you can find a package that's an excellent fit for your requirements you'll buy it, but you'll choose to build your own solution rather than compromise on quality or fit with your business.

- *Build everything:* You want it all—perfect fit with the business and tight technical integration. The only way you can get it is to build everything yourself.

Note that except for the last option (which is almost always a bad one), you'll still have to make a build/buy decision for each project. You have, however, established a strong preference in each case, so there must be a compelling argument for straying from the default decision.

METHODOLOGIES

IS organizations reflexively focus their attention on establishing system development methodologies. System development methodologies are important if you're planning to do a lot of system development. If, on the other hand, you select a design principle that has you buying an ERP suite or buying and integrating a lot of best-of-breed applications, you'll find yourself forcing the process of selecting, customizing and integrating a packaged application into your system development methodology, and that's a square-peg/round-hole situation.

The methodologies you use will depend in part on the design principle you've selected. If you've chosen a design principle of "Best-of-breed when you can," for example, you'll scan the marketplace for packaged solutions far earlier in the process than if you've chosen to use "Best-of-breed only when it fits."

And if you're going with an "ERP all the way" approach, you won't even glance at the marketplace unless you determine your ERP vendor's solution is lacking features or is insufficiently robust[8].

What follows aren't full methodologies (see the section titled "The Role of Methodologies,"). They're more like lightweight frameworks you can use as starting points for establishing practices that fit your organization.

THE ROLE OF METHODOLOGIES

The Total Quality Management crowd looked at manufacturing and figured out that the secret to quality was having predictable, repeatable processes. In doing so they took the discipline of manufacturing to a new level. They also, through no fault of their own, ruined life for the rest of us.

It happened because TQM was so successful. An army of consultants figured that what worked in the factory would work everyplace, so they simply assumed everything in the known universe worked like a factory. This led, directly or indirectly, to the creation of huge numbers of methodologies—predictable repeatable processes that lead to high quality results. It also led,

---

[8]*Translation: It stinks.*

by the way, to our failure in the Vietnam War, because the kids who ran the Department of Defense at the time were business whiz kids who believed in TQM, and especially in focusing on what is measurable. That's why the Vietnam War was run on body counts instead of strategic objectives.

But I digress.

Methodologies[9] have value in that they define processes for achieving results such as system designs and specifications. Methodologies easily get out of hand, though, because a methodology is simply a means to an end. If you aren't careful, following the methodology becomes more important than achieving a high quality result and then you have problems.

For example, if somebody asked you the last letter of the alphabet you'd probably say, "Z." And you'd be right.

A methodologist would first define a methodology:

1. Define "last letter" as any letter with no successor letters.
2. Choose a letter of the alphabet at random.
3. Determine the successor letter for the chosen letter (if the chosen letter is "B" then the successor letter is "C").
4. If the chosen letter has no successor letter, you're done. Otherwise, make the successor letter your new chosen letter and repeat step 3.

Get the picture?

Here's another way of looking at it: Methodologies are the project equivalent of paint-by-numbers kits. You'll get repeatable and predictable results, but you won't get great art.

In general, the bigger and more complex the effort and the more people involved in it, the more you'll need to define and use a formal methodology. Methodologies add overhead, but they do reduce uncertainty.

Not that many years ago, Computer Aided Software Engineering (CASE) became popular for a brief period of time. CASE methodologies required that a project team first "model the business," and modeling the business was anything but quick and easy.

continues

---

[9]*Actually methods, because methodology means the study of methods.*

continued

That was okay, but shortly afterward, modeling the business and maintaining the currency of the models became more important than completing working systems, at least in the minds of some CASE methodologists. One once said to me, "If this company is serious about CASE, it will fund two FTEs to manage the business models."

Luckily, the business wasn't serious about CASE. It was serious about serving its customers and creating a quality product, and it wanted a working system. The company executives were smart enough to know that CASE was simply a means to an end.

Be judicious in the use of methodologies, and never let anyone forget that they're a tool, not a reason for being. Take that one additional step and your methodology has become something different and terrifying.

It will have become a religion.

We'll begin with the high-level decision sequence to be followed for each of the preceding design principles. Following these we'll flesh out some of the more important steps. These frameworks amount to decision trees (see Chapter 10, "Making Decisions,"). It's up to you to develop a full-blown methodology based on them.

ERP All or Most of the Way

At the highest level, you have just one decision to make, and it's one you'll have to make separately with each business unit in your company. That's whether you will customize your ERP solution to fit how that business unit operates, re-engineer the processes of the business unit and customize the ERP solution to those redesigned processes, or use the ERP solution to define the processes to be used by each business unit.

After you make this decision, the remainder of your process is (from the perspective of this book) quite simple. That's because from this point forward, most companies will need outside help to implement an ERP solution. If this is the direction you've chosen, your next step is selecting a systems integrator that specializes in the implementation of ERP solutions. After you've selected the vendor, you'll make all the remaining decisions jointly, with the guidance of your systems integrator to help you. You'll make your remaining decisions jointly, and because there's a vendor involved you're going to be watching the meter closely. That's wise and appropriate. While you're watching the meter closely, though, don't cheap out on training and change management. No matter how good the project, it will crash and burn if you don't attend to the needs of the people who will use it every day.

Buy Best-of-Breed When You Can, Build When You Have To, or Buy Best-of-Breed When It Fits Well, Build Otherwise

These are probably the most common strategies among IS organizations right now, and for good reason. If you choose to operate under either of these principles you'll minimize risk, obtain a good match to your business requirements, and make allowances for the likelihood that a software vendor understands the business function it supports as well or better than you do. (It should, because it's supporting the function in lots of businesses whereas you're supporting it in only one.)

The only difference between these two options is how well a packaged solution has to fit your requirements before you'll consider it. In the first option, you only do in-house development as a last resort—risk minimization and speed of implementation outweigh fit with requirements as factors in your decision matrix. In the second, these priorities are reversed.

Many companies will choose to seek outside help when implementing a packaged solution. The rules are similar to using an outside integrator to help with implementing an ERP solution.

In most cases you should choose your systems integrator with your strategy already decided, or you'll go where the systems integrator is most comfortable, not where you want to go. The exception to this rule is when you've established a long-term strategic relationship with a systems integrator. If you have (and if the integrator has earned your trust) you'll be far more successful by involving your integrator from the beginning.

From the time the integrator starts working for you, you'll make your remaining decisions jointly, and because there's a vendor involved you're going to be keeping track of costs. That's wise and appropriate, and no different from the ERP scenario. As with the ERP scenario, and every other process or system implementation for that matter, training and change management are vital to your success. No matter how good the project, it will crash and burn if you don't attend to the needs of the people who will use it every day.

Your first step when buying a package is to determine your basic strategy. Here are your choices:

- *Customize the Software to Fit Your Business:* Appropriate when the business function is operating as well as you think it can and you want new software, either to automate functions currently handled manually or to replace an old system that's obsolete, unsupported, or otherwise ready for replacement.

- ***Re-engineer the Process, Customize the Software to Fit the New Process:*** This is a popular and successful strategy. Usually, if you're ready to implement new software or replace an obsolete system, you also want significant improvements in how the business function operates. Whether you prefer the term "re-engineer," "redesign," or "figure out a different way to accomplish the same goals" the result is the same: You design a new process to replace the old one, use your new process design to define system requirements, and then select the system best suited to the process you've just designed.

- ***Select the Software and Adopt Its Native Process:*** Sometimes, the way someone else does it is good enough. If the business unit is willing to take this approach, figure you're selecting both a software product and a new process. You and the business unit need to agree on the right choice, of course; the result is a "plain vanilla" installation that should be smooth and relatively easy.

The analysis that follows assumes you've selected one of these basic strategies[10] and that you find a package that's sufficient to your needs (we'll cover software development later on). Here are the basic processes to follow for each of the strategies you can follow when you decide to buy a solution.

Customize the Software to Fit Your Business

1. *Document the current process, information requirements, and integration requirements.* You need to understand the problem you're trying to solve, and you need to understand the issues surrounding integrating the new system—with other applications, with existing databases, and with your whole technical architecture. Don't forget to deal with user-interface–level integration either. Just because it can coexist with other applications on the desktop doesn't mean it's integrated—how many windows do you want end-users clicking in, anyway?

2. *Develop a Request For Proposal (RFP) or similar document; distribute it; evaluate responses; select a solution.* An RFP is the appropriate vehicle for making this decision because your requirements are well-defined (see the section "On Selecting Vendors and Products" later in this chapter). Easy and maintainable customization is an important requirement within the RFP. So is vendor stability, market-share, and mind-share[11]. Because building a solution is one of the options you're considering, include "Build" as one of the columns in your decision matrix (along with each of the vendors you've invited to respond) and assign a small team to write a response to the RFP[12] based on building a custom solution.

---

[10]*If you haven't figured out that you need to heavily involve key business stakeholders in this decision and the ones that follow, you flunk. Re-read this book starting with the Introduction—even better, from the front cover.*

3. *Select a finalist.* You should have created your decision matrix before releasing your RFP to the vendors, so this step should be straightforward. Often, you'll find that two vendors end up with nearly the same score. That's fine—you can evaluate two finalists. Just create a process for deciding between them.

4. *Investigate the finalist(s) in more depth, including the use of site visits to see the software in use.* Again, this is what you'll be using to run an important part of your company. Years ago, ads for the Packard automobile (one of the finest cars ever made in America) said, "Ask the man[13] who owns one." Asking current owners remains an excellent idea.

5. *Make final selection.* **Danger, Will Robinson!!!** (If, on the other hand, your name is Jane Smith, **Danger, Jane Smith!!!**) You started without well understood requirements and you've discovered a solution in large part based on information provided by the candidates' sales representatives. You're at risk of making a decision based on quality of presentation, warm fuzzies, and whoever happened to make the last presentation[14]. After the last vendor has gone home—preferably, a few days after the last vendor has gone home—the project team should decide on the final selection criteria and weightings, create a decision matrix, and score all the finalists.

6. *Develop specifications for customizing the software.* Based on the information you collected in Step 1, you and your chosen vendor should have no trouble determining what you need to do to adapt the software to your current business and technical environment. Remember to work the new system into your technical architecture as part of the process for creating integration specifications—new applications should either fit your existing architecture or they should extend or change it in a planned way.

---

[11]*Mind-share is the shared expectation among you and your peers in other companies that this company is, and will continue to be, an important player in the industry. Mind-share can't be quantified—you'll have to use your own judgment on this subject. Most companies only consider products from companies that have significant mind-share. Mind-share leads to self-fulfilling prophesies regarding the demise of those companies that lack it, so buying from those companies is risky, regardless of their products' technical merits.*

[12]*Dedicate them to the task—don't make them squeeze this into their spare time, because they don't have any. Also, give them a few more weeks than you give the software vendors because they have to design a solution from scratch—a high-level solution, but a solution nonetheless. As an alternative, invite your favorite systems development company to submit a response to the RFP, if you prefer to contract out major development (see the section "In-house Development versus Contracting It Out," later in this chapter).*

[13]*The Packard, if you aren't familiar with it, was a pre–feminist era automobile.*

[14]*It's a fact: Far more than half of all decisions go to the company making the last presentation.*

7. *Install, customize, and integrate the new system.* This is the standard nuts and bolts of IS—it should be your power zone. So long as you give the project team enough of the right kind of training, exercise good project management, and did a good job of creating specifications in Step 2, you should have no trouble.

8. *During an initial acceptance period, monitor and fine-tune the new system, and make sure everyone is using it as intended.* End-users understand their business. They're smart people who are accustomed to solving problems. If they're typical, they expect IS to say no to most requests and instead figure out clever workarounds when faced with system limitations. Surprise them, and save yourself some headaches in the bargain. During the acceptance period, establish a team of "floor walkers" to answer questions, look over shoulders, discover rough spots that need fine-tuning and so on. Clever workarounds might solve immediate needs, but eventually they come back to haunt everyone.

Re-engineer the Process, Customize the Software to Fit the New Process

1. *Document the current process, its information requirements, areas of dissatisfaction, and aspects of the current process that must be preserved in a new process.* Don't go into very much detail, except in documenting the process's information requirements—and you probably have that detail documented, because most of the time there's already an information system in place to support the current process[15]. You want your design team to learn just enough so its members understand the business, but not enough that they "go native," tacitly accepting all the limitations and constraints built into the existing process.

2. *Using whatever process redesign methodology you prefer, design a new business process.* You don't need to design every last detail. Heck, you probably never need to design every last detail—some things take care of themselves during the initial acceptance process. You do need enough detail, and a good enough way of presenting the design, so that everyone involved can visualize the new process in action.

3. *Using the new process redesign as a starting point, determine the information and integration requirements of the new business process.* Information requirements you need in detail. They're a key part of your system specification and product selection criteria. Integration requirements are the same as they were before.

---

[15] *You do have the data design documented, don't you?*

4. *Develop a Request For Proposal (RFP) or similar document; distribute it; evaluate responses; select a solution.* An RFP is the appropriate vehicle for making this decision because your requirements are well-defined. Easy and maintainable customization is an important requirement within the RFP. So is vendor stability, market-share, and "mind-share." As with the previous strategy, include "Build" as one of the columns in your decision matrix and assign a small team or an outside developer to write a response to the RFP based on building a custom solution.

5. *Select a finalist.* You should have created your decision matrix before releasing your RFP to the vendors, so this step should be straightforward. Often, you'll find that two vendors end up with nearly the same score. That's fine—you can evaluate two finalists. Just create a process for deciding between them.

6. *Investigate the finalist(s) in more depth, including the use of site visits to see the software in use.* Whether you're using your current business design (as in the previous strategy) or creating a new one from scratch, don't be too cheap or lazy to do this. You're betting the company on the answer, so make sure it's a good one.

7. *Make the final selection.* Everything that made sense when you were keeping your old process makes the same sense here.

8. *Develop specifications for customizing the software.* Based on the information requirements you documented in Step 1 and extended with your new process design in Step 2, you and your chosen vendor should have no trouble determining what you need to do to adapt the software to your current business and technical environment. Remember to work the new system into your technical architecture as part of the process for creating integration specifications—new applications should either fit your existing architecture or extend or change it in a planned way.

9. *Install, customize, and integrate the new system.* This is the standard nuts and bolts of IS—it should be your power zone. So long as you give the project team enough of the right kind of training, exercise good project management, and did a good job of creating specifications in Steps 4 and 8, you should have no trouble.

10. *During an initial acceptance period, monitor and fine-tune the new business process and the new software, and make sure everyone is using them as intended.* This step is much the same as when you adapted the new software to the current business process, with one important exception: The new process design won't be perfect. Your floor walkers must be adept at recognizing when end-users encounter unanticipated situations and how they deal with them. You need to figure out when to adopt their solutions and how to communicate the solutions to everyone else who might need it (and you need to add the solution to your design and document it).

Select the Software and Adopt Its Native Process

1. *Through research, interviews, focus groups, and team interactions, develop a high-level consensus regarding the goals of the new system and process.* You're in a fairly peculiar position as a business when you choose this option. The business function you're working on is important enough to merit your attention and a serious project, but you're willing to build it on a generic process design created by a vendor who's never visited your company. Oddly, this is often a good idea. It works when the business function, although important, isn't strategic, specific to your company, or a competitive differentiator. You still need to develop consensus around what you're trying to accomplish and what constitutes success, so you can choose the right vendor.

2. *Determine the leading vendors[16] for the software category in question.* Search the Web, consult the market research companies, check the advertisements, and ask your friends and peers in other companies what they use and like.

3. *Using written documentation, tours, interviews, and other interactions, make sure the vendors all have a thorough understanding of the business problem you're trying to solve.* Although this is important no matter what "buy" option you select; it's absolutely vital here. You're asking the vendor to provide the design for your business function. The vendors need to understand your business and how the business function fits into it so they can figure out how their software can help you out. Don't restrict their knowledge narrowly, either—the more they know, the more they can help you.

4. *Through a combination of written proposals and presentations, select no more than three finalists.* Find screening criteria to let you eliminate unlikely vendors quickly. You're better off learning a lot about a few packages than being less thorough about a lot of them. Remember, your goal isn't to create the fairest selection process in the land. Your goal is to implement a solution that works. If you don't use AS/400 computers and don't intend to, for example, and one of the vendors provides only a turnkey AS/400 solution, you can stop. You'll be doing both of you a favor.

5. *Investigate the finalists in more depth, including the use of site visits to see the software in use.* Again, this is what you'll be using to run an important part of your company. Especially because you'll be adopting the vendor's process, you'll want to see the entire solution in action.

---

[16]*Five or so is a good number.*

6. *Make final selection.* Everything said before makes sense here, too, and for the same reasons.

7. *Develop specifications for integrating the software.* Work the new system into your technical architecture—that should be the appropriate process for creating integration specifications. New applications should either fit your existing architecture or they should extend or change it in a planned way. You should have no surprises by now because fit with your architecture was part of your RFP.

8. *Install, customize, and integrate the new system.* This is the standard nuts and bolts of IS—it should be your power zone. As long as you give the project team enough of the right kind of training, exercise good project management, and do a good job of creating specifications in Steps 4 and 7, you should have no trouble.

9. *During an initial acceptance period, monitor use of the new business process and software to make sure everyone is using them as intended.* This step is much the same as when you started with your own process redesign—the difference, of course, being that you're using the vendor's process design instead. The new process design won't be perfect. Your floor walkers must still be alert to recognizing when end-users encounter unanticipated situations and how they deal with them. You need to figure out when to adopt their solutions and how to communicate the solutions to everyone else who might need it (and you need to add the solution to your design and document it).

PROCESS-NEUTRAL SYSTEMS

The relationship between processes and systems isn't as simple as designing a process, then designing a system that implements it. It sounds neat and easy. Unfortunately, doing things that way would hamper your flexibility as your business changes.

Processes change over time. Sometimes the changes are minor; sometimes dramatic. The business applications that support these processes have to adapt to process changes with as little fuss as possible. To achieve this goal you must design "process-neutral systems"—that is, systems that are independent of the specific business process, but which can support a variety of business process designs so long as they all achieve the same end result.

To design process-neutral systems you need to develop two complementary perspectives of your new business processing environment. One is a process-centric view. This view treats your information systems as "actors"—robots that participate in the process just as human beings do. The information system's role is to participate as a source, repository, and recipient of information.

continues

continued

The other perspective is a systems-centric view. This view treats the information system as a collection of databases, edits, transactions, and the process as source and recipient of information.

Your design is complete when you've cross-checked every point of intersection between system and process to make sure the system supplies the process with all the information needed by the process at that point, and that the process can supply the system with all the information it needs at that point as well.

In other words, when the system and process meet, the process must be able to continue and the system must be able to complete its transactions.

Making your system design process-neutral solves another problem inherent in closely linking process and system design. That's the desirability of avoiding "waterfall methodologies."

A waterfall methodology builds the whole system at once before implementing any of it. It's the classic "big project" approach to system development, and it almost always leads to failure for all the reasons described in Chapter 11, "Programs, Initiatives, and Projects."

Information systems are best implemented in small pieces. You can't, however, implement new business processes in small pieces—it isn't even a meaningful statement.

What you can do, though, is develop a process-neutral system and implement it within the old process, in modules compatible with the older system it's replacing (this is a complicated subject beyond the scope of this book—the short version is that you're going to run the systems in parallel with automated interfaces until you have enough of the new system completed to turn off the old one).

When the new system has been completed and tested, or is complete enough at least, you can then implement the new business process. Chances are, of course, that experience with the new system will provide valuable insights about how to fine-tune the new process.

Sometimes you want the system to control a business process. You can still accomplish this goal without violating the principles of process-neutral system design. You do so by establishing a separate workflow automation layer in your software.

Workflow is a distinct category of software, and you can buy workflow engines that let you define complex work branching and routing rules, "pop" particular screens on end-user's desks in response to particular conditions, and keep track of the progress of whole chunks of work—even when the work involves more than one information system.

Think of workflow as an intelligent automated dispatcher. It keeps track of the work that has to be done, the progress on that work, and the resources (human and automated) available to do the work. As with a human dispatcher, its job is to assign the highest priority work to the person best suited to its completion.

By separating the control of work into a separate software layer specialized to that purpose, you can design the information system itself to be process-neutral, use the workflow system to control the work, and change the workflow rules when you need to redefine a process without needing to make major changes to the information system itself.

ON SELECTING VENDORS AND PRODUCTS

"Oh, &$@%#, not another &%^ing RFP!"

Requests for Proposal (RFPs) are painful to create when you're buying, and painful to respond to when you're a vendor.

American business sends out a lot of RFPs every year[17]. Clearly, we've become a nation of masochists, and you have alternatives, depending on the specific circumstances surrounding your vendor evaluation.

You generally face one of these three situations: (1) you fully understand your requirements and the market, and you need equivalent information from all suppliers; (2) you understand your business, have a general understanding that technology can improve it, and want open-ended suggestions on how different products can help improve or transform your organization; or (3) you need to choose a product from a well-defined category and need something that's good enough. These situations call for different approaches.

When You Know Your Requirements

Here's when you should write an RFP. Quite a few books (including my own *Telecommunications for Every Business*, Bonus Books, Chicago, 1992) provide detailed guidance. Three principles are worth mentioning here.

continues

---

[17] *I should say something authoritative here, like, "According to the Ipshi Pipshi Group, American businesses send out a staggering 683,495 RFPs every year, inviting an average of seven companies to respond to each one." I should, but I don't know of any studies, and in this case, prefer ignorance to knowledge anyway.*

continued

First, specify your design goals, not the means by which vendors should address them. For example, if you need a fault-tolerant database server, don't say you need a system with redundant power supplies, backplanes, CPUs, and network interface cards. If you do you'll get what you asked for (in this case, a system that frequently fails from operating system bugs). Instead, ask how the vendor ensures fault tolerance. Then you'll learn one of the vendors provides mirrored servers with shared RAID storage for a lower overall cost and higher reliability than the other alternatives with designs that fit your preconceived notions.

Second, don't withhold information. If you use nothing but Windows NT servers, for example, say so in your RFP. You'll save both your vendors and yourself a lot of work.

And finally, if any vendor offers to "help you write your RFP" just laugh gently, compliment them on their sense of humor, and go onto the next vendor (who will make the same offer). Don't take offense—they're just doing their job. Don't take them up on the offer, either.

Looking for Help

Sometimes, you don't know all the questions. You know you want to phase out your nationwide SNA network, for example, but have an open mind regarding the best replacement strategy.

You can hire a consultant to help you write an RFP, I suppose—or, you can hold extensive conversations with a variety of vendors to learn what each has to offer. By doing so, you'll get a broader look at the market, and you'll also get a wonderful education in the strengths (from each vendor) and weaknesses (from their competitors) of each approach currently selling.

In this example, you might find yourself talking to a couple of frame relay vendors, a provider of Internet "Virtual Private Network" (VPN) technology, and an independent systems integrator. You'll benefit from an unstructured dialog in which each vendor can assess your situation in depth and describe a scenario of how their approach will work for your company.

When Good Enough Will Do

Let's imagine you've been asked to select a new standard Ethernet network interface card (NIC). You could write an RFP or hold extensive conversations with sales reps, but why? Read a few reviews, ask a few basic questions, insist on a few evaluation units (to make sure they work and to learn about any installation glitches) and pick one. Flip a coin if you want. It's a low impact decision.

One other factor to keep in mind when selecting products and vendors: Very few of us make decisions based on logic. Salespeople and working psychologists (overlapping groups) know we make emotional decisions and then construct logical arguments to justify them. Don't fall into this trap: Recognize your emotional preference up front, figure out how much weight you should give it, and keep it from dominating your process.

SYSTEM DEVELOPMENT METHODOLOGIES

No, we aren't going to spend much time creating a system development methodology in this book. There are already too many of them out there, and usually you won't develop anyway—you'll buy a solution using one of the preceding frameworks. And as noted in the section, "The Role of Methodologies," methodologies can easily get out of hand, turning into obstacles to success rather than enablers.

The fact is, projects fail because of bad project management, not bad methodologies. All a good methodology really does for you is to deliver a reasonably complete work breakdown structure for you to use in constructing your project plan—it defines the tasks you need to undertake to succeed.

So long as you remember the key points of good project management—keeping projects short and small; starting with as small a core system as possible; making extensive use of prototypes and delivering functionality in a succession of rolling releases; and more than anything else, *focusing everyone on the importance of getting product out the door*—you'll succeed.

IN-HOUSE DEVELOPMENT VERSUS CONTRACTING IT OUT

You have a big project staring you in the face, a history of big projects failing, and a decision to make. Do you bring in an outside systems integrator to take on the project for you?

The answer is, of course, "That depends." If you have a history of failure with initiatives of this size, you need to ask yourself what will be different this time (other than your having read this book). If you can't come up with a good answer, seek outside help, either in the form of project management consulting to help your project team learn the ropes, or in the form of an outside project team.

continues

continued

If you do decide to bring in an outside project team, get ready. Your entire IS organization will resent your decision, and explaining that you made this decision because, "We keep on failing when we try to do this ourselves," just won't make things get better, either.

Then there's the problem of who will maintain the new system when the vendor goes away, because only the vendor knows how everything works.

In other words, you lose if you try to do it yourself and you lose if you farm it out. What's the answer?

It isn't all that bad: If you decide you need outside help, insist on creating "blended teams." A blended team is a simple idea: It's a team with members from both your systems integrator and your own company.

The absolute minimum number of your company's people you should include in a blended team is the number you'll want supporting the new system when the systems integrator goes away. The maximum is as many as you can spare to do the work minus the core team required by your integrator.

In addition to the standard rules for project management, there are two requirements for making blended teams work.

First, everyone has to understand that the systems integrator's project manager is in charge. Don't dance around this point and don't cater to sensitive egos. Just tell everyone, "These people manage big projects for a living. We undertake big projects occasionally. The main reason we're bringing them in to help us is that they know how to run projects like this."

Second, make it clear to your systems integrator, and especially to the integrator's project manager, that the blended team must function as **one** team. Not as two teams, not as two armed camps that coexist with barely concealed hostility, but as a single team, focused on achieving the goals of the project.

This will be harder for the integrator's staff than for your own, by the way—consultants are always at risk of believing their own public relations, and when you're an expert for a living, it's awfully tempting to denigrate the skills and knowledge of your client.

The best way for the project manager to address this issue is head-on during the early stages of team formation. Through the simple process of listing what each team member brings to the project, everyone in the blended team will start to understand how interdependent they are.

Just one more thing: If it isn't already abundantly clear, the selection of your systems integrator is a very important issue. Check references, gain commitments on key individuals for the life of the project, and otherwise do everything you can to make sure you're working with a quality partner.

During the sales process you'll be introduced to a lot of high-powered professionals and see some awesome résumés. You can't insist on the specific team members—no systems integrator can work that way—but you can insist on the experience level and track record you can expect for each role.

PROCESS MEASUREMENT

"Either this man is dead or my watch has stopped."

—Groucho Marx

MANAGEMENTSPEAK

Our leadership team has determined that we need to establish metrics for our key processes to verify that we continuously improve.

Translation:

Let's produce a blizzard of numbers large enough to make the leaderships' eyes glaze over, although not actually measuring anything useful or informative.

We easily measured our first big successes with business computing, back in the days we called ourselves "Electronic Data Processing" (EDP). By automating repetitive calculations and the creation of formatted reports, we dramatically increased productivity. There wasn't much question about it because the computer replaced a bunch of accounting clerks who then had to find something else useful to do.

Then the personal computer happened and after we got over our initial shock and dismay, we figured increasing productivity had to be their reason for being, too.

Twenty years and a lot of angst later, the productivity largely hasn't shown up—unsurprising because very few people use their PCs to increase their productivity—and we've ended up like the kid looking for his lost quarter under the streetlight even though he lost it a block away because "the light is better here."

WHY DOES IS NEED TO BE GOOD AT MEASUREMENT?

IS needs to become very good at defining, collecting, reporting, and acting on business measures. One reason is that other people are measuring our worth, and they're doing an awful job of it, too—like, for example, searching for productivity improvements and failing to find them when that isn't the point of a lot of our effort in the first place.

We're far better off defining our own, useful measures of the value we create than letting someone else do it to us.

The second reason we need to become good at business measures is that a lot of what we do we can do better, and the first step in improving any process is being able to measure it. Otherwise, we don't make progress—we just posture and argue.

And finally, every time we modify an application or install a new one, it's for the purpose of improving our companies. It isn't always to increase productivity, but it is to improve something, and that something is usually an important business process.

The new application or application modification should lead to immediate improvements and facilitate ongoing improvement for some time to come. Process improvement can't happen without process measurement for the simple reason that without process measurement there's no way of knowing whether anything has improved or not.

Jerry Pournelle used to say that "Anything not worth doing isn't worth doing well." That seems to fit most managers' view of business measures—they don't much like 'em, but because business has become increasingly "metrics[1]-driven," they have to measure something. Just don't make it too hard.

The definition of good business measures is hard, rigorous brain-work. It requires thought, analysis, and a few iterations to get right.

EXAMPLE: MEASURING THE PC'S VALUE

How, for example, might one measure the value of a personal computer?

Let's start by dispensing with the commonplace but erroneous notion that PCs are supposed to make employees more productive. Thinking about how people use PCs leads to the conclusion that the PC makes people more capable and effective, not more productive. It might seem like a fine distinction. It isn't.

Productivity measures the number of units of something produced through the consumption of a single unit of something else. If we increase the number of widgets we produce while "consuming" a single hour, we've increased productivity. If the number of miles "produced" (traveled) while consuming a single gallon of gasoline goes down, our car's productivity has gone down and we know we might need to do some maintenance[2].

What units of anything do we produce with a PC? It depends on the task and most of us use our PCs for a wide variety of tasks. We use it to write memos, for example, but if we write a longer memo in the same period of time, we aren't more productive, just wordier.

In fact, executives now write their own memos on PCs. Their Cretaceous counterparts dictated or hand-wrote them, gave them to a secretary to be typed, and then revised them and had them retyped once or twice. They probably spent less total time in the process then than now, so the PC has made them less productive.

---

[1]*The difference between a metric and a measure is either that metrics, created as they are by consultants, sound more precise and are more expensive than measures, or that metrics are ratios whereas measures are simple quantities—miles and gallons are measures whereas miles-per-gallon is a metric. I call them measures and I say to heck with it.*
[2]*Miles-per-gallon is a familiar, easy-to-understand productivity measure. So now you're in charge of the corporate fleet and someone suggests you fuel some of the cars with propane instead of gasoline. Do you compare propane and gasoline-fueled cars by miles-per-gallon or by some other measure instead?*

Of course, where the old process took as long as a week from the time the executive wrote the first draft until the time the memo went into the mail, the new, email-based process takes less than an hour from the time the executive starts to type until the memo's recipients have it in their inboxes.

Which gives us two keys to measuring the value of the PC. The first key is that it has made people more effective, not more productive. What we need to assess whether PCs have been worthwhile are measures of effectiveness, not measures of productivity.

What constitutes a good measure of effectiveness? There is no such thing, or rather, there are dozens and perhaps hundreds of such measures. The office workers, managers, and executives who use PCs embed them in their work habits. To assess the value of the PC, "all you gotta do" is figure out what each user of a PC is responsible for, and then figure out how the lack of a PC would affect their capability to fulfill those responsibilities.

The second key to measuring the value of the PC comes from the nature of the example: It involves a single, well-defined process—writing and dispatching a memo. Measurement is about processes and process improvement. That's been known at least since W. Edwards Deming first introduced the concept of statistical process control.

Which leads us to the conclusion that measuring the costs and benefits of the PC are the wrong things to measure—measurement is about processes, not things.

DEFINING PROCESS MEASURES

In 1981, in his fascinating book *The Question of Animal Awareness,* the scientist Donald Griffin described a four-step process of scientific inquiry:

1. List all variables that might affect a system.
2. Study the variables easiest to measure.
3. Declare these to be the most important variables.
4. Proclaim the other variables don't really exist.

Many process managers go through a similar exercise. It's the wrong one[3]. Here's a better alternative:

1. Establish what's important—that is, management's goals, arranged into a thought map that relates the various goals to each other.
2. Define a mathematical expression—a measure—that corresponds to each management goal.

---

[3] *If you weren't clear on this point, perhaps a different career might be a better fit to your talents.*

3. Test each measure to determine whether it behaves properly—whether it always goes one way when things improve and always goes the other when things get worse. If a measure fails to behave properly, modify and refine it until it does.

4. Develop suitable data collection and reporting procedures.

5. Implement a process-improvement program.

The rest of this chapter details how to go about each of these steps. We'll concentrate on data center operations because that's where IS directly delivers the goods to the rest of the company every minute of every day (it's unambiguously a core process), but your business analysts can apply the exact same method to create a system of measures for any business process they help redesign and automate.

STEP 1: ESTABLISH MANAGEMENT GOALS

What's important? Connect the dots between data center operations and real, paying customers—the people who make or influence buying decisions. What's important to them about the process you're analyzing?

In the case of the data center, the answer is obvious: Real paying customers want to never hear certain phrases. High on their list of exactly what they don't want to hear are

- "I can't help you now because the computer is down."
- "Boy, the computer is slow today."
- "I'm sorry you didn't receive your refund check. We had a computer crash and they can't find the backup tape."

(Two other perennial favorites are: "I'm sorry your invoice is wrong. We have a computer glitch we've been trying to fix," and "Our systems won't let me do that for you." These aren't data center issues, though.)

Metrics weenies make a distinction between "external" and "internal" goals right about now, and it's a good distinction to remember. External goals are what people outside the process care about. Internal goals are the levers process managers can push and pull to affect the external measures.

Every good measurement design starts by establishing external goals for each core process.

No, that isn't right. Good measurement is part of good process management, and good process management starts by establishing clear external goals for each core process. Measurement design isn't possible until the process manager has defined the process goals, and often it's when we start defining performance measures that we realize we haven't established goals with sufficient clarity (or at all).

The data center is messy in this regard because the data center doesn't manage just one process. A typical data center manages a lot of them including batch processing, output distribution, intercompany information exchanges in the form of electronic data interchange (EDI) and electronic funds transfers (EFT), interactive processing, personal computer installation, end-user support, data recovery, and PC repairs. And those are just the externally visible processes. Internally there are disciplines like system and network management, change control, and system backup.

That's a lot of stuff. So now that we have a manageable example, we'll zoom in further and analyze the Help Desk in our examples.

Our Help Desk answers calls from end-users and either resolves the request during the phone call or escalates it to a suitable specialist based on the nature of the call. The Help Desk process isn't complete until the call is marked "closed" and a resolution has been entered.

External Goals

External goals are related to the products and services you offer. They are the goals whose achievement is directly visible to recipients of your products and services and that can be connected to the creation of value for your company's customers. And although the recipients of your products and services aren't "internal customers," it's still true that nobody wants a product or service—they want the result of receiving the product or service.

Car buyers don't buy cars. They pay money for luxury transportation, reliable transportation, an ego-gratifying transportation experience, a collectible investment, or whatever other result they're looking for. The object is a means to an end.

In the same way, employees who call the Help Desk have an issue they need resolved. Real paying customers want employee issues resolved because that makes employees more effective in creating customer value. Your primary external goal is to maximize the Help Desk's effectiveness by maximizing the extent to which it makes employees more effective in their own jobs.

Effectiveness has three components: Cost, speed, and quality. As the old saying goes, you can have it cheaper, faster, or better—pick two. And so long as you don't change the system you're managing in a fundamental way, these three commodities trade off against each other.

Cost

Cost means unit cost—the expense associated with production of a single unit of output, however it's defined. From the perspective of goal-setting, you always want cost to be as low as possible. The question is how much you're willing to compromise speed and quality in the process.

For our Help Desk example, the cost goal is to keep the cost of handling each end-user problem as low as possible. By doing so, we can support the largest number of end-users.

Speed

Speed is how long it takes you to deliver the goods after receiving a request. Setting speed goals is much like setting cost goals—anything longer than instantaneous is a compromise. In any system there's a natural limit to how much you can improve speed through ingenuity. There's a point at which speed improvements come through cost increases or quality reduction. The trick for you is to be a strong enough leader to challenge everyone's ingenuity without being unrealistic.

As with most process goals, the perception of the service recipient is often as important as the reality. The Help Desk's speed goals aren't hard to figure out (there are two: answering each call quickly and resolving each caller's issues with minimal delay), but it's worth going through the thought process that gets us there to demonstrate this point.

Imagine two Help Desks. The first answers every call within three rings—no caller is ever put into a hold queue—but the analysts aren't the sharpest knives in the drawer. They have a set problem-resolution routine that generally gets them to a solution, but it takes awhile to slog through it.

The second Help Desk uses a different staffing model. The best analysts in IS rotate in and out of it so everyone handles calls. This, of course, is an expensive way to staff the Help Desk, so callers usually have to wait awhile in the hold queue before they get to talk to someone. When they do, the analyst usually resolves their issue within a minute.

On the average, the two Help Desks get issues resolved in the same period of time. But which one generates more satisfaction with the end-user community? The first one, of course.

It's a psychological issue: People hate to be on hold; they're relatively patient when they perceive somebody is working on their problem. That's why speed of answer is an important process goal. It has no operational value—what "really" matters is how fast end-user problems are taken care of.

That's a fine thing for you to understand. Just don't try to sell the end-user community on it, because they'll hang you for that kind of attitude.

Actually they'll ask why can't they have both short hold times and fast issue resolution. Don't fight it—as you'll see in the next section, the Help Desk has a tangible and important impact on employee morale, and making end-users wait a long time on hold doesn't get you there.

Quality

Cost and speed are pretty tangible qualities. Quality, on the other hand, is a term so widely abused that nobody knows what it means anymore.

In Statistical Process Control circles, quality means conformance to specifications, which doesn't help all that much because it begs the question of what is to be specified, and assumes whatever you're measuring is amenable to objective measurement.

If you're manufacturing rulers, length is the most important specification (width, on the other hand, is not). In the data center, the length of your file servers is of little interest to anyone except a space planner, whereas reliability, a term that isn't very meaningful in the context of a ruler, is preeminently important[4].

Conformance to specifications has the advantage of making quality measurable. It has the disadvantage of being entirely different from how most customers (and most human beings, for that matter) use the term.

Most of us relate quality to value, not conformance to specifications. That is, we don't think, "Hey, this car is exactly as long as the manufacturer says it is!" We think, "Wow! The seats are made of genuine Corinthian leather, not imitation Naugahyde!"

Items that don't meet defined specifications are, for the most part, perceived as slipshod and disappointing. Another way to think about a failure to meet specifications is that it's *value reduction*—quality that isn't noticed when it's present, but is obvious and resented when absent, reducing the perceived value of products and services.

Ever receive an invoice that's wrong? Get a few of these and you'll be ready to find a new supplier—who can deal with the kind of idiot that can't even bill you for the right amount? You'll probably tell your friends about what an undesirable supplier this bozo is, too[5].

---

[4]*Sorry this isn't more challenging. Not everything that's important is hard to understand, though, and you don't get to try the complicated stuff until you get the basics right.*
[5]*Even when the error is in your favor, because what usually happens is that the vendor eventually finds the mistakes and then bills you for a huge adjustment when you least expect it.*

Wrong invoices reduce the perception of value on the part of most customers, but accurate invoices don't increase the perception of value. The proof: Have you ever exclaimed to a friend what a great supplier the XYZ Company is because it always gets the invoice right? If so, you must have experienced a lot of disappointment in your life.

Telecom managers are often saddled with this problem (being measured on negative quality, not on having experienced a lot of disappointment). Dial tone is expected. The telecom manager is invisible unless there's a problem, so doing a perfect job means going unnoticed (if the telecom manager defines the job as delivering dial tone).

The Help Desk needs to avoid value reduction along with everyone else. It reduces value every time an end-user problem takes too long to be resolved or doesn't get resolved at all. So long as a problem is unresolved, someone in the company either can't get their job done at all or takes longer to do it than they should. To the extent that the jobs people have are worth doing and add perceived value for real paying customers, every time the Help Desk fails, eventually it has some impact on a customer.

That gets us to the key thought process you need to go through in establishing your goals: Someone outside of your organization—either the direct recipient of your services, a real paying customer, or both—must care about every attribute of your service you plan to define as an external goal.

So—one set of goals for the Help Desk will relate to getting issues resolved. Your direct service recipients certainly care about this—it's the reason for your existence. Paying customers who can't get the service they need when employees can't function care about it too.

We've already covered the cost and speed of resolving issues. Now we need to adhere to specifications, and in the context of a Help Desk, adherence to specifications means accuracy—diagnosing problems correctly and recommending the right solutions the first time. Everything else is a mistake—it's out of spec—and reduces the perceived value of the service you provide.

Adherence to specification—the way quality experts define the term—means avoiding value reduction. The rest of us, who think of quality in terms of genuine Corinthian leather, figure quality means creating the perception of additional value. Call this property—the one that makes service recipients and paying customers happy enough to talk about you in positive terms—*value added*.

It's right about here that the quandary of the internal customer comes into the discussion. As noted in Chapter 5, "Your Role in the Business," there's no such thing as an internal customer, except through the magic of metaphor and the vagaries of internal charge-back systems. As you make decisions, you have to figure out whether you're adding value for your "internal customer" or for the company's real paying customers.

> ### INTERNAL CUSTOMERS REDUX
>
> Let's imagine you've landed on the side of truth, righteousness, and the American Way and agree that the whole idea of the internal customers is wrong. You promote your newfound understanding (or old-found understanding if you've been thinking this way for a while) to the rest of the company. The CEO disagrees with you. What now?
>
> The answer is simple—you shrug and treat employees as internal customers. That's because your real internal customers, which is to say the people you report to and want to report to, have given you work direction. Every successful leader knows when to shrug, accept a decision, and move on.
>
> Keep on lobbying for a new approach if you like. But be smart about it. Pick your spots and make each conversation on the subject a new event and thought process, not simple nagging.

Assuming you find the right answer (real paying customers) how do you figure the needs and wants of your service recipients into the equation?

We're focusing on the Help Desk for this exercise. Take a moment to connect the dots between it and real paying customers. Does the Help Desk have any opportunities to create added value as well as avoiding value reduction?

Absolutely. Customer perception is customer reality, and perceived value is value. That means if you can improve the way customers experience your company, you're adding value. Can you do that through the Help Desk?

The Help Desk has a chance to incrementally improve both the morale and the competence of each employee that calls it. The morale and competence of your company's employees, in turn, largely determines how real paying customers experience your company every time they contact it.

That means your Help Desk and the specialists who handle the tough problems it can't solve add value by being pleasant and helpful, and by looking for opportunities to show whoever they're helping a new and useful trick during every conversation.

Those are important things to do. Even better, they cost you nothing. Good manners are free, but bad manners can be very expensive.

The Help Desk, then, has two additional goals—to make every employee contact an enjoyable one, and to use every contact to increase employee skills. These goals don't take precedence over fixing the original problem, but they're important just the same.

Take a step back for a second to review the goals we've established thus far and you'll see something missing. Somewhere in all this, you ought to know what your service recipients think of you. People who receive services don't peel the onion as far as the people who deliver them, because they don't have to. That means employees don't say to each other, "Well, our Help Desk is good at keeping its costs down and responds quickly, but the percentage of calls in which it gets the diagnosis right the first time is off by a few percentage points from what I'd really like."

Nor do they say, "Our Help Desk does a fine job of meeting its defined goals of accurately diagnosing problems and proposing useful and appropriate solutions while always being cheerful and pleasant, and also helping me by suggesting new techniques I didn't know before."

They either say, "Our Help Desk stinks!" or "Every time I call them they just do a great job."

You want to know what your service recipients think of you, because if they think you stink you have *tsuris*[6].

External Goal Summary

- *Cost:* Minimize the cost per end-user issue resolved
- *Speed*

  Answer calls quickly

  Resolve issues quickly
- *Quality*

  Accurate diagnosis

  Appropriate solutions

  Enjoyable interactions

  Enhanced end-user skills

  Favorable service-recipient perception

Internal Goals

You can't always grab hold of an external outcome and just change it to suit your purposes. A lot of your influence as a manager is indirect. You push and pull hidden buttons and levers and if you do it right, the Help Desk's effectiveness increases.

---

[6]*Plenty headaches.*

For example, callers don't have any idea how many Help Desk analysts are on duty at any given moment. Callers either get through immediately or are put on hold. Callers also experience your unit costs either directly, through charge backs, or indirectly through your impact on the company bottom line. Your staffing level affects unit costs, too.

Somehow you need to strike the right balance between keeping hold times down and keeping unit costs down—you need to optimize *staffing utilization*.

Optimal staffing utilization is an example of an internal goal. So are Help Desk analyst turnover, training, morale, and lots of other issues under your direct control but invisible to callers.

As part of establishing what's important, you need to decide on your most important internal goals. For each internal goal, you need to understand which external goals it affects and how.

This is a mathematically-oriented chapter. In keeping with this slant, here's something you may remember from high-school algebra: The specifics are left as an exercise for the reader.

STEP 2: DEFINE MEASURES

One of the silliest statements I ever heard an executive make was about measures of success. Having just defined them, and having based the annual performance bonus calculation on them, he explained his expectation that managers would "do the right thing" if what was good for the business would drive the measure in the wrong direction.

Lewis's Fifth Law of Management states, "What you can't measure, you can't manage but when you mismeasure, you mismanage." You're far better off not measuring at all than measuring the wrong thing. That's because, when you establish a measure and put its graph on the wall, everyone in the company will stop moving the business and start moving the measure. If you've defined good measures, the company and the measure will move in the right direction together.

If, on the other hand, you've done a sloppy job, it's been nice knowing you.

Many bad measures come from the irrational notion that the only good measures are objective. That's ridiculous—imagine what would happen if Steven Spielberg relied on only objective measures in evaluating screenwriters, for example—he'd hire the fastest typists, not the people capable of creating drama, tension, and dialog.

Lots of what you need to measure can only be measured subjectively. That doesn't mean you should shy away from it. It means you need good judgment to measure it. Objective measures aren't bad things—they're rare, and they get increasingly rare as the quality you're measuring becomes more important, but they aren't bad things at all.

They aren't, however, the only thing.

On with the show. In Step One we established what's important in the Help Desk's processes. Now it's time to turn these goals into measures.

THE PARABLE OF THE LAWN MOWER FACTORY

To understand some of the problems associated with measurement, imagine you now run a lawn mower factory. In addition to unit cost and cycle time, you decide to measure the defect rate—a common enough manufacturing measure, and an important one because nobody wants to buy a defective lawn mower.

You buy a big roll of graph paper, post it on the wall, and chart defects per thousand lawn mowers, adding a new data point every week. Sure enough, the defect rate drops continuously from the day you put up the graph.

As it turns out, your lawn mowers are subject to two different defects: (1) Bad paint jobs; and (2) weak blades that shatter unpredictably, amputating the feet of the lawnmower pusher.

It also turns out that detecting and remedying bad paint jobs is easy. The lawn mower blades are a tougher problem. Your foremen and the people on the production line, being practical people, succeed in reducing the defect rate by concentrating on improving the paint jobs, ignoring the thornier blade problem.

The defect rate plummets and everyone is happy. Except, of course, for your "footloose" customers and your legal department, which has to explain why you care more about making the whole lawn mower a uniform shade of green.

The problem is that your initial measure, defects per thousand lawn mowers per week, failed to apply a common-sense understanding of the relative importance of different kinds of defects. Armed with an appreciation for more complex mathematics, you boldly go where no lawn mower factory manager has gone before and change your measure to:

$$\text{Defect Rate} = \frac{\sum (\text{Importance Factor} \times \text{Defect})}{\text{Lawnmowers} \div 1,000}$$

continues

continued

> It looks complicated, but all you're doing is counting some defects more than others. You assign, for example, an Importance Factor of 1 to bad paint jobs and 1,000 to defective blades. If, in one month, you produce 5,000 lawn mowers with 5 bad paint jobs and 1 defective blade, your defect rate for the month will be (1,000×1 + 5)/5 = 201 defects per thousand lawn mowers.
>
> That, of course, is awful, and what's even better is that everyone in the factory immediately understands that catching one bad blade will improve the factory's performance statistics as much as catching 1,000 bad paint jobs.
>
> The result: Fewer amputations, a better factory, and best of all, a happy legal department!

Cost Measurement

We've set a goal of minimizing the cost of resolving each end-user issue. It's easy to say this. Figuring out what it means is a lot more fun.

When you're dealing with labor-intensive operations like a Help Desk, don't bother figuring in the cost of equipment and facilities. That isn't what you're trying to improve anyway.

How about time? Time is a useful surrogate measure for money[7] and lacks some of money's complications[8]. But what time gets counted? The Help Desk analyst's time spent resolving problems? Of course, but how about those inevitable times when an analyst is present but the phone isn't ringing? Or the analysts to whom problems are escalated when the Help Desk can't handle the problem over the phone? How about end-user downtime, time on hold, and time spent on the phone working with the Help Desk? We're dealing with external goals right now, so all these factors should be included in your unit costs, don't you think?

In English, we want to add up all these cost components and divide by the number of problems to come up with the average time per problem. We arrive at the formula

---

[7]*All together now: "Time is money." Thank you.*
[8]*To track money, you'd include each analyst's salary in your computations. Even the most mathematically illiterate employee will be able to figure out whether he or she is above or below the average salary you pay. That's generally a bad idea.*

$$Cost = \frac{(HDA + EA + \sum \#EUs \times Issue\ Duration)}{\#\ Issues}$$

where

> *Cost* is the average cost of resolving a reported issue measured in staff hours.
>
> *HDA* is the number of full-time–equivalent Help Desk Analyst hours available in the reporting period (including vacation, sick time, and unproductive hours—you're paying for the time so count it in).
>
> *EA* time is the time spent by "Escalation Analysts"—anyone to whom the Help Desk escalates problems—handling issues elevated to them by the Help Desk.
>
> *#EUs* are the number of end-users affected by each reported issue.
>
> *Issue Duration* is, for a single issue, the number of business hours elapsed from the time it was reported to the time it was resolved.
>
> Σ is the mathematical symbol for summation, in this case adding things up for all reported problems.
>
> *#Issues* is the number of separate problems reported in a reporting period.

What you're doing is adding up all the IS hours devoted to Help Desk issues—all Help Desk analyst hours plus the time everyone else takes handling Help Desk issues. To that you're adding all the end-user downtime: For each problem, multiply the number of people it affects by its duration to get the total number of employee hours lost per problem, and then add all the problems together.

Add up all the time, divide by the number of problems, and you get the total time per problem.

Okay, be honest. When you saw the sigma (the "Σ") did you start to sweat just a little bit? Sorry. Measures aren't supposed to be simple. They're supposed to be mathematical expressions of what's important. When Deming started all this with Statistical Process Control, he made extensive use of multiple regression analysis—a technique that involves complex calculations and requires a sophisticated knowledge of statistics. Simple measures have nothing to do with good measures, and because when you mis-measure you mismanage, you're better off skipping this section entirely than shying away from the right measure just because it takes a bit of math.

Speed Measurement

Speed also has its complications. It might mean the "cycle time"—the elapsed clock/calendar time between the moment you start producing whatever it is you produce and the time it's finished. It also might mean the time that passes between the moment you start producing something and the moment you ship it. Think it's the same? No, you're more sophisticated than that.

We established two external Help Desk goals: Answering calls quickly and resolving issues quickly. When you experience equipment failure, the time needed to resolve the problem (the external measure) will be shorter than your measure of the time needed to repair the failed item[9] (an important *internal* measure).

It's a good idea in these situations to establish two kinds of measures—averages and service levels. Averages tell everyone what to expect. Service levels tell everyone what you consider to be acceptable.

Speed of Answer Measures

We've decided that answering calls quickly is an important goal, not because it matters in any objective sense, but because it has a lot to do with the end-user experience, which has an impact on their morale (and, as a consequence, on the whole company's perception of IS).

Average Speed of Answer

You measure the average speed of answer the way you come up with any average—add everything up and divide by the number of events:

$$\text{Speed of Answer} = \frac{\sum (\text{Hold Time})}{\# \text{ Calls}}$$

In other words, you add up all the time people wait until they talk to an analyst and divide it by the number of calls to calculate the speed of answer, measured in seconds per call.

Speed of Answer Service Level

Service level measures take a bit more doing but aren't really more complicated. Service levels are defined by the percentage of events that fall within a range. In defining the measure, you can either establish the percentage and measure what service level you're delivering to that percentage of events, or you can establish the service level and determine what percentage of events fall within it.

---

[9]*Assuming you've established a fault-tolerant architecture, a hot-backup system, or a spare-parts inventory. If you haven't—now you understand how implementing a system of well-chosen performance measures can lead you to improve your processes.*

For the Help Desk's speed of answer service level, we can start by asking what level of service 95% of the callers experience. That is, we sort the calls from shortest to longest answer time. If we had 100 calls, we'd find the 95th call on the list. The time that caller waited on hold would be the service level we're delivering.

As a formula:

$$\text{Service Level} = \text{Hold Time}_{0.95 \times n}$$

If n is the number of calls handled, $0.95 \times n$ is the call number below which 95% of the calls happened, so Hold Time $0.95 \times n$ is the longest hold time experienced by 95% of all callers.

If we chose to start with a set service level instead, we might say our goal is to answer calls within 20 seconds. Once again we'd sort the list from shortest to longest. This time we'd find the last call on the list answered within 20 seconds. As a formula:

$$\text{Service Level} = \frac{\text{\# Calls answered within 20 seconds}}{\text{\# Calls}}$$

There, that wasn't so bad, now was it?

Issue-Resolution Measures

We've already sidestepped the hardest part of establishing good issue-resolution measures. That's the trusty "calls-per-hour" metric that's so popular among incompetent call center managers.

Calls per hour is popular for a simple reason: Automated Call Distributors spit out call-per-hour statistics at the push of a button, sliced and diced in countless ways. Calls per hour doesn't tell you anything useful, and drives exactly the wrong behavior on the part of the call center staff as well[10]. It's a classic example of measuring what's easy to measure instead of what's important.

You, however, know better. You need to assess performance on resolving issues.

---

[10]*Not clear? Okay, your performance is assessed based on the volume of calls you handle. What will you do with callers who have complex, time-consuming problems? That's right! You'll dump them as fast as you can.*

13

PROCESS
MEASUREMENT

Average Issue Resolution Performance

Once again, you should probably calculate average performance and service level. That is, you should measure the average time needed to resolve a problem, and the percent of all problems resolved within an established time limit. Turning these into formulas you get

$$\text{Resolution Time} = \frac{\sum \text{Issue Duration}}{\text{\# Issues Reported}}$$

where Issue Duration is the clock/calendar time that elapsed between the moment an issue was first reported and the moment the person or people reporting the issue[11] agree it was taken care of.

Reread the preceding paragraph and you'll see one of the fringe benefits of defining performance measures. They require you to be precise in your thinking. Managers of Help Desks that aren't driven by performance measures think it's just as important to handle end-user issues quickly as you do. Establishing the measure, though, leads to definition of when an issue has been dealt with: when the end-user agrees it's been taken care of.

That will eliminate the happy practice of a technician visiting the end-user, tightening a few bolts, closing the problem, and moving on.

Issue Resolution Service Level

This works the same way as the speed-of-answer service level—you can start with either the percentage of issues or the speed and back into the other. So, your measure is either:

$$\text{Service Level} = \text{Issue Resolution Time}_{0.95 \times n}$$

or

$$\text{Service Level} = \frac{\text{\# Issues resolved within 1 day}}{\text{\# Issues}}$$

assuming, of course, that you want to discover the level of service you're providing for 95% of issues reported (first formula) or the percentage of all issues you're resolving within one day.

---

[11]*Are you wondering why we're calling these things "issues" instead of "problems"? It's because not every call to the Help Desk is to report a problem. Some are requests for advice (how do I make a word bold-face after I've typed it?") for example. So problems are just one type of issue dealt with by the Help Desk.*

Quality Measures

You'll recall we established five external quality goals for the Help Desk: Accurate diagnosis, appropriate solutions, enhanced end-user skills, enjoyable interactions, and favorable end-user perception.

How are you going to measure these?

Accurate Diagnosis and Appropriate Solutions

These are a matter of conformance to specifications. For each you should establish both averages and service levels. You'd measure the accuracy of your diagnoses, for example, by calculating the average number of diagnoses per reported issue. The service level is the percentage of reported issues diagnosed right on the first try.

The solutions measures are similar—the average number of solutions tried before issues are resolved and the percentage of issues resolved the first try.

The exact formulas are left as exercises for the reader—they aren't particularly complicated, and look a lot like previous formulas.

Employee Skill Enhancement

How are you going to measure employee skill enhancement? Hey, nobody said this was going to be easy. You have several choices here, depending on how much effort you're willing to expend.

One approach is to use an indirect measure. The more skills employees have, the more they can deal with minor issues themselves and the more they'll encounter difficult, complex problems and try difficult, advanced techniques. You can, therefore, construct a measure based on the kinds of issues employees call in over time.

To do this you need to assign a difficulty factor to each call, and also to exclude all equipment-related ones. Next you construct your measure. Because the idea is to track the average employee skill level over time as indicated by the difficulty of the issues reported, you decide to use the average difficulty level as your index:

$$\text{Employee Skill Index} = \frac{\left(\sum \text{Call Difficulty Rating}_{\text{Non-Equipment-Failure Calls}} \right)}{\text{\# Non-Equipment-Failure Calls}}$$

Another way to measure employee skills is more direct, but also more time-consuming: Ask them, and ask their managers. You could construct an employee survey ("Do you feel smarter than you did three months ago?") or a skill assessment instrument ("How do you define a new style in Microsoft Word?"). You could simply call a sample of end-users shortly after their problems have been closed and ask them if, as part of the process of getting their issues resolved, they learned anything new about using their personal computers.

Enjoyable Interactions and Favorable Overall Perception

And you thought end-user skill enhancement was subjective and hard to measure. How are you going to objectively measure whether end-user interactions with the Help Desk and escalation analysts were enjoyable and whether their overall perception of the Help Desk is favorable?

There's an easy answer to this question: You're not.

Somewhere in the evolution of human resources theory, probably in the resources of some dark, forbidding courtroom, somebody put forth the proposition that only qualities that can be objectively measured should be taken into account in assessing an employee's performance.

That's fine. Keep in mind that according to the law, witches and warlocks once roamed the land. The law doesn't provide a process for arriving at accurate descriptions of reality. That isn't what it's for[12].

End-user perceptions are subjective by definition. That makes them no less important. Quite the opposite, their perceptions are more important than anything else.

There's only one way to find out whether end-users found their interactions with the Help Desk and Escalation Analysts pleasant, and that's to ask them. Plan on surveying a sample of callers.

Employee Surveys

Several of your quality dimensions call for employee surveys—employee skill enhancement, whether the experience is enjoyable, and what the overall perception is. The best way to survey is soon after the interaction, while memories are fresh.

In constructing the survey, make sure it's brief, to the point, and asks its questions in an unbiased way. The best way to do that is to pick up the phone, call your marketing research department, and ask for its help.

They'll be delighted, especially if you agree to fix some irritating problem they've been living with for months in exchange for your help.

---

[12]*No, we won't indulge in any lawyer jokes in this book, and in fact most of the lawyers I've known personally have been fine people. It's probably one of those cases where people who are perfectly normal as individuals act in strange ways when they congregate. Let's leave it at that.*

Internal Measures

As process manager, you established internal as well as external goals for your process. You need to measure these, too. Fuel consumption per passenger mile is a key measure in the airline industry (even though no passenger cares about it at all) because fuel consumption drives margins, which in turn drive both ticket prices and some quality issues like food quality (the more fuel you burn, the less you can afford to provide other amenities).

You'll go through the same process to define internal measures as external ones—you're basically translating English to Math.

STEP 3: TESTING AND REFINING THE MEASURES

"Okay," you say, rubbing your hands with glee[13], we're ready to go out and measure!

No, you're not. You haven't yet taken an important step, which is making sure your measures behave properly. Behaving properly in this case doesn't mean they extend their pinkies while sipping coffee daintily from a cup. It means always going one way when things improve and always going the other when they get worse[14].

There are two reasons this is important: First, you plan to use the measure to find out how things are going. If it doesn't behave properly, you have no way of knowing.

Second and more important, employees are very good at making measures go the way you want them to, and they're very good at finding the easiest way to do so. If your measure doesn't behave properly, your employees might choose to improve the measure at the expense of the business (see the section titled "The Parable of the Lawn Mower Factory").

Look at each measure you've defined, putting yourself in the role of an employee responsible for improving it, and look for loopholes—actions you can take that will improve the measure without affecting real performance. Run some real-world events through it to see how they affect the measure, too. What you're doing is a lot like software testing—you want to make sure the odd situations and boundary conditions don't mess things up.

---

[13]*I'm tempted to explain that Glee™ is a hand soap popular among programmers, but that would plagiarize Richard Armour's* Twisted Tales from Shakespeare.

[14]*This, by the way, is why stock price is such an impossibly bad measure of company performance. Stock price is driven by investor expectations of other investor expectations of how the company will perform in the future. There are lengthy accounting rituals that take place at the end of fiscal periods, the entire purpose of which is manipulation of the stock price (and executive compensation). Some, such as deferring important purchases, damage the company in the bargain.*

Most of the measures defined in the previous section are flawed in some way. Let's find a few and fix them.

Refining the Cost Measure

We measured cost, you'll recall, through the formula

$$Cost = \frac{(HDA + EA + \sum \#EUs \times Issue\ Duration)}{\#\ Issues}$$

It accurately portrays the average cost of the issues called into the Help Desk. So what's the problem?

Your chosen measure makes your performance look better when end-users call in easy problems than when they call in hard ones. Remember, when you give employees a measure of success, they'll become more successful, whatever it takes. If what it takes is to discourage end-users from calling in difficult problems, they'll do that. And end-users are all too willing to bypass the Help Desk anyway.

How do you fix this glitch in the measure? Simple—give the Help Desk more credit when it fixes a hard problem than when it takes care of a simple issue. All you need to do to accomplish this is to assign a weighting factor—a Difficulty Factor (DF)—to each problem, so hard ones count as multiple easy ones. Helping a caller who's forgotten how to change a typeface gets a DF of 1. Diagnosing and replacing a defective mouse gets a DF of 2. Determining that someone has a network interface card with an obsolete driver that's flooding the network with bad packets rates a 5.

How do you apply this notion to the formula?

$$Cost = \frac{(HDA + EA + \sum \#EUs \times Issue\ Duration)}{\sum DF \times Issue}$$

where ΣDF×Issue is simply a matter of multiplying each issue by its difficulty factor and then adding the results together.

The measure still isn't entirely fixed, though, and you probably spotted the problem a long time ago: Not all problems have the same impact on the company.

This is obvious: If an end-user has forgotten how to make a PowerPoint screen object rotate, they can continue their work for an indefinite period before this lack of knowledge becomes debilitating. If the mainframe crashes, on the other hand, a third of the company might have nothing useful to do until it's back online.

Our measure already takes into account the number of people affected, so we're halfway home. All we need to do is factor in how severely they're affected and we're done. We do that by creating an Impact Factor (IF) that ranges from 1 (minor inconvenience) to 5 (destroys the ozone layer). We add this factor to our formula as follows:

$$\text{Cost} = \frac{(\text{HDA} + \text{EA} + \sum \#\text{EUs} \times \text{IF} \times \text{Issue Duration})}{\sum \text{DF} \times \text{Issue}}$$

so the time tallied for each issue is amplified by the impact.

Now we're done.

Refining Speed Measures

Our speed-of-answer measures look pretty good.

They're incomplete, of course—by themselves, they'd encourage Help Desk analysts to answer the phone and immediately hang up without providing any help of any kind. That's okay, though, because we have other measures that this kind of behavior would destroy. For the purposes it was created for, though, the average speed of answer and the speed of answer service level measures do what they should[15].

How about the speed of resolution measures? Our formula, you'll recall, is

$$\text{Resolution Time} = \frac{\sum \text{Issue Duration}}{\# \text{Issues Reported}}$$

Look good? Again, think about what kinds of behavior you want to encourage. Here's the magic question: Do you want the Help Desk to give all issues equal priority?

Of course not, but that's what this measure does. It's easily fixed. We simply need to take into account the number of people affected by each issue and its impact (we already defined an impact factor). Add these to the formula and we get

$$\text{Resolution Time} = \frac{\sum \#\text{EUs} \times \text{IF} \times \text{Issue Duration}}{\#\text{Issues Reported}}$$

[15] *I think. It's still worth your while to try to poke some holes in them.*

That leaves us with one more question: Do we want to apply a difficulty factor to this formula as we did with the cost equation? In my opinion, it's a good idea, and for exactly the same reason it made sense when we calculated average cost: Without it, the Help Desk analysts have an incentive to discourage end-users from calling in difficult issues.

That yields the following as our measure of average resolution time:

$$\text{Resolution Time} = \frac{\sum \#EUs \times IF \times \text{Issue Duration}}{\sum DF \times \text{Issue}}$$

You should apply similar corrections to the service level measures we defined earlier.

Other Measurement Glitches

By now you should be self-sufficient, so revisit your quality measures and see if you need to apply the same weighting factors to them as we did to the cost and speed measures.

Once again, don't forget your internal measures. They might not be visible to service recipients or customers, but that doesn't make them unimportant. Oxygen isn't visible either.

DATA COLLECTION, REPORTING, AND USE

So far we've indulged ourselves with an exercise in applied mathematics. It's been fun, but it doesn't get us anywhere until we start to collect real data, tabulate it, and do something with it.

Systems Impact

If you hadn't already noticed, many of the measures we just established will require a lot of effort to collect and tabulate. So much effort, in fact, that you'll probably throw up your hands and throw in the towel.

Process measurement requires excellent process management systems that have data collection and performance measure reporting built into them. The process we went through in defining performance measures should generate a much better understanding of system requirements, in fact.

To take an example, many of the measures we just defined require us to track issues rather than calls. This is harder than it might seem at first glance. A moment's reflection tells you there's a many-to-many relationship between calls and issues: A caller can report more than one issue in a single call, many callers can report the same issue, and one end-user can make several calls to resolve a single issue.

Memo to system selection committee: Add "Ability to independently track calls and issues," to the RFP.

Process measurement is important, but if it becomes too time-consuming, your managers will spend too much time dealing with numbers and not enough time dealing with people. It isn't *that* important.

So make sure you build the data collection, computations, and reporting into your process management systems. This will prevent the measurement process from unduly interfering with your management goals.

IMPLEMENT A PROCESS IMPROVEMENT PROGRAM

It's time to remember the point of it all. Why are we putting ourselves through this agony?

The answer, of course, is that we want to improve our performance over time, and if we don't know how we're doing and how it compares with how we used to do, we won't know if we've improved or not.

Implementing a process improvement program isn't terribly complicated. It has three basic components:

1. Establishing benchmarks or baseline measures.
2. Tracking performance over time.
3. Creating opportunities to improve the process.

Establishing Benchmarks and Baselines

Benchmarking has taken its rightful place as a Recognized Consulting Buzzword. It's the process of comparing your results to how everyone else performs.

Benchmarking can be quite useful if you're faced with a recalcitrant or overly arrogant bunch of employees who figure they're already doing things just as well as it's possible to do them. Give them a benchmark that clearly shows they're under-performing and it's easier to break the logjam.

Benchmarking has a few problems, though. The first is that it only works for commodity processes—ones that have similar dynamics and goals in every company that contributes results to the benchmark. Sometimes this fits the situation—for example, when a company calculates the cost per check for payroll operations. More often, though, it doesn't. Even with a seeming commodity process like payroll it's important to make sure the benchmark you use has been segmented so it only includes similar companies. For example, a company with a lot of labor unions and a mixture of hourly and exempt employees will have a higher cost per check than one that pays all employees a straight salary.

Benchmarking can also undo some of the work we just did in this chapter. At the risk of being tactless, most business measurement is done poorly, sacrificing suitability for simplicity and ease of data collection. Do you really want to figure out how to apply a poorly constructed benchmark?

Baselines—The Easy Alternative to Benchmarks

"Baseline" simply means "How we did when we first established the measures." Baselines are wonderfully useful because when you've established them, you always know whether you're getting better.

You face two hazards in establishing baselines. The first is choosing the right data collection period. If the process you're measuring has seasonal variation, for example, you'd better spend a year establishing your baseline.

The second hazard is another example of making sure employees don't manipulate the measure. When everyone knows you're going to assess improvement over time, they have a stake in doing a mediocre job while the baseline is being established. This is hard to combat. Do your best, though, and be sure not to tie any financial incentives to first-year process improvement. It's a short-term problem, but an aggravating one.

SERVICE LEVEL AGREEMENTS

It's become fashionable in IS to negotiate service level agreements (SLAs) with the end-user community. An SLA is nothing more than a contract between IS and the rest of the company that commits IS to providing a level of service and that commits the rest of the company to finding that level of service acceptable. The Help Desk, for example, might establish an SLA that says 90% of all calls will be answered within 20 seconds; an onsite technician will arrive within an hour of a call to the Help Desk for 90% of the calls that require it; and 95% of all problems will be resolved within one day of the problem being reported.

An SLA, in other words, is something of a cross between a benchmark and a baseline.

Don't be surprised when you find the end-user community not caring about your SLAs the day after you establish them, though. SLAs are useful for IS. End-users want their problems fixed, and although they might understand and agree to something less than the instantaneous resolution of all problems, they no more define their satisfaction in terms of your meeting a set of SLAs than you define satisfaction with Kellogg's, Post, or General Mills cereals as keeping the insect part count below the FDA-approved levels.

Although SLAs are good measures for you to use in managing the process, you're better off treating them as internal measures. When you communicate your performance to end-users, they'll probably care more about the averages and a discussion of the three events in which you performed the worst than they'll care about the service level you provide.

Tracking Performance Over Time

This is pretty easy. On whatever schedule makes sense for each measure, grab its value and add it to a chart or graph to see how you're doing. The benchmark or baseline you established becomes a horizontal line on the same graph, which tells you whether you're getting better or not.

Choose a small number of key measures, both external and internal—no more than five. Make these the ones you most want employees to improve. Put a big chart on the wall someplace everyone will see it every day, and graph these five or so crucial measures on it.

Think of this as a dashboard. You don't see every possible driving measure on your dashboard, either—just the handful you need, like engine temperature and fuel supply, to keep you from getting into trouble.

You might hear a bit of grumbling about the chart, especially at first. Stick with it. Employees generally love these things, so long as the meaning of the measures is clear. It tells them how they're doing and gives them something to shoot for.

You don't need to post the formula, although you should make it available to anyone who's interested. Just post something like "Average Weighted Issue Resolution Time" and make sure everyone knows you're factoring in the difficulty of each issue and its impact.

Also, print the words "Good" and "Bad" on the vertical axis. Don't make 'em guess.

Create Process Improvement Opportunities

First we had Suggestion Boxes. Then we had "Scientific Management" where professional time-and-motion analysts had all the good ideas. Now we have empowerment, and once again understand that the people who actually do the work often have some useful ideas.

Make sure it's easy for employees to convey those ideas to you, and make sure you suitably compensate employees for providing good suggestions that lead to tangible performance improvements.

This leads into a subject we'll deal with in more detail in a later chapter: Do you compensate the individual or the team? For process improvement ideas, my own preference is usually to compensate the team, for two reasons.

First, it's often difficult to track down just who had the good idea, and often you don't want to. Imagine a team brainstorming session on how to improve processes where you have to write down who has each idea and who refines it. Also, imagine spending time adjudicating disputes over who had an idea first, because in facilitated brainstorming sessions people take turns presenting ideas.

And of course, if you compensate individuals, everyone will spend their time and energy lobbying for their ideas rather than for the best ideas. They have money at stake, after all.

The same problems hold true if ideas come through suggestion boxes, email, phone calls, or private conversations. Compensating individuals for improvement ideas encourages the theft of ideas, "protection of intellectual property" (a bizarre notion when applied to a workgroup) and other dysfunctional behavior.

Another suggestion: Don't promote this compensation as an incentive. As you'll see later on, that can lead you down a number of unfortunate blind alleys. You compensate people for improvement ideas as a matter of simple fairness. They stick their necks out and the company benefits. You probably benefit too because your bonus is usually tied to performance improvements.

Why shouldn't the employees who make things improve get something for their trouble as well?

All You Gotta Do Is...

We're at the end of the measurement road. It's been a long road, with some twists and turns, and by now you probably wish you'd never heard of performance measurement. How are you going to get this done along with everything else you need to do, especially given the number of different processes you have to manage?

That's why it's a good idea to define process owners. Depending on how you're organized and how many processes you're accountable for, you might be the process owner yourself, you can assign a manager to each process, or your managers can assign two or three people to cooperatively manage each process.

Performance measurement is a major effort, and must be built into how you manage processes or it's without value. Divide and conquer, or you won't conquer at all. It's a great opportunity to hone your delegation skills.

THE COLUMBO EFFECT AGAIN

Oh yeah, just one more thing.

Don't apply the discipline of performance measurement to individual employees. You're managing and measuring processes, not people. It's an important distinction.

Yes, there are times you can measure individual employee performance using mathematical measures. It works for employees who have just a single, repetitive organizational role, like assembly-line workers and—and—hmmm, nobody else comes to mind.

The moment you try to apply the discipline of performance measurement to the measurement of employee performance, several things happen, all unfortunate:

- Employees refuse to do any work except for work that favorably affects their performance measures.
- Employees try hard to pass off difficult and thankless work to each other to bolster their individual performance statistics.
- You defenestrate teamwork (or as Pogo said, you can do something even worse and throw it out the window).
- You demoralize and tick off everyone.
- You entirely miss lots of good work employees do, or at least used to do, because you're looking at the measure instead of the person.

Don't do that.

Remember that although it's true that if you can't measure you can't manage, if you mismeasure, you mismanage.

It's also true that management is about processes, not people. As Ross Perot pointed out a long time ago, you manage processes but lead people.

And nobody ever said leadership requires measurement.

THE HUMAN FACTOR

A consultant of my acquaintance once explained to a client, in my presence, that figuring out the business issues is the hard task. "Technology," she commented, "is the easy part."

"Technology is the easy part for you," I pointed out after the client had left, with considerably more patience than I felt, "because you never have to deliver it."

Delivering working technology is hard, tedious, precise, demanding work. It requires that rarest of commodities, exact, logical thinking. That many executives, who seem obsessed with being more important than the rest of us, hold an attitude of "I can buy and sell people like that," is unsurprising, but it isn't just executives. Most Americans have given up on exact logical thinking as something other, socially inferior people have to do, but not them. They have Important Concepts, and better things to do with their time and energy than to think things through at multiple levels to make sure everything really will hang together.

Somewhere in the last couple of decades, the belief has grown up that to be successful, CIOs must be businesspeople, not technicians. Technicians, we've been told with enough repetition to turn our brains to butter[1], spend the corporate coffers buying and building technology for technology's sake, not for any good business purpose.

---

[1] Or margarine, if you're watching your intake of saturated fats.

You hear this tripe every day, and like so many "facts" that "everyone knows," it flies in the face of our daily experience. Back when the head of EDP was a former programmer who still kept his hand in the game, we built the legacy systems that still run our companies. We delivered, in other words, working code so good that three decades later our companies can't survive without it.

The more we've put businesspeople in charge of IS who have never learned COBOL, FORTRAN or C++, the more unsuccessful we've become at delivering working systems[2]. If that weren't true, we'd have long-since unplugged our ancient legacy systems, since most of them are an obstacle to progress.

Why did we abandon a pattern that worked for one that continues to fail miserably? Because to succeed, CIOs need to be part of *The Club* (see Part I if you've forgotten what *The Club* is all about). Even the best of the lead-dog techie EDP managers didn't relate well to the members of the executive committee. While they delivered top-notch results, they weren't able to explain what was going on, why it all cost so much, why the company needed to buy a bigger computer, an operating system upgrade, or a DBMS.

The problem, in other words, was social, not business.

Somewhere in my management career my peers pigeonholed me as a "techie." My strength, they informed me kindly, lay in handling the technical aspects of IS management. I wasn't oriented toward handling the people issues.

Shortly after this conversation, one of my peers (to be fair, one who hadn't shoved me in the pigeonhole) asked for some help. It seemed she was having some problems with one of her best programmers and communication had broken down. Since I had a reputation for being more technical, she thought I'd have a better chance of connecting with him.

If you're wondering, it was a tough, largely unproductive conversation. Not once, though, did the programmer suggest I didn't understand his problems. Quite the opposite. He became frustrated with me because I understood them very well, but still didn't offer the one solution he insisted on. On the other hand, he stayed in the organization and remained a valuable employee, so maybe it wasn't a total loss.

The point? To be a good CIO, you must be able to lead technical people.

---

[2]*If you're a non-technical businessperson who's now faced with running IS and you're feeling thoroughly offended—think of this experience as an exercise in awareness-building. You face the same handicap running IS that an accountant would face if put in charge of Marketing. With luck, this book will help you deal with the challenges you're facing.*

It's possible to lead people effectively without a gut-level understanding of what they go through every day. It's possible, but just as soldiers figure generals who haven't seen combat are more likely to get them killed, so programmers figure CIOs who have never designed a system or written a line of code are more likely to make commitments that turn into death-march projects.

If you're a CIO with no technical background, don't despair. You can succeed in your job without it. You do, though, have a lot of learning to do and a lot of credibility to earn. You do that learning by listening to every member of your IS organization—a lot—so that deep in your spleen you can understand how they do their work, think about their work, think about each other, and think about the business[3].

Sit down with your best programmer and ask her to show you what she is up to. Ask lots of dumb questions, like, "What's the problem you're trying to solve?", "What's your plan of attack?" and "What's a 'general protection fault'?"

If she asks why you want to know, give her an honest answer: "I'm leading this organization, and while I have a pretty good sense of what we need to be and where we need to go, I don't really understand what you do. My choices are to either learn how you and the rest of the programmers in this organization work, or to make some questionable commitments."

Technical people have an engineering mentality. Unlike most of the population, engineers figure every problem is simply a puzzle. They can solve it, if they simply have enough time, enough ingenuity, and a big enough CPU[4].

Unlike most of the population, engineers also understand the value of good design. Unfortunately, they understand it so well they can't articulate it, so it ends up sounding like technology for the sake of technology. The way they look at it, bad design is immoral.

Engineers take the load requirements for the building, calculate what's needed, and then double it just to play it safe. They're artists who understand people will interact with their creations, so they want them to be elegant and durable. Engineers don't buy substandard concrete to save a few bucks.

---

[3]*Yes, they do think about the business. Some have probably thought about it at a level of detail beyond anyone else in the company, in fact.*
[4]*People who assume all problems can't be solved are always right, by definition. Engineers, who assume all problems can't be solved, are sometimes wrong. Given a choice, I prefer to associate with the ones who are sometimes wrong. Wouldn't you?*

Engineers will also hook their stereos to a meter to look for distortion. Even if the distortion can't be detected by any biological ear, a true engineer will try to reduce it further. Engineers aren't big on laws of diminishing returns.

If you're a technically literate CIO, don't sit there with a smug look on your face. While you were busily entering the ranks of management and climbing the executive ladder, you lost track of the specifics and you'll never get them back again. Management, I'm afraid, has ruined you for useful work—or do you think you could still spend an entire week with your head buried in a computer screen writing code[5]?

The hardest part of being CIO isn't the technology. It isn't the business issues, either. It's the relationships, because you have to relate, on an empathic level, with your technical staff one minute, and the company's executives the next.

It's a lot like switching back and forth from English to Urdu, and it's harder than any other leadership role in the company.

This section is about all of the human factors associated with leading an IS organization. It's about people, skills, culture, motivation—dealing with those unpredictable humans who make the process of leadership so hard.

And so rewarding.

---

[5] *I don't think I could either, but there are times I miss those days. A lot.*

STAFFING AND SKILLS

"Personnel? That's for idiots!"

—Dirty Harry

MANAGEMENTSPEAK

I see you involved your peers in developing your proposal.

Translation:

One person couldn't possibly come up with something this stupid.

Back when my hair fully covered my scalp, Bell Labs was a legendary place. Even a biologist like me knew two of its successes: Arno Penzias and Robert Wilson discovered the cosmic background radiation there, giving powerful support to the "big bang" theory of the universe's origin; and John Bardeen, Walter Brattain, and William Shockley gave birth to the transistor in the same labs.

Bell Labs had a magical aura in those halcyon days. It was in the business of hiring geniuses and letting them be brilliant, figuring you don't have to invent the transistor too many times to pay for a sizeable research facility.

Makes sense to me.

Somewhere in all of this, Bell Labs' leadership asked a good question: What makes a star performer?

To answer this question, most companies would put its executives in a room to participate in a facilitated brainstorming session. Everyone's thoughts would get equal weight and the resulting bulleted list would go to human resources to be incorporated into the next year's performance evaluation system.

Bell Labs, with lots of research scientists in its leadership, developed a more reliable research protocol. Step One for its investigators was to have managers to list their star performers. Next they had nonmanagerial employees do the same thing.

Step Two was even shrewder than Step One: The investigators asked the employees who showed up on both lists about their work habits.

Ask yourself two questions before reading on: (1) Would you have come up with the Bell Labs approach, or would you have had a bunch of managers brainstorm a list of characteristics? (2) If you went through the Bell Labs procedure, what percentage of names would appear on both of your lists[1].

In the case of Bell Labs, just half the names appeared on both lists. It's a useful exercise, by the way—it won't take you much time, and the discussion you have with your leadership team afterward, when you all figure out why so few names appear on both lists—will more than pay for itself.

So will the next discussion you ought to have. Bell Labs, in the business of commercializing its research, distilled the traits its top performers had in common (traits like keeping track of assignments and building a strong internal network) and created a training program around them, figuring you can never have too many star performers.

---

[1] *A third question is also worth asking: Would your brainstormed list of characteristics match what star performers really do?*

You may benefit by at least publishing the list of traits your star performers come up with and encouraging employees to develop them, too.

Just as you can never be too rich or too good-looking[2], you can never have too many star performers either. It's mystifying to me that this point is controversial, but many people in leadership roles misunderstand this proposition and argue with it. They point out, for example, that when the job is pushing a broom, you don't need a nuclear physicist. Sometimes, they say, all you need is an average person. I guess that means you shouldn't bother having performance appraisals for janitors, or if you do have them, you should encourage average performance, penalizing those janitors whose performance is better than the minimum standards you set.

No?

Nuclear physicists make lousy janitors. That doesn't mean you don't want star janitorial performers. It means being a star is contextual, and people who shine in one role may not shine in others. It's commonplace that the best managers in baseball were often barely adequate as players; the reverse effect, made famous as *The Peter Principle[3]*, also demonstrates the point.

You want star performers. Three decades ago Harold Sackman researched the gap between different programmers. He found that the best ones were able to write programs 16 times faster and debug them 28 times faster than those created by programmers in the pack, and that when they were done their programs were six times more compact and ran five times faster[4].

Nothing in my experience suggests anything has changed. So here's another little question for you: Do you pay your best programmers even five times what you pay your worst programmers?

Probably not. Most companies base compensation on value as determined by the job market, not by the value employees create for the company. Should you? There's a thorny question. Ignore the question of "What's the right thing to do," at least for the time being, and be pragmatic: Will market-based compensation keep your best employees in your employ and happy to be there?

The answer isn't a simple one (I'll cover this subject in Chapter 15), nor are the answers to all the other questions related to attracting, hiring, and keeping a great staff.

14

STAFFING AND
SKILLS

---

[2]*Actually, you can: Either trait can turn you into a nut-case if you aren't careful.*
[3]*The Peter Principle, Laurence J. Peter (William Morrow & Company, Inc., New York, 1969)*
[4]*You'll find more about this, and lots of other fascinating ideas, in the classic The Mythical Man-Month: Essays on Software Engineering, Frederick Phillips Brooks (Addison-Wesley, 1975)*

This chapter is about acquiring the right employees and making sure they have the skills they need to succeed in your organization (which presumably involves their doing what you need them to do). It's about hiring, training, and providing opportunities for professional growth.

In a leadership role, you achieve through the work of others. This chapter is about making sure you have the right "others" around to do it.

HIRING THE RIGHT PEOPLE

In his excellent book *Ask the Headhunter,* Nick Corcodilos points out that the hiring process is broken. The process we've been told to go through—place an ad in the paper, ask applicants to send their résumés to HR, have HR screen the résumés for the best skill-to-task matches, and interview the survivors—doesn't work.

If it did, why are fewer than 20% of all open positions filled this way? If you don't find this evidence compelling, reread the section on performance measures, because you missed the point of it.

The standard hiring process is horrible for both the applicant, which it dehumanizes, and the hiring manager, who is completely alienated from it.

Like so many other leadership tasks, hiring the right people isn't especially complicated. Difficult, yes, but complicated? To hire the right people, you must define who you're looking for, find people who fit the bill, and persuade them to join your organization.

This isn't complicated. So why do so many hiring managers get it wrong? You'll see.

Start with the Right Attitude

Too many managers think of the hiring process as an tedious, time-consuming chore to be handled with as little effort as possible. A moment's thought tells you otherwise: Because leaders succeed through the efforts of others, hiring is as important to leadership as selecting great coffee beans is to Starbucks, or great clothes is to Nordstrom's.

Want to know why outsourcers win big deals that displace internal IS departments? Most outsourcers understand that their employees are their product, and that winning business starts with having a great product. Hiring is a core competency for an outsourcer. It is for you, too—do you act like it?

Still not convinced? Not hard-headed enough for you? How about this: Every time you hire an employee it costs you between $50,000 and $75,000. Admittedly, the people who calculate numbers like these have a tendency to throw everything into them they can. Okay, divide by two—it's still an expensive proposition, and every time you make a hiring mistake you spend it again.

This is a process where it pays to do it right.

Defining Who You're Looking For

Define *who* you're looking for, not *what* you're looking for. The difference between the two is immense.

Too many hiring managers toss a set of requirements over HR's transom and then wait for a list of qualified applicants to appear.

Human Resources has been led astray by its desire for objectivity and intellectual legitimacy. Overwork has led it to seek help from automation as well. The result is skills-to-task matching. This is a practice that equates job applicants to bags o' skills, the open position as the only role an applicant will ever play in the company if hired, and easily defined skills as the most important factor in an applicant's potential success.

The good news about skill-to-task matching is that HR can automate it. The bad news is that it leads you to hire only the candidates you want the least.

The least? Absolutely. You know from your own history that ambitious employees, the ones who are looking for their next career step, usually work harder and show more initiative than the ones who want to retire with the same title they hold now. Why anyone would want to hire an applicant who shows no sign of ambition is a mystery. But an applicant who has all the skills you're looking for and still wants the job you're offering is either coasting, desperate, or both, and in the job market that exists as these words spring onto the computer screen[5], desperation is its own warning sign.

The best applicants are stretching. They'd never accept a position they were fully qualified for.

When you define your requirements for an open position, figure you're bringing into the company a person who will, over many years, be asked to take on a wide variety of roles. The employee's responsibilities will increase over the years as will his or her impact on the organization, and with each new role the skills that employee will need in order to succeed will change.

How important is it that the database administrator you're trying to hire have at least five years of Oracle experience?

Hire people, not résumés and not bags o' skills. Be as general as you can about the specific skills you need right now. ("Expertise in data design and administration and a demonstrated ability to integrate the data designs of packaged software solutions into an existing legacy environment.") Be willing to train a new hire who has the right experience, knowledge, and aptitude in specific technologies if you have to.

---

[5]*In 1998, the demand for skilled IS professionals greatly exceeds the supply.*

Avoid the trap of urgency: "We need someone who can hit the ground running." The wrong employee never will run, and you're better off covering an open position with a contractor while the new hire comes up to speed than you are hiring for the short-term.

Most important of all is how you work with HR. It's easy to make HR the bad guy in all of this, but the problem with HR is your laziness. Make sure HR understands what you're looking for—what you're really looking for—and insist it screen applicants on that basis and not on what's easy and objective.

What are you looking for? Important, transferable skills far more than experience with particular products. Character far more than a well-written résumé[6]. And most of all, a clear track record of success.

Recruiting

You don't do recruiting. HR does recruiting. Why cover it here?

The average HR analyst has 40 hours of meetings scheduled each week and several open positions to recruit for. He or she has been steeped in HR lore for a decade and really believes in skill-to-task matching. Because it makes his or her job possible, he or she believes that you can find the right candidates using *Resumix* to automatically search a résumé's database.

When you take a hands-off approach with HR, you'll allow the recruiting industry to prevent you from meeting your best potential employees.

The most important thing to remember when working with HR is that you're delegating, not collaborating. Chapter 10, "Making Decisions," covered delegation; now might be a good time to go back and review the subject.

That's what's most important when you work with HR. When HR is recruiting on your behalf, you and your recruiter must take two principles into account:

- **Recruiting Principle #1:** Most of your best candidates are gainfully employed by someone else.
- **Recruiting Principle #2:** That doesn't mean they're happy.

Raiding other companies may seem unsavory and unethical to you. I don't know why, but it may. If you're in this quandary, take a moment to review the basic precepts of capitalism. Our entire economy is built on competition. Your attempt to recruit staff from other companies is no less ethical than attempts on the part of your sales and marketing organizations to recruit customers from your competitors.

---

[6]*Unless, of course, you're looking for a professional résumé-writer. Otherwise, why does the quality of the résumé matter to you?*

Still waffling? One more shot: The candidates you want won't be interested in your offer if their current employers are treating them well. The nerve of those rotten scoundrels, treating your potential employees so badly! It serves them right to lose such great people to you!!!

There. Feel better?

Recruiting Principle #3: Get Your Hands Dirty

HR needs to actively recruit from other companies as well as running employment ads in the paper. You need to actively recruit as well. Yes, you. The one peering at this book.

When people are looking for work they're told to build and use a personal network so there are lots of eyes and ears helping in the search. Why wouldn't that be good advice for you, too? Tell everyone you know that you have an open position and describe the kind of person you're looking for.

What's the worse they can say? "I have her and I'm keeping her." Now—go back and reread Recruiting Principles #1 and #2.

Recruiting Principle #4: You Don't Have to Hire

You can lease cars with an option to buy. You can rent houses with an option to buy. There's no reason at all you can't do the same thing with an open position.

Many of your best potential employees are independent contractors. People become independent contractors for quite a few different reasons—some just like the variety, others have trouble getting job offers for one reason or another, and a third group just figures the pay is better.

Regardless, you can interview independent contractors at the same time you're searching for candidates, and you can ask the independents if they'd entertain a job offer after three months, assuming the work and the relationship are working out on both sides.

Try before you buy is a great selling strategy, and in this situation, both parties are selling and buying.

Last Comment on Recruiting

You're better off screening résumés yourself than having HR do it for you. Make sure HR knows that's your preference. You do want HR to screen out applicants who have no real chance of succeeding. You don't want HR to forward only the "short-list" because its short-list is too likely to be defined by skill-to-task matching, no matter how much preaching you've done.

Interviewing

Ah, the good old days! Applicants entered your office, nervously twisting their hats into strange and contorted forms as they stammered a greeting. You secretly enjoyed their discomfiture as they desperately tried to find some reason you should hire them.

Being the boss used to be fun.

Some companies still believe in the "grill 'em" theory of interviewing, figuring it's a good way to see how an applicant stands up under pressure. If you're in this camp, good luck to you, and thank you for persuading so many qualified job applicants that your company is the wrong place to work. It gives the rest of us a shot at them.

Interviewing well isn't difficult, but it also isn't automatic. Given the plethora of resources available to you on this subject (including the aforementioned *Ask The Headhunter*), in this section I'll let a few tips suffice:

- *Prepare:* We all know we ought to, and somehow time gets away from us. Next time don't make excuses. Make sure you know what you're going to ask before you walk into the interview room. What should you ask?

- *Ask relevant questions:* Relevant questions take the form, "Describe a situation in which *x*. How did you handle it?" or "Let me describe a situation—What would you do about it?" The situations you're asking about should have some bearing on what the applicant would be expected to deal in your company.

- *Ask character-related as well as work-related and questions:* It's as important to get a sense of how an applicant would deal with (for example) a conflict of interest as with a server crash.

- *Probe for specifics. Probe more. Keep on probing:* It's easy for even bad applicants to give a glibly plausible answer when dealing with generalities. Probe for specifics. Fakers and incompetents give themselves away in the details, usually by being unable to provide any.

- *Let the applicant ask questions, too:* This is just as big a decision for the applicant as it is for you, so it only makes sense to let the applicant ask you questions about the position. Not only that, but the kinds of questions applicants ask will give you more insight into their character than any of their answers to your questions.

- *Give honest answers:* Not brutally honest, but honest. If the job sometimes calls for weekend work, say so. If it calls for weekend work every week of the year, say so, and then explain that your company rewards this kind of behavior with stock options (if it does), and bonuses (if it does). Or, explain that the people who succeed in a job like this are the ones who view it as a great place to gain valuable experience. Or something. You gain nothing by tricking someone into coming on board; you also gain nothing by discouraging great candidates.

Last Thought on Interviewing

There comes a time in many job searches when you have to decide whether to settle for a candidate who may be good enough or hold out for a really great one. This is a tough choice, and as with most tough choices there's no one right answer.

In the real world of staffing, the old cliché about half of everyone finishing in the bottom of their class is a fact of life. It's easy to say you only want to hire the best and you're willing to hold out until the perfect job-seeker shows up. Unless you're offering top compensation, the work you'll be asking of the new employee will be a source of unending joy, and your company is a wonderful and rewarding place to work, producing an end to world hunger as its principle product—well then, you have to ask yourself why the best in the business will want to work for you.

Figure out what you really need, and the kind of person you're likely to attract given the position you have open and the tangible and intangible benefits of working for you. In most IS shops it makes sense to staff a small number of key positions with the best people it's possible to hire, compensating them accordingly and giving them whatever perquisites[7] are likely to attract them and keep them in the fold. For the rest, staff with journeymen and apprentices, not masters of the craft, relying on their character and work ethic, great processes, and strong leadership to maximize their effectiveness.

TEAM INTERVIEWS

The team interview—in which three (two is too few and four is intimidating) members of a workgroup interact with a candidate separately from your interview—is a popular feature of today's employment environment. It's popular because it's a very good idea. Why? Why not? After all, the candidate you hire will work a member of this team.

Your team has a stake in hiring someone who will be an asset to it. It might hurt your ego to hear this, but your team understands its day-to-day work and its team dynamics better than you do, unless you're *far* too involved in the details. The people who work for you will do a better job of making sure the applicant will be an asset to the team.

continues

---

[7]*I could have said "perks" but I thought I'd impress you.*

continued

Team interviews have another advantage. Candidates want to understand what it will be like to work for your company. Your team is in a better position than you are to help a candidate evaluate whether they'll like the job you've defined and the experience of working for you. Even if a candidate is a perfect fit from your perspective, and from your team's perspective, if you hire a candidate who later concludes working for you is a mistake, you have to go through the whole process all over again.

The job has to be a good fit on both sides or you lose time and money. Team interviews can help both sides avoid making an expensive mistake.

Team interviews aren't, however, a panacea. First of all, interviewing doesn't come naturally to most members of work teams—their expertise is in doing the work and interviewing is a leadership skill. The solution to this is simple: Train them. Shortly before candidates start to appear, take some time in one of your staff meetings to explain how to interview. Have team members role play it with each other, and critique their performance. Buy them each a copy of this book and have them read this section[8].

Team interviews will give you excellent information to help you make the hiring decision—such good information that some experts think you should delegate the hiring decision to your work team.

Your author's opinion is that this is a mistake, for two reasons. First, except for very strong teams, most employees prefer mediocre candidates, and it's the strongest members of the team who will feel most threatened by a talented new hire. Beware of this tendency. You can't eliminate it, but you can ameliorate it by coaching interview teams on the benefit to them of hiring the strongest possible candidate and by listening carefully when you debrief the team after all interviews have been completed.

The other reason it's a mistake to delegate the hiring decision goes back to the basic principle, expressed earlier in this chapter, that you're hiring someone who will take on more than one role over time. Your team will, as a general rule, have a narrower (albeit deeper) focus than you will, so avoid the temptation to completely delegate the task.

Instead, ask two peers, perhaps from other parts of the company, to participate with you in a leadership team interview. You'll get a better picture of the candidate this way, it will help the candidate gain a broader picture of your company, and it will set a very good tone with each candidate about the kind of company they're talking to.

---

[8]*Buy your mom a copy too—she'd love it. It makes a perfect gift for the holiday season as well, so pick up a few extra copies!*

And oh, by the way, in this day and age it's always a good idea to not be alone with a job applicant. Sexual harassment is a reality; so is the possibility of unwarranted accusations. This isn't why you make every interview a team interview, but it's a fortuitous fringe benefit.

WHAT HAPPENS NEXT?

Onboarding

You've recruited. You've interviewed. You've made an offer and the applicant accepted it. She just showed up for her first day of work, and went through the standard HR orientation program. What next?

In a lot of companies, her manager shows her to her cubicle, apologizes that procurement hasn't yet delivered her PC, and hands her a stack of documentation to read and become familiar with.

What a great way to start out a long-term relationship.

How you handle an employee's first week on the job sets a tone that will last a long time. A well-defined orientation program goes a long way to ensuring the tone is a good one. As always, form follows function and the function in this case is to help each new employee become an effective team member as fast as possible. What do you need to accomplish this?

You need your new employee to feel welcome. You need the existing team to become comfortable working with the new employee. The new employee needs to start building a network of resources, gain knowledge of your technical environment, work practices, methodologies, and culture.

All the *stuff* that differentiates long-term employees from newcomers.

The starting point of any orientation program is to assign a buddy—an experienced employee responsible for showing the newcomer the ropes. Buddies introduce newcomers around the department, make sure they don't eat lunch alone, and point them to the people they need to meet to succeed in their jobs.

The second component of a great orientation program is a series of scheduled chalk-talks. The most experienced staff-members (not managers) in your organization meet one-on-one with the new recruit, describing whatever seems important. It might be methodologies, it might be the network architecture, and it might be Help Desk procedures. The specifics depend on the individual. What's important is to create a framework within which a newcomer can interact one-on-one with experienced employees, so each gets to know the other as an individual.

It's the staff-level introductions that will help newcomers the most. To make the newcomer feel like a valued member of your organization, though, you should also make sure each one has a chance to meet one-on-one with every member of your leadership team (including you). Where staff-level interactions reveal what's really going on, leadership interactions reveal what you'd like to see happen.

Your orientation program should include written reference material as well. The written reference material isn't the orientation program, though, because the orientation program is as much social as anything else. Its first goal is to create interactions between the new hire and the employees with whom he or she will need to work. Only secondarily is its goal to provide useful information.

Skills Management

"Okay, wise guy," you may be thinking by now. "When do I get someone who can actually get the job done? It's a great theory but[9] at the end of the day I still need an experienced Oracle DBA."

Yes, you do, and you should get one right away, too.

Some consultants recommend maintaining a formal skills inventory. Similar in many respects to the technical architecture methodology described earlier in this book, you would define a sort of warehouse of skills you need, inventory the skills available in your staff, and compare the two to create a gap analysis[10].

If you're willing to go through the effort of creating and maintaining a skills inventory, more power to you. Be careful before you commit to the process though. Skills inventories get stale very quickly and it takes effort to maintain them, even if you have every employee maintain their own records.

Unless you maintain the skills inventory and use it frequently, it's simply an expensive academic exercise with limited practical application, other than as a defensive tool to protect you against mindless cost-cutting. "Here is the list of skills we need to keep IS running," you imagine yourself saying triumphantly to your boss, brandishing a thick computer printout. "If we eliminate the positions you asked for, we won't have them all anymore."

---

[9]*"It's a great theory, but…" is ManagementSpeak for "I disagree." It's a silly thing to say, though, because great theories accurately predict the behavior of the real world and have a lot of practical use.*
[10]*ConsultantSpeak for "Compare the two," if you're unfamiliar with the term.*

Don't bother. It won't work. You'll hear one of two responses: (1) "Make it work or we'll find somebody who can"; or (2) "Fire everyone and hire fewer, more highly skilled replacements."

The other problem with a formal skills inventory is the frequent need for several skills to occupy a single head. Yes, you could create a database structure to represent these needs—like most inventories, you'd need to create bills of materials—but you'll spend energy managing the database you should be spending leading people.

Most IS organizations are better off without a skills inventory, instead figuring out how to acquire new skills as the need arises. Figuring out how to acquire the new skills isn't a complicated proposition. You have exactly three choices: Train, hire, or contract. Pick whichever one or whichever combination seems most attractive and move on.

Train

This is the option preferred by existing staff, who selfishly want to keep their jobs rather than altruistically throwing themselves in front of buses for the good of the company.

They have the good of your company at heart, too, because training them is far cheaper than any of your other alternatives. When you figure recruiting costs you as much as $75,000 per head and contractors charge enough to cover their needed profit margins, the economics are clear. Training is dirt cheap.

Training gives you loyal employees who know both the new technology and your installed base. What's not to like?

What's not to like is that training doesn't give you hands-on experience with the new technology. No matter how good the training course, a few years of experience count for plenty and newly trained employees will make mistakes on your nickel. The question is, how expensive are those mistakes?

Hire

Hiring is, of course, expensive. It's the opposite of training—it gives you the new skills you need packaged in an experienced practitioner. That practitioner, though, has neither proven loyalty to your company nor experience in your existing technology. And, as already mentioned, recruiting is expensive.

Hiring has another hidden cost if it's all you do—it creates resentment among current employees who'd like to acquire new skills to complement what they already know. That resentment will be reflected in morale, and it will make the onboarding process slower and more painful than it needs to be.

Contract

Contracting is like hiring, except instead of high up-front recruiting costs, you pay high ongoing contracting rates. You get an experienced practitioner who, like a new hire, doesn't know anything about your internal systems. The contractor, though, has even less loyalty to you, and has even less incentive to learn about your internal systems. If contracting is your sole skills-acquisition strategy, you'll create even more resentment than hiring from the outside.

If, on the other hand, you need more people for a relatively brief, well-defined period, contract labor can be just the ticket. You can bring them onboard faster than new recruits because the contracting company is responsible for their competence and productivity, and if they don't work out, replacing them is fairly bloodless.

The Right Mix of Training, Hiring, and Contracting

Here's a recommendation: Make training the centerpiece of your skills management program. It's good for morale, it's relatively inexpensive, and the people who get the skills can practice them in the context of your existing systems, too.

Sometimes, staff members resist change, or a new technology requires more than training can provide. Object-oriented analysis and its predecessor, client/server computing, called for new ways of thinking about application design foreign to traditional mainframe programmers. Recruiting one or two experienced practitioners provides not only skills but thought leadership inside your organization. Think of recruiting as a complement to training, not as an alternative.

If the situation calls for immediate experience in the new technology, but staff members are eager to acquire the new skills, contractors may be an effective way to bridge the gap. Or, if you need to hire one or two experienced practitioners but expect the search to be protracted, hiring contractors lets you get started immediately so that recruiting is no longer a barrier to progress.

Growth Opportunities

Send employees to training. Give them opportunities to grow. They're two different goals separated by a common technique: Education.

Where you define particular skills you need to have on-staff, employees define their own career goals and the skills they'll need to achieve them. Some employers try to prevent employees from acquiring skills that will help them move on to new roles and challenges, figuring they end up paying for both the training employees and the cost of replacing them. Recruiters like this kind of company—each one is a constant source of talent eager to find new jobs.

Wiser employers realize that an employee who's ready for a new challenge will find it. The employer's choice is whether to retain a valuable employee, albeit in a new role, or whether to give away valuable employees to other companies.

The best thing you can do is to give employees control of their own destiny. Give each one an education budget—perhaps four days and enough money to pay for one out-of-town class. Let them choose which conferences or seminars to attend.

The next thing you need to do is make sure every employee has the time to take advantage of this program. It's easy to set some number of days as your standard. It's another to schedule them in the press of daily work and project deadlines. Make sure that if employees feel any pressure, it's pressure to use their education budget every year.

Education is fine. It simply isn't as fine as on-the-job training. Look for creative ways to let employees grow on the job, gain new experiences, and try new challenges. Help them find mentors who will help them grow and gain new perspectives. Give each employee growth assignments for which they aren't fully qualified, or perhaps aren't remotely qualified—a great learning experience for highly talented, cocky employees who don't recognize anyone else's value or any limitations of their own.

Failure can be an important growth opportunity, so long as it's managed right.

Most important of all, avoid the creation of a one-dimensional career ladder. In too many IS organizations the standard career path is programmer→programmer/analyst→systems analyst→project manager→department manager→CIO. Progression to systems analyst is relatively smooth, but because there are only a limited number of management positions, the only way for most systems analysts to advance their careers is to leave the company, or at least to leave IS.

Not smart.

For that matter, how smart is it to define "career advancement" as "stop writing code"?

Creating multidimensional career options is one of the most important steps you can take to retain your best employees and keep them productive. This whole subject is entangled in the related subjects of promotions and compensation, which is the subject of the next chapter.

Read on.

> ### TRAINING AND THE RISK OF DEPARTURE
>
> "What if I spend a lot of money to train an employee and a recruiter pulls him away to another company?" a CIO whined to me not long ago.
>
> "What if you don't and he stays?" I asked in reply.
>
> When you train someone in a valuable skill, their market value increases. Most companies peg salaries to market rates, so the act of training an employee in a new skill generally means paying them more as well, after they've demonstrated the ability to apply that skill on the job.
>
> For some reason, otherwise rational corporate executives find this morally distasteful, figuring employees should feel enough gratitude for the favor of being trained that they'll forego compensation commensurate with their market value.
>
> What's especially fun is that the executives who feel the least compunction over laying off loyal, productive employees for no good reason except to please Wall Street analysts feel the most outrage. Apparently, loyalty is a fine quality—for other people.
>
> This is a classic case of what happens when you ask the wrong question. "What if I train an employee and he leaves?" is just such a wrong question. "What's the most cost-effective way to build a team with the right mix of skills?" is the right question.
>
> You need to take a businesslike approach to this whole issue. If you want a team with the right mix of skills, you'll have to pay for it, one way or another. Training current employees is simply more cost effective than any other alternative, even when you factor in the cost of the salary increase you'll incur so they're still compensated at market rates.
>
> Pay people what they're worth, regardless of the process that made them worth it. Treat them well. Give them challenging, rewarding work to do.
>
> Why would they ever leave, anyway?

LAST THOUGHT

If you remember nothing else in this entire book, remember one piece of advice from this chapter: You hire people, not résumés, and you lead people—you don't manage bags o' skills[11].

You need skilled people, of course—making sure you have them is the single most important factor in your own long-term success.

---

[11]*Astute readers will recognize that I'm plagiarizing Grace Hopper. Always steal from the best— that's my motto.*

COMPENSATION, REWARDS, AND CAREERS

"Ah, what do the experts know?"

—Spiro T. Agnew

MANAGEMENTSPEAK

We're looking for someone who is dynamic; a self-starter, and highly motivated.

Translation:

We're looking for someone we don't have to pay as much.

Let's do some math. Begin with an average programmer's salary: Make it $50,000 in annual wages. Add benefits, like life and health insurance, a dental plan, and all the tax overhead the company kicks in. On the average that comes to about 20% of the base salary, or another $10,000.

Now, add the cost of all the facilities the programmer needs to be productive, like floor space (even if you're cheesy, a cubicle occupies 64 square feet of office space, and you need to factor in the employee's share of conference rooms, bathrooms and so on) cubicle construction, furniture, telephone, personal computer, and so on. Even if you're stingy that will easily total another $20,000 per year.

Add it all up and your $50,000 per year programmer costs you about $80,000 per year.

Now add the hurdle rate. If you did without this programmer, you'd have $80,000 to invest. For simplicity, we'll put our money in tax-free municipal bonds earning 6% per year, which means we're doing without $4,800 in income.

Your programmer needs to return all of this cash in real value to your company—about $85,000—or you're losing money.

Every employee has to make the numbers, and the numbers suggest at least 70% in total overhead over an employee's salary. Call it the 70% Solution.

Very few employees are aware of the 70% Solution, but they should be. An employee who makes the numbers is helping the company turn a profit and should feel fairly secure. An employee who isn't making the numbers is a money loser and should feel…exposed.

Except for the sales force and billable consultants, few employees can demonstrate the value they add to the bottom line. The 70% Solution isn't a prove-it-or-lose-it exercise. It's more a matter of soul-searching.

It's also a good question to ask an employee during performance appraisals: "In your own estimation, what have you accomplished during the past year that has generated $85,000 in value for the company?"

It's a good question to ask, but only if you prepared the employee for the question 12 months before, and only if you ask it in a joint-problem-solving way. If you approach performance appraisals the way Perry Mason approached cross-examination, you're making a number of mistakes, not the least of which is that you have a lot to do with whether an employee makes the numbers.

But we'll get to that because that's part of what this chapter is about. It's about compensation, promotions, and of course the dreaded Performance Appraisal.

It's about the financial tools you have at your disposal as you barter with employees for their talents, efforts, and attention.

But first…

THE EMPLOYMENT CONTRACT

Every employee has a set of defined responsibilities. They're generally enshrined in a document called a "Position Description" which is a conspiracy between managers and Human Resources to conceal what the company will actually ask employees to do. In most cases, at least half of an employee's time each year—easily 1,000 hours—is spent doing "Other duties as assigned on a time-available basis."

So let's disallow that phrase and imagine just how awful life would be if your employees only worked on the tasks laid out in their position descriptions. *Everything* would fall through the cracks.

You and your employees have an implied contract. Never mind the legalities—we're talking about employee psychology now. In this, the only contract that matters if you want to get the work done, you give the employee money in the form of salary and the employee performs the work described in the position description at a pace just fast enough to keep up with the herd.

That's all the employment contract requires—doing the base job at an average pace in exchange for the employee's base salary.

Do you want more than that from your employees? The employment contract includes provisions for this. In exchange for a variety of other forms of financial and nonfinancial incentives, employees will work harder, take on unassigned tasks, show initiative and creativity, and in general keep the company running despite the best efforts of the company's leaders to kill it through dumb decisions and poorly chosen management fads.

Some of these incentives are tangible things you can point to. They're the subject of this chapter. Others are intangible, the stuff of leadership. They come later on.

These incentives are the levers you have at your disposal to influence employee performance. You have a lot of them, and knowing which ones to pull and when is as much your responsibility as knowing which dials to turn and switches to throw and when is the job of the engineer in the control room of a nuclear[1] power plant.

---

[1]*Humor me. How do you pronounce this word? If everyone who reads this book takes care to pronounce it "new-klee-are" instead of "new-cue-lar" then I'll have accomplished something useful in this life.*

There's nothing quite as pathetic as a manager who complains about the useless people who work for him and how little they're willing to work. Superstars are the exception. Worthless nebbishes are the exception, too. Most employees excel or fail in proportion to the quality of leadership they experience. Do you have an underperforming team and can't figure out the root cause of the problem?

Look in the mirror and you'll see the most likely source of difficulty.

COMPENSATION[2]

Employees get all kinds of money from their employers. There are wages, spot bonuses, annual bonuses (also known as at-risk pay) stock and stock options (which all serve the same purpose), and the collection of stuff known as benefits. Companies call this heterogeneous collection of monetary outflows "compensation", but what is it compensating employees for?

Each of these items has a specific role to play in delivering financial well-being to employees. While it's probably impossible to construct a compensation plan employees will actually like, they'll gripe about the plan less if you think of each component as a separate tool designed for a distinct purpose and restrict your use of each tool to the purpose for which it is best suited.

Here's a rundown.

Wages

Wages are a fair exchange of money for services rendered. They're a fee for services rendered. That's all they are. The heart of most employee discontent about compensation stems from trying to use wages as a performance incentive as well. So here's the most important piece of advice in this section:

Don't try to use the annual salary increase as a performance incentive.

To understand the problem, start with how companies set wage levels: Most resort to salary surveys in order to pay "market rates" for each position. Paying market rates, which are established through the law of supply and demand, is fine, and in fact there's no practical alternative.

If you pay employees less than the market will bear, the only ones who stay either (1) can't leave; or (2) *really* want to work for you for some reason or other. Paying too little is bad for the company.

---

[2]*My serious thinking about this subject began when I read some of Alfie Kohn's work. While I don't completely agree with him, he makes far more sense than most traditionalists and is well worth reading. Get yourself a copy of Punished By Rewards: The Trouble With Gold Stars, Incentive Plans, A's, Praise, And Other Bribes (Houghton Mifflin, 1993).*

If you pay employees more than the rate established by the market, they'll take home more money and be less likely to leave your employ, both good things. Sooner or later the bookkeepers[3] will figure out the company can obtain the same services for less money, and out go your overpaid employees, trying in vain to find a job that pays as much. But they won't, because you paid them more than the market will bear, which means their standard of living will drop and they'll be more miserable than if they'd never received the money in the first place.

Overpaying employees also makes the 70% Solution harder for them, and as already mentioned, any employee who doesn't make the numbers is in a fragile situation.

Overpaid employees always hang by a thread, whether they know it or not. Paying more than market rates doesn't work.

Now…try to reconcile paying market rates with using wage increases as a performance incentive. It doesn't work.

Give it a try. Take an employee who's making the average but excels in performance. Give that employee as big a raise as the guidelines allow—call it 10% instead of the 4% average endorsed by human resources. Do the math and you'll find that for a $50,000 per year employee who's paid twice a month, that translates to about $80 per paycheck in actual take-home pay. That's the best you can do, and it isn't a realistic incentive for being a top performer.

Take someone who's been a top performer for a few years and watch what happens—the employee hits your company's wage ceiling. The only increase you can give someone who's hit the top of the market range is the amount the range changes from year to year. Up to a point, you can promote the employee (a subject covered later in this chapter), but unless you've constructed nonmanagerial career paths, that eventually dead-ends as well (and in most cases the kind of non-managerial career path you'll have to build strays out of territory defined by the market).

Take someone who's been a top performer for a couple of years but then loses steam for some reason. You're now paying someone who's working at mid-market levels a wage far more than the market average. Not healthy.

The Solution

Don't make wage decisions based on performance. If you're serious about pegging wages to market rates, change wages as employees demonstrate proficiencies that change their worth in the marketplace, change their wages to reflect what they'd be able to earn in the market, and explain all wage changes in this context.

---

[3] *The only word in the language (except "bookkeeping" which has the same root) with three double letters in a row. It's important insights like this that make a book like this worthwhile.*

That should be the beginning and end of all wage discussions. In many cases this will result in larger wage increases than the ones based on HR's guidelines; in other cases the increases will be smaller. If your HR organization is populated with traditionalists, you'll find yourself fighting a lot of battles if you try to institute this kind of practice one employee at a time, so you're better off renegotiating the whole compensation program in advance. (Wait until you finish the chapter before you reach for the phone.)

One more time: Wages reflect an employee's market value, and should be adjusted regularly (once a year is traditional) to address how the employee's market value has changed.

COMPANIES PAY A STANDARD OF LIVING, NOT MONEY

We work for the government until about May of each year, or so we're told. What would happen if the government were suddenly far more efficient and they cut your taxes as so many politicians promise?

Nothing.

You don't think you'd keep the tax cut, do you?

Raises are pegged to changes in the cost of living—the payroll department issues guidelines every year telling you how big a raise you should give an average employee. The amount may be directly based on the consumer price index, or it may be based on how market rates have changed. If it's market-based, market changes result from changes in the cost of living.

Reduce taxes, and the cost of living increases less. A smaller increase in the cost of living means a smaller raise.

Employees don't get to keep a tax cut. Employers keep them. This isn't a bad thing, but it's a different thing.

You pay employees a standard of living. Their wages are a means to that end. Still not convinced? Ask an employee to move from Sioux Falls to New York City and watch what happens: You'll add a cost of living adjustment to the salary you'd been paying.

Which brings up the question of why companies provide benefits like life, health and dental insurance, retirement plans and so on. They provide them because they pay a standard of living and these are common elements in how adults think about their standards of living. Both employers and employees simply spend less when the employer provides benefits directly than if employees received the equivalent value in cash and then bought their own insurance and funded their own Individual Retirement Accounts.

Employers spend less because they get to buy the goods wholesale, as it were—large corporations especially are able to negotiate very favorable rates for group insurance. Employees spend less because employers couldn't afford to provide enough cash to cover what employees would spend for individual insurance policies, especially since most noncash benefits aren't taxed, but a corresponding salary increase would be.

You don't have any control over benefits, so you don't have to spend a lot of time and energy managing their allocation among employees. They're still part of the total compensation package, though, so from time to time you'll be called on to explain to employees why they are what they are, and why they're not what they aren't.

By the way, while companies count vacation and sick time as benefits, they aren't benefits at all, because vacation and sick time cost the company virtually nothing. Think about your last vacation. You worked extra hours before your vacation began to clean up your desk, and when you got back, you worked more extra hours to clean up the work that piled up in your absence. During your vacation your co-workers or staff pitched in to handle anything that came in and couldn't wait for your return.

Vacation and sick time aren't benefits—they're simply a special case of flex time.

Spot Bonuses

Wages are a fair exchange for doing the basic job. Let's get to the core question: Since form *follows* function, what are you trying to achieve with spot bonuses?

The traditional way of looking at spot bonuses is that you're creating a financial incentive for employees to work harder. It sounds convincing. Unfortunately, when researchers dig into this question, it always turns out that once you pay people a comfortable wage, money is far from the top of what most of them consider to be highly important to them.

Pop Quiz!!!

Question: What do you call a payment in cash to a public official that's designed to get that public official to do what the payer requests?

Answer: A bribe. Yes, you got it right! Psychologically, when you resort to paying employees an incentive to do what you want them to do, it smells a lot like a bribe. It feels kind of cheap.

Is the Right Answer No Spot Bonuses?

No, that's the wrong answer too. As with a lot of the law, intent counts for everything here. If your intent is to motivate better performance, you'll get into trouble. If your intent, on the other hand, is to keep all of your messages consistent, you'll be fine.

What do you tell employees you value? Probably you use words like creativity, hard work, dedication, risk-taking, and "going beyond the call of duty." Okay, you say you value it. Prove it, buddy.

Spot bonuses prove it. They put your money where your mouth is[4].

As my Grandma Claire used to say, actions speak louder than words and a spot bonus is a very loud action. The best use of a spot bonus is as an act of communication to reinforce with employees the kind of attitudes and behavior you value. Thought of this way, a spot bonus isn't an incentive, nor is it a reward. It's simply a memorandum of commendation, printed on *very* expensive paper.

This also means that when you give an employee a spot bonus, you need to be the one doing the thanking, not the employee. You're recognizing that the employee went above and beyond, exemplified the kind of behavior and attitudes you look for in the company, and through those actions the company benefited.

Since the employee went above and beyond, expressing gratitude is nothing more than good manners. Since the company benefited tangibly and significantly, the expression of gratitude would be suspect if it consisted of mere words. Hence the bonus.

A bonus should be immediate, following the event that triggered it as quickly as possible. When somebody does you a favor, you say thank you right away, not months later. The same should be true of bonus checks.

And…bonuses should be given privately. Praise should be public; what kinds of performance you reward with spot bonuses should be public. There is no problem with your creating an expectation—this is a way of saying thank you, and expectation of good manners is useful in a civilized society of any kind. The alternative is an expectation that you will hand out spot bonuses capriciously, and that's worse than avoiding the practice altogether.

The bonuses themselves, on the other hand, should be private. A public bonus makes the recipient feel good and makes everyone else feel good for the recipient too, so it's a good thing.

---

[4]*Strictly speaking, they put the company's money where your mouth is, but that's okay because when you're leading employees, your mouth is a surrogate for the company, too.*

It's a good thing until the next day, that is, because the next day every other employee will start to wonder when it's their turn. Watching someone else get a check creates competition between employees rather than encouraging cooperation among them. Keep it private.

Annual Bonuses, Stock, and Stock Options

Most companies handle annual bonuses pretty well and lots more are getting on board with the sensible practice of delivering some of this benefit in the form of stock or stock options. The purpose of an annual bonus is to communicate a message, only it's a different message from spot bonuses. The message delivered by annual bonuses, whether given as cash or as negotiable equities[5], is that employees are part of the company, not just hired help. Stock really does make an employee a legal part of the company—put enough stock in the hands of employees, and a significant block of shareholders will vote for practices tied to the company's long-term health rather than to short-term improvements in the price of the stock[6].

Most people want to feel like they're part of something larger than themselves, and that they're making a contribution to it. Good leaders encourage that desire and attach it to the company.

In the old days, companies had management bonuses and everyone knew it. Nonmanagerial employees heard "win one for the Gipper" speeches from these executives and reached for the Pepto Bismol[7] while the executives reached for their bonuses.

Most companies are more enlightened these days, realizing that in order to ask employees to act for the good of the company instead of with pure self-interest, executives have to share the annual bonus as well. Anything else is an exercise in hypocrisy, and employees smell hypocrisy as well as any cat smells tuna.

Typical annual bonus plans, also called performance sharing plans or "putting some compensation at risk" are based in part on the employee's individual performance, and in part on the company's performance. As employees gain influence in the company, more of their compensation should be at-risk, and a higher proportion of their at-risk pay should be tied to the company's performance. After all, they have more influence on it.

---

[5]*Don't phrases like "negotiable equities" make me sound like I know what I'm talking about?*
[6]*It's a mixed blessing, though, because employees are less likely to embrace painful changes than faceless, uninvolved shareholders. As with every other issue in the known universe, balance is everything.*
[7]*No, I haven't received any product placement fees, more's the pity.*

How Much Pay Should Be at Risk?

If you reward performance through salary increases, you reward performance with an annuity. Perform well once, receive the benefits forever.

If, on the other hand, you recognize performance through the annual bonus, it's a one-time payment—something that must be earned in order to be received.

Not only that, but it turns out that one-time bonuses can be about three times as big as an annual increase and through the miracle of discounted cash flows, the company comes out even. Earlier in this section we worked through an example that showed a top-performing employee would only see about $80 more per paycheck than an average employee. Psychologically that's an unimportant amount, even though it totals about $2,000 in cash if the employee put every dime in the bank.

Imagine giving the same employee a check for $6,000 after taxes. In terms of personal impact, there's simply no comparison.

And the company breaks even.

Promotions

Early in my leadership career I judged it was time to promote a systems analyst to senior systems analyst. HR stopped me in my tracks. I hadn't demonstrated the need for a senior systems analyst in my department. In my eyes, this promotion was nothing more than recognition that the analyst had achieved a higher level of performance, while in HR's eyes it meant creating a new position while eliminating the old one.

Some companies still do silly stuff like this, but the trend is toward a system called "broad-banding", which is HR-speak for "The way managers thought about the subject was right all along." In broad-banding, there's a single description for systems analysts; levels within that broad band (hence the name) are established based on an employee's level of achievement within that category of work.

That's a good thing, because moving from analyst to senior analyst isn't really a promotion. It's just recognizing that someone's market value and contribution have increased because they're operating at a higher level. They're part of the process of increasing wages—the part not tied to cost of living increases.

Real promotions are job changes, where an employee is asked to take on not only more responsibility but a different kind of challenge as well. Real promotions can be awkward, because employees have been taught to expect a fair and open process for all open positions and resent any instance in which an employee is inserted into a new responsibility without an open competition.

This expectation is, of course, ridiculous. There are times when open hiring is the right thing to do and there are times when it isn't. Imagine, for example, that you've decided to reorganize IS (a common enough occurrence, but wait until the next chapter). Throwing all of your existing managers out of their jobs and forcing them to apply for the new positions in an open competition isn't merely degrading, it ensures they'll wait until two weeks after Hell freezes over before they voluntarily participate in a similar exercise ever again.

If it's time to give a high-performing employee a new set of challenges, and you have an appropriate new set of responsibilities in mind, don't pretend and don't apologize. Announce the promotion with pride.

Don't, however, make the mistake of using promotions to avoid the headaches of recruiting. If you're creating a new position because there's a new job that needs doing but it isn't one you've built around the talents of an employee you've already decided to promote, open the position to all internal applicants. Some employee you've never met may just surprise you.

PERFORMANCE APPRAISALS

Remember your high school physics? Quick—what are the three laws of thermodynamics?

It's okay, I can't remember them either. What I can remember is their social equivalents, which I can then backtrack into the actual physical laws. These laws are

1. You can't win.
2. You can't break even.
3. You're not allowed to quit the game.

Performance appraisals are like that too. Of all of the processes for which leaders are held accountable, none is as universally disliked as the performance appraisal, and it's disliked equally by manager and employee.

Figure this one out—managers hate them *and* employees hate them, and it doesn't make any difference. We still do 'em.

Why does everyone hate performance appraisals? There are lots of reasons. One is simple—they call for honest communication between manager and employee. Who wants that? Sure the employee gets some strokes for his accomplishments, but beyond doubt he'll get to relive a year's worth of errors, failed assignments, and all the other negatives that are part of any honest discussion of performance.

And underlying it all is the expectation most employees have, which is that what matters is how much the boss likes you. No matter how well or poorly an employee performed, the boss gets to choose which points to emphasize and which ones to ignore.

Recognizing that performance appraisals are subject to this kind of bias, some companies try to build the assessment process around objective criteria. Too bad that's an impossible goal.

There are a few performance dimensions where objective measurement is possible, but only a few. Even something as seemingly concrete as "number of lines of code written" fades into oblivion when you remember that you tapped some of your programmers to participate in some nonprogramming special projects. Then you remember that while some programmers were tasked with creating Yet Another Cobol Merge/Purge Program, others were asked to learn how to build object-oriented GUIs in C++.

360° feedback is another popular strategy for making managers less important to the process. The theory is that an employee's peers and "internal customers" have something useful to say about the employee's performance.

And so they do. If it weren't for the very human tendency of each employee to suggest those peers and service recipients most likely to say nice things, you could even expect objective information from 360° feedback questionnaires.

There are two other issues with 360° feedback systems. The first is that they create a lot of overhead. Fully implemented, every employee in the company will end up assessing the performance of between four and eight other employees, each of whom is assessing them as well. Think there won't be some mutual back-scratching among the awesome amount of paperwork it creates?

Which leads us to the biggest issue with this system: It creates popularity contests, which means leaders will think twice about making unpopular decisions, including giving poor performance appraisals.

This isn't to say 360° feedback sessions are a bad thing, only that they're just as subjective as a manager's opinion.

The fact is, every step of a good performance appraisal is subjective, relying on the judgment of each employee's manager. It's time we all stopped pretending and embraced this reality. The issue is creating better leaders, not de-emphasizing their role in the process.

Performance appraisals require another assumption: That managers know what each employee does over the course of a year in enough detail to assess it. The fact is, they don't, and the better the employee, the less the manager knows about the specifics.

What to Do About It

Exactly what your performance appraisal process looks like will depend on the nature of the work you ask employees to perform. In some cases, managers will be able to work with each employee to create a plan for the year—what the employee will be asked to accomplish, what skills the employee should acquire, and so on.

In other cases, where you often don't know what you'll need employees to do until just a few weeks before it happens, an annual plan is a meaningless document.

Sometimes, employees will work on assignments you give them. Other positions call for employees to respond to work requests without your direct involvement.

How you establish the criteria you'll use to assess each employee will depend on the specifics of their job.

What's important is this:

- *Establish your expectations in advance:* Whether it's specific accomplishments or better work habits, make sure employees know early what you expect them to achieve during the assessment period. In a performance appraisal, an expectation that's a surprise is a serious breach of leadership responsibility.

- *Give frequent feedback:* The performance assessment is just the last step in an ongoing process. All of your employees should know, all the time, how well you think they're doing, and they should be free to let you know when they think you're looking at their performance wrong.

- *Put employees in control of the process:* Employees should have a lot to say about the goals you establish for the appraisal period, they should be made responsible for keeping track of their performance against those goals, and they should be held accountable for accurately assessing their own performance. The best performance appraisals have employees assessing their performance for their managers, whose role is critiquing the employee's self-assessment.

There is no way to make performance appraisals a pleasant experience. Employees know there's money and ego at stake, after all, and at some level they know how they rank as performers. Top performers don't really need to go through a process like this…they know how they're doing better than you do, and their self-assessment will be tougher than any assessment you give them. Everyone else knows they aren't a top performer.

That's why they pay you the big bucks.

TO SUMMARIZE

Compensation includes three components that are under your control: Wages, spot bonuses, and annual bonuses. You're best off using wages to make sure you pay each employee what they're worth in the marketplace so they don't leave for financial reasons. That includes giving them raises when their competence and ability changes the kind of position someone may want to recruit them for.

Use spot bonuses to communicate your appreciation of an employee's hard work, dedication, creativity, or other contribution that's benefited the company. You give spot bonuses because employees earn them, not to demonstrate your largesse.

The annual bonus builds a sense of being part of the company and sharing in its successes. As with the spot bonus, it's a communications tool.

With few exceptions, money doesn't do much to motivate employees to excel, so don't use it that way. It does, however, do wonders to prove your sincerity.

ORGANIZATION AND POLITICS

"Never underestimate the power of a schnook."

—Boris Badenov

MANAGEMENTSPEAK

My mind is made up. I am adamant on the subject. There is no room for discussion. But if you want to discuss it further, my door is always open.

Translation:
&%^$ you.

I'm going to write a science fiction novel someday about the colonization of Mars. Here's the set-up: In 2021 we establish the first Martian colony. Five years later, in 2026, the first Martian corporation opens its doors for business. Ten years after that, every corporation on Earth is out of business, unable to compete with their Martian counterparts.

Why? Mars takes about twice as long to orbit the sun as Earth. That means that Martian corporations have only half the number of year-end closings as their terrestrial counterparts. This gives Martian corporations an overwhelming competitive advantage.

Companies do incredibly stupid things during year-end closings. Sometimes they defer important expenditures to make profits seem higher. Other times, budget managers indulge in a year-end spending spree because if they leave money unspent in this year's budget they'll find next year's budget reduced[1]. All because the Earth has reached an entirely arbitrary position in the sky.

Pacioli invented accounting in Renaissance Italy, and in doing so helped the United States lose the Vietnam War, and also nearly killed off American business. It wasn't his fault, though: Pacioli never pretended to be doing much more than keeping the books. It was American business leaders who tried running entire businesses using only the accounting system and nothing else. (And it was someone from the business community, Robert McNamara, who tried to win a war the same way, relying entirely on what he could tangibly measure—body counts—to assess progress in the Vietnam War.)

One of the most unsettling aspects of modern accounting is the way it deals with people. Have you ever heard a business executive describe employees as an important corporate asset? The next time you hear this utterance, ask how the accounting system treats this "asset." The answer, dictated by Generally Accepted Accounting Principles (GAAP), is that every time the company pays employees, the cash account is reduced and the labor expense account is increased. GAAP treats employees as a loss in the Profit and Loss statement.

How does this compare to computers? When you buy a computer, accounting decreases cash and increases assets. Computers are an asset on the Balance Sheet—something of tangible value, although that value diminishes over time. Employees are not an asset—if they were, they'd appear on the Balance Sheet too.

Imagine how business would treat employees if every one were listed as a corporate asset, and with every increase in skills and experience the value of that asset increased. Would that change how you treat your employees?

---

[1] *I guarantee you that if the federal government would fix this one rule, rewarding budget managers for coming in under budget rather than penalizing them, the result would be at least tens, and more likely hundreds of billions of dollars a year saved.*

This chapter is about leadership. In a sense, it's about making sure your employees are assets to your company and treating them like assets to your company. It's about motivation, corporate culture, establishing and managing reporting relationships, and dealing with corporate politics. These, of course, are all means to an end, which is to make employees as effective as possible. Making employees as effective as possible is, if we're honest with each other, a means to an even more important end: Your own effectiveness, because your effectiveness and your ability as a leader are one and the same thing.

ARE YOU LEADING?

If you've been in management for very long, you've read dozens of accounts of what it means to be a leader. Mostly, they're feel-good, inspiring, entirely useless descriptions of self-sacrifice and charisma. They're fun to read, and give you no guidance at all in how you need to behave in order to succeed as a leader.

Never mind all that. Here's what it means to be a leader:

Other people look to you for approval.

That's it. When someone looks to you for approval, you're leading them. When they don't, you aren't.

This, of course, says nothing about whether you're leading them well or badly, whether you've chosen a good direction or an awful one. It's simply the litmus test of leadership—the quick and easy indicator of who's running the show.

Leadership, Manipulation, and Morality

Leading people is a matter of getting them to achieve what you need them to achieve. In becoming an effective leader, you have two choices. You can follow your instincts, or you can learn and make use of specific techniques that increase your ability to shape the behavior and attitudes of those around you.

The former is called "charismatic leadership," the latter "manipulation." The former is also called "trusting to blind luck"; the latter is also known as "being smart and effective."

Self-deception isn't a good starting point for effective leadership. You need to recognize that leadership *is* manipulation. To lead people, you need to consciously determine what is most likely to get them to move in the right direction, work the right way, solve the right problems.

To lead you need to manipulate. If the word "manipulate" makes you uncomfortable, substitute a euphemism, like "consciously and deliberately shape their behavior and attitudes."

Coming to grips with this reality is just one step in a difficult personal process every good leader must go through in order to be effective. That's the difference between the morality your mom taught you and the ethics of leadership. The simple fact is that when you're a leader, good intentions alone will lead both you and everyone who reports to you to perdition. "Let your conscience be your guide," is horrible advice for a leader.

Machiavelli analyzed this dilemma centuries ago in renaissance Italy[2]. Machiavelli recognized that being an ineffective leader is immoral and leads to the likely consequence of being replaced by someone more adept at acquiring and maintaining power. Maintaining authority is a prerequisite for leadership, but some of the actions leaders must take to maintain their authority may be unsavory. Not taking those steps doesn't make you more ethical, said Machiavelli, because all that accomplishes is letting someone worse than you take over.

SCENARIOS IN ETHICS

To understand why the ethics of leadership are different from day-to-day morality, here are two dilemmas you'll face all the time:

Dilemma #1: Staying in Power

You're a department manager in IS and the CIO just left the company. You and one of your peers are the strongest candidates for the position, and you know for a fact that while your rival has a strong track record of success (so do you), he also abuses his employees in one-on-one meetings when nobody is looking and stabs rivals in the back. Promoting this character to CIO would subject the entire IS organization to his dysfunctional personality.

So...do you stay above the fray, presenting yourself in the most favorable light you can, knowing your rival will work hard to discredit you and also knowing if he gets the job, you won't be the only one whose life he makes miserable?

Or, do you need to take some steps of your own?

The answer may seem obvious...that the ends never justify the means...but that oversimplifies your choices. Every action you take is both means and end. That is, everything you do has immediate consequences and longer-term consequences. When you're in a position of influence, you need to balance all of the consequences of your actions, including the consequences of letting the "bad guys" win, and also including the consequences of diminishing yourself in your own eyes and in the eyes of those around you.

---

[2]*One wonders if Machiavelli ever bumped into Pacioli and if so, what they talked about.*

Returning to the scenario we're analyzing, do you suffer the slings and arrows of this pinhead, or do you sling some arrows of your own?

It depends. It depends on how big a schmuck your rival is, whose ear you have...but remember, in corporate America there's nothing particularly ethical about failure.

Dilemma #2: Maintaining Trust

In America in the late 1990s, business doesn't have to be bad for layoffs to happen. A merger may lead to consolidating operations in a different city, your employer may outsource some business function or other (although most outsourcers hire the current staff), or the stock may just be underperforming.

Your company is planning to downsize and relocate one of its business functions, and quite a few people will lose their jobs. If word gets out prematurely, the business consequences will be severe as morale plummets and employees find new employment as fast as they can. Secrecy is a matter of survival right now.

As CIO, you're heavily involved in the planning because the relocated operation will use a new computer system. A friend of yours is a manager in the affected area, and probably won't survive the experience. In conversation one day he asks you "if the rumors are true." What do you answer?

Sure, you can say something that gets you off the hook like, "Now Ben, you know I couldn't answer that question even if there was something going on." You could, but if Ben isn't a very dense human being, he'll know exactly what you meant.

When secrecy is called for, your choice is either to lie or to violate a confidence. Which is the right thing to do? If you think there's a simple, black-and-white, one-size-fits-all answer, you may not be ready for a leadership role. The whole point is that as your influence and scope of responsibilities increase your choices become harder. Part of leadership is being willing to make hard decisions.

THE FOUR RELATIONSHIP DIRECTIONS

You're leading when the other person looks to you for approval. They're leading when you seek approval from them. This rule applies to every relationship you have, not only to those who report to you.

In any organization, you manage relationships in four directions: Down, to those who directly or indirectly report to you; up, to those you directly report to, "left" to your organizational peers; and "right" to everyone who receives services from your organization.

Very few people are good at managing relationships in all four directions. Most are either good at managing down and to the right or up and to the left.

If you're in the first group, you're good at getting the job done but handle politics and manage your career poorly. You're an admirable person but a loser. If you're in the second group you land on your feet and get ahead…but what have you actually accomplished?

To be an effective leader you have to lead in all four relationship directions. To do that you need everyone in those roles to look to you for approval. How?

Understanding the answer is part of the larger question of how to motivate people.

MOTIVATION

Marketing gurus[3] recognize six great motivators: Fear, greed, guilt, avoidance of boredom, need for approval, and exclusivity. These are the big buttons marketers push to get prospects to buy from them. You can push them too, becoming more effective in motivating those around you as you do so. (Another ethical dilemma: Are you motivating people or manipulating them? What, other than the goal you're trying to achieve, is the difference? Either way, you're making conscious use of learned techniques to modify behavior. The goal of this book is to make you more effective. It's up to you to use your newfound powers for good…

These six motivators aren't created equal. Each has specific uses. Knowing which to use in a particular situation calls for understanding each motivator, accurately assessing circumstances, having experience in using each motivator, and developing insight into each individual's psychology.

All this book can help you with is the first item—understanding each motivator, how to use it, and how not to use it.

Fear

Fear motivates humans more powerfully than any other emotion. That isn't exactly a blinding insight, of course. Anyone who has ever experienced true, serious, panicky fear remembers the feeling and just how much they would do to escape the source of the fear. Scare a middle-aged, out-of-condition human enough and you'll watch Olympic records fall in tatters.

---

[3]*To be precise, I learned this at the knee of the direct marketing guru Herschell Gordon Lewis, with whom I share quite a bit of genetic material. HGL has been like a father to me…a good thing, under the circumstances.*

Many managers apparently experienced fear sometime in their careers and figured it's a perfect example of something that's more blessed to give than to receive. Otherwise, why would they expend most of their managerial energy bullying those around them? This kind of managerial behavior is worse than immoral. It's ineffectual.

There are legitimate uses for fear in a leader's motivational toolkit. It's an appropriate response to insubordination, for example—sometimes an employee just won't accept the idea that you're the boss until you gently explain that the two possible consequences of undermining your authority are a very unpleasant work environment and being forcibly removed from the work environment altogether.

If you find yourself dealing with a lot of insubordination, though, don't respond by losing your temper more. Losing your temper is unprofessional and a poor way to motivate through fear. But that isn't the reason. If you have to quell a lot of insubordination, you haven't established yourself as a leader. You're reacting rather than setting the pace and have other changes to make.

Fear is most useful in establishing a sense of urgency. "You're underperforming, Jones, and if you can't keep up with the rest of the team you won't leave me with many choices," may be exactly what Jones needs to avoid losing his job. You certainly aren't doing Jones any favors by soft-peddling the situation.

"If the company can't get the new product line out the door by June, there's a good chance we'll have to close our doors, and we can't release the product line until this system is done." Think that will give your team a greater sense of urgency than, "We have a May deadline and I'm sure you'll all work hard to make sure we finish on time"?

Fear is the best motivational tool you have for creating a sense of urgency. If you need hard, fast work, don't shy away from it. If, on the other hand, you need creativity, good judgment, and initiative, fear is the worst tool for the job. Avoid it. Scared people aren't creative and avoid taking risks. They simply want to get away from whatever it is that's scaring them just as fast as they can.

The guidelines for using fear as a motivator:

Fear Is Like Tabasco

You're better off using fear sparingly than too much because a little goes a long way. Too many good employees will simply leave.

The Consequences You Describe for Failure Must Be Real

Lying makes you the boy who cried wolf, and you won't get a second chance. Only use fear as a motivator when there's something to be legitimately afraid of.

Fear Is Focused on Consequences, Not You

Unless the issue is insubordination, making employees afraid of you is not in your best interests. If they're afraid of you, they'll avoid you as much as they can. Even when forced to interact with you, they'll give you as little information as possible and sugar-coat the rest. Think you can succeed as a leader when you don't hear about problems until it's too late to do anything about them?

Bullying employees, making them afraid of you, creates a poisonous atmosphere. People in leadership roles who intimidate their employees may think they're leading, but they're wrong. It isn't the bully who's leading. It's fear of the bully that leads employees, and that's different. Leadership involves setting direction, but when fear is the driving motivator for employees, there is no direction, only a lot of activity intended to avoid provoking the bully. Since the boss is a bully, provocation is a given, of course, so what happens is that employees keep their heads down, hoping the boss's anger will fall on someone else this time.

Bullies think they're leaders. They give orders and their victims obey. Employees react quickly, they don't argue, and they do things the "right way," which is to say, how they think the boss would do it.

Employees are reacting to fear rather than following a leader, which has several unintended consequences for the bully.

- Since all decisions are potential provocations, employees prefer to wait and ask the boss. Initiative is dead.
- When employees do make decisions, they're trying to second-guess what the boss would do, not figure out what's best for the company. Bullying leads to bad decisions.

By bullying employees, bosses create an unhealthy, addictive symbiosis. The boss, needing a sense of dominance, depends on employees to provide an outlet. Employees in their turn have a ready excuse for every failure—the boss's temper.

Depending on the psychology of those working for you, it may be important for employees to understand that you can be intimidating should the situation call for it. You can't be a doormat for employees either.

When in doubt, though, find a different solution.

Greed

Greed, avarice, the desire for material things—among the deadly sins, it's a favorite, and a cornerstone of capitalist economics besides. It motivates people to buy lottery tickets, fly airlines they don't like on inconvenient routes, and marry people they aren't particularly fond of.

Why not use it to motivate employees?

You can, but it's dangerous. We covered some of this ground when we talked about the use of spot bonuses. Here's one more dimension of the problem with using greed as a motivator: Like any addictive drug, satisfying a craving for money results in habituation, which is to say the addict needs regular hits, and each hit needs to be bigger than the last one to have the same effect.

"Get this project done on time and there's $5,000 in cash in it for you," you say to the project team. They bust their humps, get the project done, and get the cash. Now you have another project that needs doing. Think they'll work hard without the potential for a cash incentive? Not on your life. You've set the pattern.

So okay, you offer another $5,000 reward. Think they'll work as hard as last time? No, they won't. Since you created the expectation of a $5,000 reward, that's now money they're entitled to. Psychologically, it just became part of each employee's base compensation. You'll need to offer more to have the same effect.

There are some situations where you can and should cater to greed. If you're part of a cash-poor start-up and are trying to attract great employees you can't afford, holding out the hope of wealth in exchange for up-front economic sacrifice can work well. Lots of start-ups succeed by giving employees stock options in lieu of salary for this exact reason. Keep in mind that this appeal to greed has a lengthy pay-out, though. Even better, as long as the employees haven't exercised their options, they can make the pay-out even bigger by continuing to help the company succeed.

Greed also works with sales professionals, who are accustomed to receiving a significant proportion of their compensation in the form of commissions. Sales professionals aren't typical employees, though—monetary gain is higher on their list of priorities, and their performance is assessed in a single, easily measured dimension.

Catering to greed has one other, obvious drawback: It's expensive. Compared to every other motivator available to you, it has the biggest budget impact. Why use it when other alternatives are available?

Compensate employees fairly and wisely. As described in the previous chapter, think of your compensation system as a communications medium, not as a motivator. Catering to greed is a dangerous game, as likely to backfire as to work well.

Guilt

As every mom knows, guilt is a wonderful way to get children to do what they ought to do. "You don't call, you don't write—I don't think you love your mother!" gets the kids to call and write. Even when the kids are in their 60s, they'll squirm and feel uncomfortable—like they did when they first went off to college.

When you use guilt as a motivator, you place yourself in a parental role and employees in a child role, and not in a way that creates a positive interaction either. In the workplace, you want employees to think and act as adults, not as children. If guilt has a role to play in the modern workplace, it's a tiny one.

The only time guilt ever makes any sense at all as a motivator is as an alternative to fear in regulating inappropriate behavior among employees. "Think about how you just made her feel," is probably a more effective way to get an employee to stop acting inappropriately than, "Do that again and I'll kick your posterior very hard."

Probably.

Don't make a habit of instilling guilt in employees. You need grownups working for you, not kids.

Avoidance of Boredom

In the early 1990s, Harry Newton (of computer telephone integration fame) pointed out to me that just as service had become an important product differentiator, entertainment was growing into a similar role.

Look around you and you'll see it's true: How else do you explain McDonald's Happy Meals, not to mention the Disney Store?

Entertainment succeeds as a marketing dimension because in this day and age, people can't cope with being bored. Whether you look at this phenomenon as avoidance of boredom or a desire for entertainment, it's an important motivator, and one you can use to your advantage as a leader.

Look at it from the boredom-avoidance side for a second and you'll see the immediate imperative that follows from this motivator: Employees who find their work boring won't work as hard as those who find it interesting, and they'll be more likely to leave for positions where the work is more fun. Employees who find themselves working in a boring, stiff, stifling corporate culture will leave for companies that embrace the concept of having fun on the job.

And—pay attention now—employees who work in companies where sending a joke over the corporate email system is grounds for termination will bolt for companies with a more reasonable attitude the first time someone is stupid enough to enforce the policy.

There are two ways you can make use of the need to avoid boredom in motivating employees. The first is environmental, making the workplace itself an enjoyable place to be. Small businesses have a huge advantage over large corporations in this regard because they can get away with practices that would cause the HR director of any large corporation to keel over. I've known of several small companies over the years that brought in a cooler full of beer Friday afternoons, for example. The beer served as a conversational lubricant, and the tradition helped create a relaxed, informal atmosphere in which employees communicated better and felt more a part of the corporation.

Try that in a Fortune 500 company and see how long you last.

Since beer is probably out for you, feed employees at staff meetings instead. Bring in motivational speakers (they're mostly entertainers who tack on a message to warrant their fees). Encourage liveliness in progress reports. And so on.

You can make use of this motivator in disciplinary situations, too. For example, several supervisors and teams I've known have instituted some variation of the Cookie Penalty. (Sometimes it's the Donut Penalty or the Bagel Penalty. Unless you run IS for a health food store it must never be the Tofu Penalty.)

The Cookie Penalty is simplicity itself. If someone on the team commits a minor infraction of the rules—like showing up late for a meeting, flogging a dead horse[4], or using *ad hominem* arguments[5] instead of sticking to the issues—a jury of their peers convicts them in a kangaroo court (no point wasting time on finicky details like rules of evidence) and passes the sentence: ***Bring cookies to the next meeting!***

It's a great technique. It gives team members a way to communicate their dislike for a peer's behavior without ego damage or confrontation, it raises morale instead of lowering it, and it builds a sense of team identity by establishing a tradition.

---

[4]*An employee of mine, responsible for taking the notes for one of our weekly staff meetings, distributed a sketch of all of us, whips in hand, surrounding a horse that had recently expired. We all complimented him on how accurately he had recounted the meeting.*

[5]*If you're unfamiliar with the term, here's an example: Employee #1: "2+2=4". Employee #2: "How can you say that! Hitler once said the exact same thing!" In ad hominem, arguments you try to win through name-calling instead of logic, and it's poisonous. Terms like "bleeding-heart liberal" and "knee-jerk conservative" have the same effect, and have pretty much eliminated useful political dialog in the USA.*

And it keeps you from overreacting to minor irritants in the bargain, while still serving to dissuade employees from behaving in undesirable ways.

Fun isn't only useful in disciplinary situations, of course. It's also useful when constructing rewards. A lot has been published regarding "non-cash rewards"—things like T-shirts, coffee mugs, team bowling nights, and so on. All of these are good things to do, and always for the same reason—they establish the office as an enjoyable place to be. Yes, there's a minor appeal to greed, but employees really won't work extra hard because of the expectation that they'll get a free T-shirt.

Non-cash rewards, like spot bonuses, work because they evince sincerity when you say thank you. They're much more effective than the equivalent amount of cash because they reinforce an atmosphere of fun in the office.

Again, there are two ways to use avoidance of boredom as a motivator. The first, which we just explored, is creating an enjoyable, casual atmosphere. The second is to make sure the work itself is fun.

No, it isn't possible to make all work fun all the time, any more than it's possible to make education fun all the time. "Edutainment" is a recognized neologism, ungraceful as it is, because educators have finally realized how much better students learn concepts when the concepts are packaged in ways that hold students' attention. You should recognize that this insight is just as valid when you construct work assignments.

Sometimes, an employee's primary responsibility is fun and interesting, at which point you're done. If an employee's current primary responsibility is pretty dull, though, give her a second responsibility she'll find enjoyable and interesting.

Here's how it works: It's human nature to work harder on things you like. Assign someone a task they'll enjoy doing and they'll work hard on it.

It's also human nature to want to get past the dull stuff to work on the interesting stuff. So long as you also hold employees accountable for their dull work, they'll do that as fast as they can so they can get to the more entertaining responsibility.

You win twice.

Some managers think it's fine to say, "That's why they call it work," and ignore this easy-to-use motivational tool.

How sad.

Need for Approval

Leadership, you'll recall, is determined by who looks to whom for approval. The need for approval is nearly universal among human beings. Through the simple expedient of delivering approval, you'll establish yourself as a leader.

Remember the four relationship directions? You can turn yourself into a leader in all four of these directions by catering to other individuals' need for approval while carefully managing your own need for it.

This isn't a complicated proposition. Think for a moment about how you feel when someone you respect gives you a compliment. Feels good, doesn't it? Guess what—other people feel the same way. They like it. They'll work harder if they think their hard work is appreciated. They'll show creativity if they think someone will notice. All manner of good things happen when you give a compliment, and it costs neither you nor the company a dime.

WHY BAD MOODS ARE CONTAGIOUS

Why do so many leaders forget to give compliments? It's because of a fascinating psychological phenomenon pointed out to me years ago in a sales training seminar: Most people, most of the time, don't feel all that good about themselves and their lives, and they think they can feel better by giving away their ill feeling to someone else.

Think about how much this explains. Why does someone act like a jerk? They don't like themselves, they don't like their lives, and they want to feel better about it all. Of course, when they act like a jerk they just feel worse about themselves, so their behavior doesn't improve, and when they act like a jerk they make someone else feel worse. That person now has some ill-feeling to give away, too. Like a nuclear chain reaction, the process of giving away ill-feeling can create an explosive situation.

Crabbiness is contagious.

If you aren't the introspective sort, go to a mirror and look in it. Tell the person you see looking back at you that he or she is vulnerable to the same syndrome. Tell him or her to work hard at stopping the contagious spread of grouchiness.

Listening as a Form of Approval

Why do you have two ears but only one mouth? So you'll listen twice as much as you talk. It's an old joke but it's good advice. Listening has lots of benefits. Among them:

- People usually appear more intelligent when listening than when talking.

- Your chances of learning something are much better when you listen.

- Listening to someone is a compliment—you're signaling them that their thoughts are worth hearing.

Asking for Help as a Form of Approval

Asking for help has a lot of the same characteristics as listening. When you ask someone for help, you compliment their abilities. You also get their help—advantage number two.

Best of all, when you ask someone for help and they agree, you've delegated work to them. Now if you delegate work to someone else, that means you're giving them work direction. I once knew an end-user who was adept at using the company's computer query and reporting tools. He adamantly refused to help any of his peers use the computer, though. When I asked him why, he explained that once he started down that road, he'd get a reputation as a worker instead of a manager because he'd be doing the work of others for them, instead of the other way around.

Learning to say no is hard—we're all taught the virtues of helping others. So don't say no when others ask you for help, but make sure you're helping them do the work rather than accepting an assignment.

How to Give Compliments

When you compliment someone, you cater to their need for approval. By complimenting them you both motivate them and establish yourself as a leader in their eyes.

Okay, better go out there and give as many compliments as possible. Even better, establish a process performance measure for yourself: Compliments per Listener per Hour.

Regrettably, it doesn't work that way. When giving compliments, less is frequently more, for several reasons.

The first is how good most people are at spotting phony compliments. "Hey, Jim, I like that pinstriped tie you're wearing. It looks *great* with your plaid suit!" Even if Jim believes you, nobody else in earshot will be fooled, and the next time you give one of them a compliment, everyone will assume it's insincere, too.

Don't give phony compliments. Change the subject, listen rather than talking, and if the situation calls for it, be diplomatic but honest. Just don't lie, especially when the lie is so easily detected.

Another reason to be prudent in how you give compliments is the problem of grade inflation. When you praise work as excellent when it's merely pretty good, you take away the motivation to excel. You're better off giving a more restrained compliment that balances your appreciation with recognition that the performer can do better. "You did a good, solid job, Carol," you might say. "It should work out well. I especially like how you laid out the screens—they're clean and easy to navigate. Now tell me, what do you see as the strongest part of it, and where would you do it differently next time?"

A couple of points about the preceding dialog are worthy of notice. First, the compliment was clear but not effusive. A "good, solid job," is something to be proud of, but leaves lots of headroom for next time. Second, the praise was specific. Specificity is the hallmark of a sincere compliment. "It was great," means, "I read somewhere I'm supposed to give compliments, but I never actually looked at your work, Carol."

And finally, the discussion about performance improvement began with a question—Carol gets to guide it. Chances are, she'll be harder on herself than you'd ever be. With your guidance, she'll understand where she needs to improve to get a better grade. And, as part of the discussion on how she needs to improve, you get to give more compliments, like, "That's a good insight, Carol." When someone is criticizing herself, a compliment helps pave the road.

Why else should you give compliments sparingly? Another reason is periodic variable reinforcement. This is a phenomenon first noticed by B. F. Skinner in his research into operant conditioning. What it means is that if you feed a pigeon a food pellet every time the pigeon pecks a bar, the pigeon will rapidly lose interest. If you feed the pigeon every three pecks, you'll hold its interest better.

If, on the other hand, you feed it randomly and unpredictably, but still only when it pecks the bar, it will go into a pecking frenzy, pressing the bar far more than with the other types of reinforcement.

Periodic variable reinforcement explains a number of mysterious human behaviors, like why people play golf. If you play golf you should recognize the phenomenon—it's the occasional great drive, pinpoint chip-shot, or long putt that brings you back to the course.

Give compliments like this. Don't be overly stingy with them—just be a tough grader, and only give compliments when situations calls for them. You want to motivate excellence, and that means reserving your strongest compliments for the best work only.

Give compliments publicly, too. There's an ancient rule of leadership that's still some of the best advice you can get on the subject: Compliment in public, criticize in private.

One more tip—scale your compliments to the abilities of the recipient. It's their achievement you're complimenting just as much as it's your objective assessment of their work.

Complimenting Peers and Superiors

Complimenting subordinates is expected. Complimenting service recipients is an easy thing to do, too. Complimenting peers and superiors may seem to be an unnatural act, though. After all, your peers are your rivals and don't report to you, and the person you report to is supposed to give you compliments, not the other way around.

Except it doesn't work that way. You get promoted to leadership positions when it's obvious to everyone you have "leadership potential." That means the people who decide these things see you as a leader. They see you leading. Most importantly, they see others looking to you for leadership. Now how can you get them to do that?

Get people in the habit of looking to you for approval and you're their leader. It may seem manipulative, but it works, and since someone is going to get that promotion, why shouldn't it be you?

When you compliment peers, the compliments must be sincere and legitimate. "I admire the way you handled that situation, Glenn. How'd you come up with that approach?" gets Glenn on your side, gets Glenn explaining to you how he thinks, gets Glenn looking to you for compliments. And, of course, you learn how Glenn came up with his innovative approach.

Compliment Glenn a few times and he'll start looking for you so he can brag about his next new success. He's looking to you for approval, and in doing so, has subordinated himself to you.

The same techniques you use with peers also work with your organizational superiors, only you have to be even more careful about how you deliver compliments to this group. When you compliment your boss, you're walking a thin line between legitimate praise and brown-nosing. The best executives are past masters at giving compliments themselves. They're also pretty good at spotting sycophants, and they won't respect you for trying to manipulate them through flattery.

The best way to compliment anyone who's higher in the pecking order than you are is to ask them for help or information. You gain identity with them in the process, learn something, and give them compliments both more subtle and more significant than slapping on the back and saying, "Hey, nice job!"

Exclusivity

What makes *Homo sapiens* unique? Use of tools? No, other animals make use of tools. Use of fire? No, the jack pine's seeds can't even germinate until they've been exposed to fire. Language? Koko the gorilla participated in an Internet chat session.

No, what makes us unique among organisms is our desire to be unique, special, part of something that makes us stand out from the faceless crowd. Each of us is a unique individual; more to the point, being a unique individual, and being treated as someone special, is important to each of us.

Marketers call this the need for exclusivity. Have you visited the Dilbert Zone on the World Wide Web? Did you join Dogbert's New Ruling Class (DNRC)? Once you joined, did you click over to the Dilbert Store to buy some merchandise to show off your membership in this exclusive group?

See how it works?

If you want a cheap, sure way to motivate employees, remember their names. Remember something about them. Make it clear you care about them as individuals.

Ask about how George's daughter fared in her first semester of college. Ask Brenda if her mother is fully recovered from the flu. If Jill's dog is sick, ask if she needs an afternoon off to take the dog to the vet, rather than saying, "If you put your dog to sleep, you could pay more attention to your job," as one manager of my acquaintance pointed out to an anxious employee.

Treating people as individuals rather than as part of a faceless group makes them feel good about themselves and good about you, and helps instill a sense of loyalty to you. Loyalty is hard to earn and easily lost. Calling someone "Hey, you with the face," isn't a good way to start.

There's a second, trickier dimension to exclusivity as a motivator. People want to feel like they're part of something special—something bigger and better. Part of DNRC, perhaps, or some other elite group. If you want a team to plow right through brick walls, nothing does the job like persuading them they're part of the "A" team, the Navy Seals, the Delta Force, the Top Guns—or even the Dirty Dozen.

When you build a strong sense of team identity like this, all kind of good things flow from it—*esprit de corps,* energy ,and trust come to mind. So what's tricky about it?

What's tricky about it is that creating a strong sense of team identity has a dark side. Depending on the social context, that dark side is expressed as xenophobia, elitism, arrogance, and a misplaced emphasis on team goals over the goals of the whole organization. I'm part of a special group and *you're not!* So you *can't possibly understand* the special stuff we do, and couldn't do it as well as we do, even if you tried.

The very process you've used to build a strong, motivated, cohesive team isolates that team from the rest of the organization, and isolation builds mutual distrust.

If you need any more convincing, go outside the business world for a moment and think of all the groups in the world that consider themselves the sole repositories of "the truth." How many don't visualize people outside their special group as real individuals? Whether it's those who carried the "White Man's Burden" two centuries ago, religious extremists (regardless of their particular god), or, I'm sad to say, lots of modern American business executives, the act of belonging to an elite group dehumanizes everyone who doesn't belong to it.

Think about how IS and end-users interact. In far too many companies, IS professionals swap dumb end-user stories while end-users gripe about pencil-necked geeks who just want to play with toys. Is there any doubt what the source of the problem is? It's the human desire for exclusivity that makes each group strangers, and therefore less human, to the other.

There's one more danger to creating a sense of elitism in your teams, and that's the danger of success. In particular, your success.

What happens when, due to the exceptional leadership skills you've shown, you receive a promotion? The very people you've described as being not as good as your elite squad suddenly report to you, and they know you've portrayed them as second-rate. Think you'll gain their trust very quickly? It doesn't work that way.

Go Ahead Anyway, But...

The hazards of catering to exclusivity don't outweigh the benefits. Just be careful how you construct the sense of team identity. Do everything you can to avoid creating a sense that it's the team against the rest of the company. Never disparage any other group, and foster an understanding that every team in the company has its own special characteristics that, while different, are just as valuable in their own way to the company as a whole.

Emphasize interdependence. Construct as many situations as you can where members of your team interact with members of other teams throughout the company. If you can, create cross-team "internships" where you and other teams swap employees for a month at a time.

Most important of all, make sure your team reserves its competitive instincts and its sense of rivalry for your company's competitors, rather than for the rest of the company.

The Most Important Motivator

Fear, greed, guilt, avoidance of boredom, need for approval, exclusivity: Which is the most important motivator available to you?

None of them. The most important motivator is the need for self-esteem.

The need for self-esteem lies underneath the need for approval and the need for exclusivity. You can't reach it directly, which is why marketing gurus don't use it as a selling tool. Members of the "self-esteem movement" often try to use external approval as a tool for improving self-esteem, a fundamentally flawed approach.

Your route to fostering self-esteem is to focus each employee on achieving something worthwhile. Focus individuals and teams on achieving an important goal. Help them understand why it's important and how their work contributes to it. If you can do that, employees motivate themselves and each other.

A data center manager once wrote to ask how a concept like this might apply to a group of "unimportant" employees, for example, the people who maintain the tape library. It's easy when you're dealing with application developers, he implied, but tape-hangers?

The answer, of course, is that it's the tape managers who protect the whole company from going out of business. It's the tape librarians who protect all customer records, ensuring orders don't evaporate into bit heaven. Without the tape librarians, real paying customers would experience real, annoying problems. They're essential, and while doing their jobs well may not be glamorous, it is important.

People who produce more than they consume have abundant self-esteem. They know their own worth as human beings and know that the way to continue feeling good about themselves is to continue to produce more than they consume. In a leadership role, you have an opportunity to help the people you lead achieve this state of mind. By doing so, you'll have achieved something important.

When you do, you'll get to feel good about yourself, too.

Last Thought on Motivation

Most crimes are defined by intent. If you cause someone's death, for example, the charge depends on whether you planned it in advance, committed the act in the heat of passion, killed them by accident, or were defending yourself.

When you use the techniques described in this section, you're either manipulating people or motivating them. Which it is depends entirely on your intentions. If you sincerely believe you're leading great people who deserve excellent leadership that works hard to create a stimulating, motivating environment—if, when you give a compliment you're sincere in your praise, and when you express interest in an employee, you really are interested in that employee—then you're doing what you're supposed to do, which is providing the best leadership you can.

If, on the other hand, you think, "Okay, I'm supposed to give Karen a compliment in this situation. Oooh, I hate giving compliments. I don't even know what she did, really, but I have to come up with something," then you're being manipulative.

It's really pretty easy to tell.

Summary of Motivators

You have, to recap, six primary motivators: Fear, greed, guilt, avoidance of boredom, need for approval, and exclusivity. Each is a useful leadership tool; each has specific purposes to which it is best suited; most have drawbacks if used improperly. Table 16.1 summarizes them for you as a quick reference.

TABLE 16.1 SUMMARY OF MOTIVATORS

Motivator	Best Use	Hazardous Side Effects
Fear	Creating a sense of urgency	Diminishes creativity and initiative
Greed	Achieving a well-defined goal	Turns teammates into competitors; amounts needed to motivate constantly increase
Guilt	Regulating inappropriate behavior	Turns adults into children
Avoidance of Boredom	Increasing energy and enthusiasm	None significant
Need for Approval	Establishing yourself as the leader; inspiring hard work; fostering creativity and initiative; achieving excellence	Creates perception that you are a phony or sycophant
Exclusivity	Inspires loyalty; hard work; team trust	Creates an us versus them attitude; antagonizes the rest of the company

CORPORATE CULTURE

Culture, according to the division of anthropology known as ethnoscience, is how people behave in response to their environment. If you want to change culture, you either change the environment, or you find a way to change the behaviors people exhibit in response to the same environmental stimuli.

In a corporation, the environment to which people respond is mostly the behavior of other people, so the way to change the environment is to change behavior.

To change culture, you either change behavior or you change behavior.

Put it a different way, the only way to change the culture is to change the culture. Sounds like a vicious circle, doesn't it?

Of all leadership issues, culture change is the one that's the most misunderstood. Hard-nosed business executives, focused on the bottom line, think of culture as nothing but warm fuzzies, not worthy of their attention. Many experts in corporate change teach executives to avoid trying to change the culture because it's too hard to do, and too often unsuccessful.

They're not only wrong, but dangerously wrong. Establishing a desirable corporate culture isn't a warm fuzzy. It's the essence of leadership. If changing the culture is too hard for you and too risky, you're not prepared to lead—it's as simple as that.

As with so many topics in this book, the first key to success is to think. Changing the culture is a warm fuzzy if you don't start by assembling your leadership team to discuss, in concrete terms, what kind of culture you want. While it's acceptable to start with generalities like, "We want employees to trust each other," and "We want employees to be comfortable taking risks," you'll get nowhere if you leave it at that.

You may decide to talk over what you don't like about the current culture. There are worse things than a frank discussion of your organization's weaknesses among your leadership team. Unfortunately, discussions of this sort usually cause some members of the leadership team to react defensively, which slows things down.

The best way to start a culture change is to tell stories around the campfire. Go off-site for a day or two, prohibit cell phones and pagers except during breaks, and sit everyone down in a comfortable setting, but with a whiteboard and a tape recorder.

Since culture is how people behave in response to their environment, ask everyone to take turns describing a specific situation and how they'd like an employee or team to behave when faced with it. Following the description, ask each member of your leadership team to comment. Ask that comments be specific, because as when giving approval, "That was great," means, "I wasn't paying attention."

Criticism is fine; insist that it always be followed by a recommendation. You may hear a recommendation like, "I'm not sure how to do it better, but I didn't find this approach at all satisfying, because of *x*. Does anyone have an alternative?" If so, you've just heard from a team member with lots of leadership potential.

Depending on your leadership team, you may find an imbalance in the scenarios team members are willing to bring forward. If so, have a list of your own to present. Make sure to include scenarios that would directly involve members of the leadership team. For example, include one in which one of your leaders insists that a team do something stupid.

Include ethical dilemmas, and make them difficult choices, not mere temptations. For example, it's easy to agree that accepting a bribe from a vendor is difficult. It's harder to choose a course of action when you see hints of someone in a leadership position accepting gratuities and favors from a vendor, but you aren't sure.

Why campfire stories instead of discussing the issues? Storytelling has descriptive power orders of magnitude more effective than dry discussions of principle. Also, principles are less convincing in the real world than in the abstract. "Lying is always the wrong thing to do," sounds like you're taking the moral high ground. Now, think about something as simple as a poker game. A bluff is deliberate deception. Are you really willing to say that a poker player who resorts to bluffing is an immoral person, or is acting unethically?

It's easy to paint ethics as a matter of stark contrasts between "good" and "bad." Easy, but not helpful. Your leaders will be faced with difficult choices—not just choices that are hard to make, but choices that are hard to evaluate. Part of your job is to keep your team on the hook.

After between ten and fifteen of these campfire stories, start analyzing them to find common threads. Having dealt with real-world scenarios, you're now ready to deal with the underlying principles. When you construct the principles, test them against some more real-world scenarios. Hey, you test software, don't you? Why wouldn't you test these?

The specifics are up to you. They're a matter of what behavior and attitudinal traits you and your leadership team want to foster and which ones you want to discourage. When you're done, encapsulate the results in a series of brief, bulleted statements that establish the values and style—the culture—you wish to establish in your organization.

Two suggestions:

1. *Keep the list short.* God managed with ten commandments; Buddha managed with an eightfold path[6]. Brevity is a virtue, and even if you can't be quite as good as God or Buddha, keeping your list short helps everyone internalize it.

2. *Include statements about all four relationship directions.* To lead, you need to deal with those above you in the organization, those who report to you, those who receive your services, and your peers. Since culture is the behavior employees exhibit in response to other employees, and since "other employees" all fall into one of these four categories, it's a reasonable way to make sure you've covered your bases.

Okay, you've decided what you want in the way of corporate culture. You're done, right? After all we've been through together by now, you know better. You still have to implement. So how do you foster your values and style?

Changing the Culture #1: Communication

You have three tools at your disposal for changing the culture. The first is communication. Spend time presenting and explaining your values and style in all-hands meetings, in departmental staff meetings, in one-on-one communication. When an employee acts in a way that exemplifies what you're describing, make sure everyone in your organization hears about it. Search out examples of this kind, in fact, so every employee hears examples that involve fellow employees—not just peers, but friends.

Part of communication is orientation and training. Record your campfire stories. As opportunities present themselves, replace or augment them with real-world counterparts. Publish them in notebook form and make sure every employee, and especially every new employee, owns a copy.

Remember the buddy system for orienting new employees? Make sure buddies know part of their responsibility is making sure new employees know your values and style matter to you.

How about new members of your leadership team? They need a buddy too. This should be a peer, not you. It's easy for people in leadership positions to short-change responsibilities like this in the press of daily events, so make sure you do some load-balancing when bringing in a new manager.

---

[6]*You'd do worse than organizing your values and style into the same form as Buddha. Right views, right thought, right speech, right action, right livelihood, right effort, right mindfulness, and right meditation pretty much cover the subject, don't they?*

Also, make sure new managers receive training. You can give new employees the notebook and ask them to read it. You should personally walk new leaders through the notebook to make sure they understand the thought processes underlying the culture you promote.

One thought you must—sorry, you ***MUST*** communicate to everyone—is that fostering a common culture isn't the same as turning everyone in the organization into the Stepford Nerds. Your goal isn't to create an organization of pod people, and individuality is still something you value. That's true at the staff level, and it's true at the leadership level. Employees should expect leadership that's consistent with the values and style you promote. They shouldn't expect leaders to behave identically or to be interchangeable.

Changing the Culture #2: Modeling

To change culture, you either change behavior or you change behavior. Of these two choices the latter works better.

Not clear? Try it this way: You can tell employees to change their behavior, or you can go ahead and change your own.

Culture is the behavior people exhibit in response to their environment. Most of their environment is the behavior of other people. Not all of those "other people" have the same impact, and the people with the most impact are those in leadership positions. Don't like the culture you see in your organization? Chances are, the problems start with you or a member of your leadership team. If they start with a member of your leadership team, they still start with you because why don't you know you have a problem?

Make it clear to your leadership team that modeling the culture you've all agreed to isn't optional. Fostering the desired culture must be a tangible goal for leadership performance assessment, part of the compensation formula, and a regular discussion point in leadership meetings. It's awfully easy to fall into a *laissez-faire*, everything's-fine-as-long-as-the-work-gets-done attitude.

Modeling the culture isn't complicated. It's incredibly hard, but it isn't complicated. You just have to avoid inconsistency.

Oh, that's all.

Just as a male moth's antenna can detect a single molecule of pheromone from a female moth, so employees hypocrite detectors can detect even the tiniest trace of inconsistency between the culture you say you want and your actual behavior.

You have two ways to deal with this. The first is to be as consistent as possible. That's pretty simple, isn't it? Act in ways that are consistent with the culture you want.

The second is to acknowledge when you goof.

Changing the Culture #3: Technology

Culture is the behavior people exhibit in response to their environment. *Most* of their environment is the behavior of other people. Technical change also changes the environment and can lead to a change in the corporate culture, too.

The obvious examples of how technology change leads to culture change are voice mail and electronic mail. Electronic messaging has had an awesome impact on corporate culture in most companies. Much of the impact has been positive, democratizing companies, speeding up decisions, and making the physical location of employees far less important than it used to be.

Electronic mail has also led to difficulties, largely because creating an unambiguous message using only written words, without the body language that comprises about half of all communication, is hard for many employees. Email has led to many misunderstandings, which in turn have led to anger and flame wars.

Electronic mail also dehumanizes both participants in an exchange, so people who wouldn't dream of hurting another person's feelings face to face are willing to write appallingly rude statements in an email message.

And we haven't even begun to probe the problems voice mail introduced in organizations that inadvertently created "voice-mail jail" by using the new technology to eliminate large numbers of receptionists. Making it hard for customers to reach live human beings isn't exactly an improvement in your corporate culture.

Technology can change culture. Unplanned, the change is rarely an unmixed blessing. Don't avoid technology because of its potential pitfalls though. Remember who you are—you're leading an organization responsible for improving the corporation through the optimal use of technology.

Once you've determined what you want your culture to be, spend some time figuring out which technologies, properly applied, can help you get there, and then implement them.

PERSONAL COMPUTERS

As a generality, IS resents the PC.

IS ignored the PC when it first entered the organization because "you can't do serious computing on a toy like that." Despite their complete lack of utility (from the perspective of IS), PCs leaked into most organizations the way water leaks into a sieve.

continues

continued

End-users loved PCs because they had power over them. End-users didn't need to ask IS for resources or permission before creating a new application. They simply built a spreadsheet or created a personal database and that was that.

Once IS saw what was going on, the reaction was swift and stupid. "Look at all of these uncontrolled applications!" we wailed to internal audit, finally our ally after years of being its victim. "We need to get our arms around them—for the good of the end-users, of course, who aren't intellectually equipped to manage them properly."

If all else failed we cried, "What happens if the person who created the application is hit by a bus!" (For some reason, we all find the thought of someone being on the wrong end of a confrontation with public transportation far more appetizing than someone accepting a job offer from a competitor.)

This is stupid. Employees did their work using pencil and paper long before the advent of the personal computer, and did it without asking IS for advice, guidance, or permission. When calculators became cheap, these same employees bought calculators, still without asking permission from IS.

The personal computer doesn't change anything. It's a tool end-users employ to do their jobs better and more effectively. It also happens to be a tool used by IS to deploy enterprise applications, which means it's a multipurpose tool.

Just because IS also makes use of corporate PCs to deploy enterprise applications, that doesn't mean IS should forbid end-users from using it as each one sees fit.

How IS supports PCs reflects deeply on the culture of your IS organization. Either you see your role as helping every employee use technology to become as effective as possible, or you see your job as a preventive one, keeping employees from messing up their PC and causing headaches for the PC support group.

However you characterize your culture, part of it should be to establish the following as your mantra: "We're paid to have headaches."

Employees should recite this phrase the way school children recite the Pledge of Allegiance, at the start of every meeting. They should repeat it over and over again instead of counting sheep when they suffer from insomnia. They should write the phrase on the blackboard 50 times.

How you decide to support PCs, and how well, is an excellent indicator of how your employees view their role in the company.

One suggestion on how to make PCs more manageable: Rather than trying to create a single standard for everyone, establish multiple standards tailored to the needs of different work patterns. Highly mobile workers, for example, need different configurations than those who mostly do data-entry. Data analysts have different requirements from managers.

By defining multiple profiles, testing them, and keeping them up to date, you'll greatly reduce the need for individual customization. By solving a problem once, you keep employees from having to solve it repeatedly and uniquely.

Since you'll be able to implement each configuration in a controlled, tested way, the number of problems arising from rogue applications will be greatly reduced, which means your workload will be reduced as well.

Which leads to another valuable cultural attribute: Recognizing the superiority of doing things right compared to doing them over.

Last Words on Culture

Sometimes, the best way to summarize is to repeat, so let me repeat:

Establishing a desirable corporate culture isn't a warm fuzzy. It's the essence of leadership. If changing the culture is too hard for you and too risky, you're not prepared to lead—it's as simple as that.

Everything you do, every success you can achieve, happens through your behavior and the behavior of the employees who work for you. A strong, positive corporate culture simplifies leadership because employees will understand, at a gut level, how they're supposed to act.

A strong, negative corporate culture is poison. No matter how well you do everything else, a poisonous culture will destroy any hope you have of accomplishing anything worthwhile.

YOUR CAREER

That brings us at last to the final topic of this book: Your career.

When I began in this business, we were still EDP and we had a single, linear career path. Trainee programmers became programmers, programmers became programmer/analysts, programmer/analysts because systems analysts, who became project managers, who then graduated to full-fledged managers. In the fullness of time and with luck, one EDP manager would end up in charge of the whole shebang.

There's only one reason to become a CIO, and following this connect-the-dots approach to career development isn't it. There are lots of easier career paths. Probably, they're all easier.

Don't automatically fall into the trap of "wanting to be at the top.". Define your career goals in terms of achievement, enjoyment, and what will improve your sense of self-esteem, and you'll experience a more satisfying career.

Even more important, don't plan your career the way Gary Kasparov plans his chess game. Sure, you can look six moves ahead, figuring out the major possible variations to make sure you "win." The problem with this approach is that if you fail to achieve your career goals, you'll hate your career, while if you do achieve your career goals, you'll still hate your career.

Yes, if you make a five-year plan for your career, you're really preparing to hate life for the next five years. You'll learn subjects you don't care about, you'll take jobs you don't enjoy, and you'll grit your teeth and grimly climb each rung of the ladder, probably alienating everyone you know and yourself as you do. When you're done, you'll hold a job you probably won't enjoy, because you simply have no way to know what a job is like until you're very close to it[7].

Go ahead and set a five year goal. That gives you a direction, which is always important.

Now, figure out what jobs you can take on that will move you in the right direction that you'll enjoy doing, and that you'll be good at. Every job you take should qualify in all three of these dimensions, or you shouldn't take them on.

Life is just too short.

If you want to be the CIO, you'd better love technology the way other people love cars or sports. When you're CIO, the whole job is about delivering technology, making it so useful to the organization that you get to do it again tomorrow.

If you want to be a great CIO, every time you contemplate the Internet you should get goosebumps. Corny? Maybe, but you should. The Internet shouldn't work. It's an unmanaged network bigger than anything created through centralized design. It's the technological equivalent of market economics, regulated through an invisible hand.

It simply works. Its ability to eliminate location as a factor in human interaction is a thing of wonder.

---

[7]*A personal example: I wanted to be a research scientist very badly when I was young. In graduate school I discovered most scientists work long hours for low pay, with a large proportion of their time writing grant proposals, and a relatively small proportion of their time spent in the laboratory. Too much of the job is drudgery and too little is spent in research. When I got close to it, I realized I lacked the genius that would place me in the top tier. I also discovered I enjoyed building tools far more than I enjoyed using them. And so, I changed careers.*

16

The Internet? How about the telephone? You own that too, and there's no greater miracle than our ability to call anyone in the world at any time and have the call go through. You own a piece of that miracle because the folks who manage your PBX report to you.

When you read the trade publications, you need to cast a jaundiced eye at the vaporware described in all the press releases that have been massaged into published articles. While you're in love with technology, you don't get to lose any of your objectivity or skepticism. Our industry is chock-full of BS (bushwah, you'll recall) and if you don't have a first-class BS detector, you won't get very far.

As you wade through the BS, though, every new capability somebody has dreamed up should fire your imagination, because among all of these new capabilities are possibilities for giving your organization both a temporary competitive advantage and something very cool, too.

Don't disparage coolness. Business is business, but if you're going to work the long hours being a CIO requires, you'd better enjoy the process too.

And don't be discouraged by the word "temporary." Any technology your company can deploy can be deployed by your competitors, too. It's an unending arms race, so all advantages are temporary and you don't get to stop. The only difference is that the end-results of this arms race are better products and better service so customers are better off, instead of global thermonuclear destruction.

It's a better gig.

If you're already a CIO you know all of this. Presumably, you've read this book to pick up some pointers and new techniques.

If you're not CIO but want to be, you've had one of two reactions to this book. Either you realize the job is about as much fun as it's possible to have, or you realize that by taking the job you're entering migraine city, never to leave again.

The two aren't mutually exclusive.

A few years ago, *The Economist* ran a special issue on technology (September 28, 1996). In it is an astonishing conclusion: Over the course of centuries, virtually every bit of economic growth, and as a result, all improvement in the human standard of living, is the result of technological change. Investments in capital, in labor, in anything else, really don't matter. It's technological change that has driven economic growth; nothing else.

As CIO, you are, or will be, an agent of implementing new technologies in ways that make organizations more effective in delivering goods and services.

It's nice work if you can get it.

LEADERSHIP

"Your mouth is open. Sounds are coming out. This doesn't look good."

—Buffy (the Vampire Slayer) Somers

MANAGEMENTSPEAK

The customer service department is here to stay.

Translation:

We're gutting the customer service department. This is your two weeks notice.

As the result of a reorganization, I inherited a new team. This team consisted of union-ized technicians who maintained the hardware for a bunch of mission-critical systems. The team's supervisor walked me through their work area and I shook hands, giving a firm handshake, trying hard to remember names—all that good stuff.

Most of the techs got up from their work as I approached, standing and at least pretend-ing interest in meeting me. One, however, stayed at his post, working to get a Macintosh back on its metaphorical feet. "Hey, Don," the supervisor called over to him. "Come over here to meet Bob Lewis. We report to him now."

Don didn't get up. He turned slightly and looked me over. "I've seen managers come and I've seen 'em go," he commented. "The last guy who ran this place is making salads over at Daytons."

Since Don had a clear understanding of both his priorities and the nature of reorganiza-tions, I laughed, thanked him for his expression of confidence, and we both went about our business.

While a few people work alone, most work in groups. And while a few souls manage to go through life without ever having a boss, most of us report to someone. Even the CEO reports to the board of directors, and if the board does a good job, the CEO deals with a harder reporting relationship than any other employee.

Most people work in groups, and in a corporate environment everyone reports to some-one (yes, we could try thinking out-of-the-box on this subject, but if there's any way of reaching a different conclusion it hasn't yet been found). As leader of the club that's made for you and me, you're responsible for figuring out how to turn both of these inevitabilities into factors that contribute to your success.

Working in Groups

What's the difference between a group and a team? In a team, we're all smarter than any of us are. In a group, we're all stupider.

Groups do dumb things. Groups turn into mobs and do ugly, dangerous things. As K (Tommy Lee Jones) said in *Men in Black,* "A person is smart. People are dumb, panicky, dangerous animals."[1] A big part of leadership is turning groups into teams.

What's the secret of turning groups into teams? There isn't one, there are several. Whole books—heck, whole executive seminars—have been written on this subject. Never mind all that. The following tips are what you really need to know:

---

[1] *Who says the movies don't teach us valuable lessons?*

Tip #1: Teams Have a Leader

No, not the "team leader." Most teams will end up having a natural leader—someone inside the team who has leadership potential and to whom the rest of the team instinctively looks for guidance. That's a good thing[2].

This "team leader" can't be the team's leader, though. If the team reports to you, you have to be the team's leader. One of the tools you have for this job is to co-opt the team's internal leader. Let this individual know you recognize his or her leadership potential and will help develop opportunities for personal growth and advancement. If the team leader is on your side, turning the group into a team and keeping it that way will be relatively easy. If the team leader isn't on your side, you have three options:

1. Convert the team leader to your side.
2. Get rid of the team leader.
3. Lose your ability to lead.

When you have an insubordinate team leader, life becomes awful and gets worse for you, for the team, and for the team leader. Don't let it happen.

This internal team leader provides informal coaching and advice, helps get the team moving, keeps it focused—all that good stuff. You, on the other hand, must be perceived by every member of the team as the team's Leader.

It has to be you, not the informal team leader, who establishes goals and sets direction. Both of you may cater to team members' need for approval; your compliments should be less frequent, should be results-oriented, and must mean more.

Every team must have a leader in fact, not just in title, and that leader must be the person to whom the team reports.

Tip #2: Teams Have a Purpose

Remember the Mission Statement? The idea of creating team mission statements has become commonplace to the point of tedium. Despite the triteness of the sentiment, it's nonetheless valid. Teams need to understand their reason for existence.

---

[2]*Sometimes a team will have two people like this. No, that isn't twice as good. It's a disaster. Just as fast as you can, find a way to transfer or promote one of them. They both deserve a chance at leadership; neither deserves to be the cause of team fragmentation.*

In part because employees have become hugely cynical about mission statements, and in part because the idea of teams choosing their own mission is, when you get right down to it, just a bit odd[3], you're better off following a process much like the creation of a project charter. You and the team should jointly draft a document that describes the team's high-level goals, tangible products and services, how those products and services lead to achieving the goals, and why those goals are important to the company.

Why is this a group effort and not just your wisdom? That's an easy one—you aren't the source of all wisdom. The team may have good ideas on how to modify your stated business goals in ways that give the business more than you'd envisioned; its members will probably have excellent ideas on how reshaping its products and services can achieve the goals better than anything you thought of by yourself.

In a team, we're all smarter than any of us.

Tip #3: Teams Evolve

Back in 1965, Tuckman[4] described the stages through which every team must progress from the time it forms until it becomes effective. The stages are based on two key factors: Alignment and trust. Here's how they interplay.

- *Stage 1—Forming:* When teams form they have a high level of trust but a low sense of alignment. Enthusiasm is high; everyone has great expectations[5]; but although everyone thinks they're working on the same thing, they're wrong. Human communication isn't that accurate, and although everyone thinks they've agreed, in reality the agreement on words masks significant differences in concept.

- *Stage 2—Storming:* As team members start working together, their differences emerge. Where originally each member trusted the others, now factions emerge as individuals begin to recognize their disagreements. The low initial alignment has led to low trust, which in turn leads to arguments and anger. Team members hate life, each other, and especially you because *it's all your fault.*

- *Stage 3—Norming:* Arguments and anger, while unpleasant, lead to an honest exploration of what everyone really means and how concepts differ. Assuming a team reaches the norming phase, its members work through their semantic differences[6] and become aligned to a common purpose. The worst is over.

---

[3]*You decided the team should exist. Don't you know why? If so, why aren't you willing to share this important information with the team? If you aren't...disband it.*

[4]*Tuckman, B.S., 1965. Developmental Sequences in Small Groups. Psychological Bulletin, vol. 63: pp. 384-399.*

[5]*Hey, that's a good title for a book!*

[6]*Never equate "semantics" with trivialities. "Semantic issue" means "we don't understand each other yet."*

- *Stage 4—Performing:* Through the process of working through their differences to find common ground, team members restore their trust in one another. With high trust and high alignment, the team is able to deal with whatever you throw at it effectively and achieves the purpose for which you chartered it.

This sounds like a bunch of theory, and the hokey names for each phase teams go through don't help instill managers with confidence in the validity of this model.

Nonetheless, every team goes through these stages. Every one. The only help you can give a team is to prepare everyone for the storming phase so members aren't caught off-guard when it happens, and to facilitate the storming-stage discussions when they inevitably happen. If you've prepared the team well, someone will comment, "Hey, this is the storming stage, isn't it?"

"Yes it is," you should respond. "I'm glad we got here this fast."

Tip #4: Teams Require Maintenance

Robots do nothing except work and break down. When they break down they require repairs. The alternative to repairs is preventive maintenance.

Teams also require preventive maintenance. Human beings, not having been designed for the purpose for which the team has been formed, need more maintenance than robots.

In team interactions, individual members sometimes have personal needs that must be addressed or they'll opt out of the discussion, the meeting, and sometimes the team. It's the responsibility of every team member to help address every other team member's personal needs so the team can get back to business.

A personal need may be as basic as a short break to restore the kidneys; it may be a sense of not having been properly understood; or it may be a need to break the tension. Regardless, other team members must validate and address these personal needs.

Wearing your group facilitator help, you're responsible for recognizing these situations and focusing the team on addressing them. All you have to do is identify them in public and create an opportunity for the individual involved to express the need verbally. "Jeanne, you seem to be seem to be stuck on something. Can you help me understand the issue?"

Individual team members need preventive maintenance. So does the team as a whole. Teams in the performing stage require a high degree of trust; people trust each other through complex interpersonal dynamics. Whether you plan for it or not, a significant part of any team meeting will consist of banter, gossip, and other apparently nonproductive discussions that nonetheless reinforce each member's sense of team identity.

You don't need to do anything to make team maintenance happen. It happens all by itself. Just don't interfere when it happens and everything will be fine.

Final Tip on Teams

A high-performing team is a thing of wonder. Every so often, when a team you've helped create is really humming, you'll feel the team's energy in an almost extrasensory way. When you do, don't say anything. Just lean back and revel in the experience.

It's something very special.

The Organizational Chart

Everybody has to report to somebody, if for no other reason than for the administration of salary increases and performance appraisals. Employees also find it helpful to know what they're supposed to be doing when they show up for work. Your loyal author once spent three months in an office with no assigned boss and no assigned responsibilities, and from first-hand experience he can report: It wasn't any fun at all.

Most employees are part of a team; each team reports to someone. The result is called an organizational chart. For some unaccountable reason, this has led many managers to conclude that if an organization isn't performing well, the problem must lie in how they've organized.

Managers reorganize expecting the reorganization to solve performance problems. Regrettably, reorganizations rarely solve performance problems, but they always cause them.

Reorganizations create winners and losers. At the management level, the winners are in charge of the new organizational units; the losers aren't. At the staff level, the winners report to the good managers; the losers report to the bad ones.

What's the logical response to a reorganization? Keep your head down and watch who gets shot to see where the bullets are coming from. Frequent reorganizations make skill at surviving reorganizations a core competency and turn risk-taking into a memory.

There are lots of ways to organize IS. You can separate major development from maintenance and support. You can organize around groups within the company. You can organize around technologies, or around major applications.

Pick one.

You do need to keep operations separate—the only given in IS is that you need someone running the data center, including the networks and servers.

Also, it's often a good idea to make PC support its own area as well, since the dynamics of supporting PCs in the enterprise are different from everything else. The old idea of having an "Information Center" still makes good sense in a lot of companies.

Aside from that, pick one. Then don't reorganize again.

What to Do Instead of Reorganizing

Do everything you can to cause employees to ignore the organizational chart just as much as you can. Here's why.

Take a copy of your organizational chart and place it on your desk. Now draw a stick figure inside one of the boxes on the org chart. The stick figure represents an employee.

Next, draw a circle around the whole organization and inside the circle write, outside any one box and in big letters, the word "WORK." What do you see?

The organizational chart creates boundaries separating employees from work.

You may think you've assigned all of the work that needs doing to one box or another in your organizational chart, but that's because you only know about the big chunks of work. No matter what you may think is going on, in IS there's always a bunch of uncategorized *stuff* that needs to get done. If you emphasize the organizational chart and insist that employees respect it, you'll create the equivalent of a restaurant with snooty servers. When any work outside an employee's boundary shows up, the employee will say, "Sorry, but that isn't my table," and walk away.

Is that how you like to be treated when you dine at an expensive restaurant? No, it isn't, and you're running a restaurant far more expensive than any you go to for special meals.

Everyone has to report to someone; everyone has responsibilities assigned to them. Don't let that establish any boundaries at all.

Do everything you can to ensure that everyone in your organization—*everyone*—has personal ownership of your organization's goals. Go back to the culture you said you want to establish, and if this isn't part of what you've established as your goal, reformulate your goals so it is.

CORPORATE POLITICS

Remember the social laws of thermodynamics? We talked about them in the last chapter:

- You can't win.
- You can't break even.
- You can't quit the game.

These do match up to the physical laws, by the way: Energy and matter can't be created or destroyed (you can't win); in every reaction some energy is lost to entropy (you can't break even); the laws of the universe are the same everywhere (you can't quit the game).

Which brings us to corporate politics, to which the three laws of social thermodynamics apply.

A wise man once commented to me that the only thing worse than having to play stupid games is losing them. Since you can't escape the game of corporate politics, you may as well play to win.

Politics has a bad name, which is too bad because politics has two faces, and one of them is a very positive thing.

The good politics happens because companies are composed of individual human beings. Each has a different set of personal goals; each has opinions shaped by years of experience; each has organizational responsibilities. When you need to get something accomplished, politics is the art of figuring out how to shape your program so it fits into each individual's personal ecology in a way that's positive so everyone affected (or enough to carry the day) will support it.

Politics is an important skill for you to develop because arguing facts and logic doesn't get you very far very often. Salespeople know this. In sales school they learn that human beings make most decisions emotionally and use their intellect to construct rationalizations for their emotional decisions.

Politics is, in part, selling.

Politics is an important skill for you to develop because if you want to accomplish anything, you first need to sell decision-makers on the idea, and that means understanding how to motivate each decision-maker to get to the decision you think is the right one. That, in turn, means understanding that decision-maker's experiential background and thought process. It also means doing what the pros do in Congress: figuring out who will automatically be on your side, who will automatically fight your idea, and who is amenable to persuasion.

Politics, however, isn't only sweetness and light. Corporate back-stabbing does happen. It can happen to you no matter how nice a person you are. Since the third law of thermodynamics applies, you don't get to be above the fray. All you get to do is to keep your eyes and ears open, figure out who may be trying to undermine you and how, and plan your own countermoves to neutralize an organizational antagonist.

If you want to win at corporate politics, you must keep one thought in mind at all times: It's just a game.

Yes, it's a game with stakes that are potentially high. Your job, for example, may be at stake. That doesn't change anything—high-stakes poker is still a game of poker. If you aren't willing to play high-stakes politics, you may want to rethink your career decision because being CIO means being a politician.

You don't get to not be a politician if you want high office. All you get to choose is what kind of politician you choose to be.

THE THREE DANGER ZONES

If you want to become expert at politics, read Machiavelli. It's an intriguing subject on many levels, and worthy of study.

Even if you'd rather spend your efforts elsewhere, there are three situations with special risks you need to know how to handle. These three danger zones are when you take over a team, when your team has been reassigned to a new manager, and when you find yourself on the wrong side of a losing battle.

Here are some guidelines for each of them.

1. Taking Over a Team

Whether you've just been hired or promoted to replace a departed manager, or a reorganization has placed you in charge, the first few months of leading a preexisting team are risky. You may, because early impressions are important, decide to establish yourself as a decisive leader by making immediate changes. That, you may think, will ensure everyone knows who is in charge.

Resist the temptation. When you first take over any leadership role, you're wading through a swamp in the dark. Before you take action, you need to learn where the alligators live, where the sinkholes hide under the surface, and where you can find high ground.

Spend at least a month listening and getting a feel for the situation. Meet with every direct report weekly. Meet with everyone who reports to you at least once. To the extent possible, structure these meetings so they share their knowledge with you and not the other way around.

Why? First of all, before you make a bunch of changes you ought to find out what needs changing, but that isn't the most important reason. The most important reason is that chances are, not everyone wants you to succeed.

It's sad but true. Perhaps someone reporting to you also applied for the job. Perhaps your predecessor, removed for political reasons or for being ineffective, was popular with the team, so they want you to fail. Perhaps your predecessor was a tyrant, and team members unconsciously transfer their resentment and distrust to you.

continues

continued

By listening for a month or two, you'll learn the situation. Someone will tell you. When you get people in the habit of talking to you, they won't all keep secrets, and you'll eventually build their trust.

The best you can hope for is to inherit a disaster area filled with troublemakers. You almost can't help improving it. The team will have a sense of identity (built around an us-versus-them attitude, true enough, but not one of your making); troublemakers usually have some talent to go along with their bad attitude; and whatever the team is supposed to create for the company, it's now failing at. How can you not show improvement?

Gain the team's trust by listening but not judging. Don't cater to the us-versus-them attitude but don't fight it immediately, either. Make it clear delivery must improve, but ask the team to tell you how it will improve things. The only two answers you must reject are (1) it's as good as it can get, and (2) it's someone else's problem to fix.

If someone reporting to you wanted your job, you have a special problem. Even without overt insubordination, it's a rare person in that situation who has the character to provide leadership while still respecting the reporting relationship. Resentment, or at least disbelief that you're more suited to the position, is the common response.

Some experts assert that firing or transferring your erstwhile rival is the only prudent course of action. Often, it is. You're probably best off, though, having a frank conversation and giving it a chance. What you have to do is to establish your recognition of the difficulties intrinsic to the situation. Make it clear that the employee has only two options. Support you and you'll do your best to provide career opportunities. Or, you'll help arrange a transfer to another department right now.

Have this conversation as soon as possible after learning of the situation. It's just too volatile to wait. The moment the team sees you allowing insubordination, you'll lose their respect, and with it your ability to lead.

The worst situation to inherit is a smooth-running, high-performance team that had been led by a popular manager. What can you do, other than to make things worse?

Your best bet in this unfortunate circumstance is to establish a new challenge for the team, to stretch it and make it even more successful. As you do, though, remember the Hippocratic Oath: Above all, do no harm.

2. When Your Team Has Been Reassigned

The danger of inheriting a new team pales in comparison to the danger of having someone inherit your team.

If your new leader is smart, she'll follow the above recommendations. The more you display your insights and initiatives, the more she may see you as a possible rival; the more you keep your head down, the more she'll perceive you as a nonentity.

Do your best to listen rather than talk, keeping in mind that your new boss will be very good at this game, too. Most important, become adept at translating questions into suggestions. "Do think we should do *x*?" often means "I think we should do x," regardless of the disclaimers. You're best off analyzing the advantages and disadvantages of each position, establishing your knowledge of the subject. Rather than give your opinion of the right answer, recommend a process to arrive at a good answer, and suggest your new boss either sponsor or lead the process personally.

When you get a new boss, figure out which way the wind is blowing before you show your strength. When you think you have your new boss figured out, you can decide whether you will support her or not. And if not, leave. No other course of action will accomplish anything other than to ruin your enjoyment of your work while simultaneously making you look bad.

3. Fighting Losing Battles

Sometimes you'll find yourself leading or sponsoring something that simply isn't going to happen. Either you didn't sell the idea to the right executives, it's politically unpopular, someone vastly underestimated the effort needed to make it happen, or it was simply mismanaged.

If you're in this situation, take some wise advice once given to me: Find the most public spot you can, hold the project in front of you, and put a bullet in it. If it's going to die, execute it yourself.

Business isn't the place to emulate Don Quixote, nor is there some corporate patron saint of lost causes. If someone else kills the idea, you're associated with a losing cause. If you kill it, you're someone who can make tough decisions.

MANAGEMENTSPEAK

In 1996, shortly after I began writing the *IS Survival Guide* for *InfoWorld*, I proposed starting my columns with either a pithy quotation or an example of "ManagementSpeak" and a translation. My editors worried that I'd run out, in the process creating an expectation that I wouldn't be able to live up to. Since I had a total of six examples, their concerns weren't entirely unwarranted.

In my January 22, 1996 column I asked readers to send me suggestions. In response I received a deluge. There appears to be no end to the ingenious use of language employed by managers trying to avoid saying what they mean, and no end of IS Survivalists with acute ears to record and translate them.

Below are the examples of ManagementSpeak that appeared in the pages of *InfoWorld* in 1996 through 1998. In *Infoworld*, each entry is followed by the name of the person who provided it (unless that person requested anonymity). I haven't followed that pattern here— submitters didn't know I'd be writing this book when then submitted their entries and getting all of the permissions just wasn't practical.

What follows, in order of publication, is the result of hundreds of acute listeners. My sincere thanks go to every one of them, and not only for providing a tremendous amount of enjoyment for me and several hundred thousand IS Survivalists. I've recognized an uncomfortable number of entries as things I've said myself over the years, so along the way, ManagementSpeak has improved my own speech.

I hope.

MANAGEMENTSPEAK

ManagementSpeak: I don't disagree.
Translation: I disagree.

ManagementSpeak: The upcoming reductions will benefit the vast majority of employees.
Translation: The upcoming reductions will benefit me.

ManagementSpeak: You need to see the big picture.
Translation: My boss thinks it's a good idea.

ManagementSpeak: I'd like your buy-in on this.
Translation: I want someone else to blame when this thing bombs.

ManagementSpeak: Empower (verb).
Translation: Freely blame your subordinates for your problems.

ManagementSpeak: We're still practicing empowerment, but only on a need-to-know basis.
Translation: Pay attention, dummy.

ManagementSpeak: Human Resources.
Translation: A bulk commodity, like toilet paper.

ManagementSpeak: We're going to follow a strict methodology here.
Translation: We're going to do it my way.

ManagementSpeak: We want to deliver a quality product.
Translation: The product will be late and over budget.

ManagementSpeak: I don't totally disagree with you.
Translation: You may be right but I don't care.

ManagementSpeak: My mind is made up. I am adamant on the subject. There is no room for discussion. But if you want to discuss it further, my door is always open.
Translation: &%^$ you.

ManagementSpeak: You just don't understand our business.
Translation: We don't understand our business.

ManagementSpeak: You have to show some flexibility.

Translation: You have to do it whether you want to or not.

ManagementSpeak: That's a good question.

Translation: I never thought of that, and I need to stall.

ManagementSpeak: Value-added.

Translation: It costs us ten cents but nobody will guess when we sell it for $100.

ManagementSpeak: All of our customers are satisfied.

Translation: If you're not satisfied, please take your business elsewhere.

ManagementSpeak: We have to put on our marketing hats.

Translation: We have to put ethics aside.

ManagementSpeak: Opportunity (noun).

Translation: Problem that needs immediate attention and resolution.

ManagementSpeak: I'm glad you asked me that.

Translation: Public Relations has written a carefully phrased answer.

ManagementSpeak: That's a great idea, but it's out of sync with our corporate culture.

Translation: I'm not sure how I can take credit for this idea.

ManagementSpeak: You needed to be more proactive.

Translation: You should have protected me from myself.

ManagementSpeak: It's a no-brainer.

Translation: I don't have a brain.

ManagementSpeak: I didn't understand the email you said you sent. Can you give me a quick summary?

Translation: I still can't figure out how to start the email program.

ManagementSpeak: Help me to understand.

Translation: I don't know what you're talking about, and I don't think you do either. Street Translation: You're an idiot.

ManagementSpeak: Individual Contributor.

Translation: Employee who does real work.

ManagementSpeak: We need to syndicate this decision.
Translation: We need to placate egos.

ManagementSpeak: You obviously put a lot of work into this.
Translation: This is awful.

ManagementSpeak: There are larger issues at stake.
Translation: I've made up my mind, so don't bother me with the facts.

ManagementSpeak: We're going to save money, no matter how much it costs!
Translation: None needed.

ManagementSpeak: Cost of ownership has become a significant issue in desktop computing.
Translation: We want everything done for free.

ManagementSpeak: Your project is on hold.
Translation: Your project is dead.

ManagementSpeak: That's very interesting.
Translation: I disagree.

ManagementSpeak: In a perfect world…
Translation: We don't try for perfection.

ManagementSpeak: I'll never lie to you.
Translation: The truth will change frequently.

ManagementSpeak: We have to leverage our resources.
Translation: You're working weekends.

ManagementSpeak: We want you to be the executive champion of this project.
Translation: I want to be able to blame you for my mistakes.

ManagementSpeak: We need to upgrade.
Translation: We need a different set of bugs.

ManagementSpeak: It's not possible. It's impractical. It won't work.
Translation: I don't know how to do it.

ManagementSpeak: I appreciate your contribution.

Translation: @#%* you!

ManagementSpeak: Our new organizational strategy addresses these goals (recognizing differing customer needs) by moving accountability, authority, and resources closer to local markets and local caregivers, where it belongs.

Translation: We want to shift the blame.

ManagementSpeak: Wrong answer.

Translation: You didn't tell me what I wanted to hear.

ManagementSpeak: I never argue with decisions made by senior management.

Translation: Never mind what they say—do it my way.

ManagementSpeak: If you put your dog to sleep, you could pay more attention to your job.

Translation: If you put me to sleep, you could pay a lot more attention to your job.

ManagementSpeak: I see you involved your peers in developing your proposal.

Translation: One person couldn't possibly come up with something this stupid.

ManagementSpeak: Our business is going through a paradigm shift.

Translation: We've no idea what we have been doing, but in the future we shall do something completely different.

ManagementSpeak: He has a different business model from the previous CEO.

Translation: Get ready for downsizing.

MIS-Speak: We can't release any development tools for use until we develop and fully document a robust, secure platform.

Translation: We're going to committee this thing to death, keep doing things the way we've always done them, and hope the delay makes you go away.

ManagementSpeak: (In response to the question, "Are you looking forward to your new assignment here?") Consultant: "It is an interesting project with a very aggressive schedule. It should be a real challenge."

Translation: No.

ManagementSpeak: I feel strongly both ways.

Translation: I am clueless, but I don't want to feel you made my decision for me.

Alternative Translation: If I side with you, I'll tick off someone else, and it isn't worth it.

ManagementSpeak: Our leadership team has determined that we need to establish metrics for our key processes to verify that we continuously improve.

Translation: Let's produce a blizzard of numbers large enough to make the leadership's eyes glaze over, while not actually measuring anything useful or informative.

ManagementSpeak: You will be fully empowered to make decisions on this project.

Translation: You'll get no support from me.

ManagementSpeak: I always try to match people's interests with the work I assign to them.

Translation: You'll do what I tell you to do.

ManagementSpeak: …in a fun and healthy workplace.

Translation: Young, inexperienced non-smokers work here.

ManagementSpeak: We want you to be happy.

Translation: We expect you to be happy doing it our way.

ManagementSpeak: That's an interesting idea. I would like to see it in writing.

Translation: Forget it!

ManagementSpeak: It's strategic to the organization that we have a coordinated effort, and as such we don't want to interfere with the good work that's already been done by our internal research department.

Translation: Ted is still not back from vacation yet, and nobody can move until then.

ManagementSpeak: Your statements are emotional and immature.

Translation: I disagree, and I'm a bigger cheese than you are.

ManagementSpeak: We see no changes in management at this time.

Translation: We're planning a bloodbath.

ManagementSpeak: The system has to be flexible.

Translation: We don't know what the devil we want.

ManagementSpeak: The technology is the easy part.

Translation: I don't have to do the technology part.

ManagementSpeak: It's just a proof of concept.

Translation: This is something I wanted to work on, but I knew you would say no if I asked.

ManagementSpeak: I understand your idea, and I think it may be of use to us in the future.

Translation: Forget it.

ManagementSpeak: Your continued inputs to the document editing process are appreciated.

Translation: I'll continue to ignore your suggestions.

ManagementSpeak: We're on a tight schedule.

Translation: You're working weekends for the duration.

ManagementSpeak: We can't use freeware because there's no support for it.

Translation: We won't be able to blame the vendor.

Alternate *Translation:* We never do anything we haven't done before.

ManagementSpeak: That only happens once in a blue moon.

Translation: We'll worry about it when one of our big name accounts brings it up.

ManagementSpeak: Next week we will have a retreat for our management team and key employees.

Translation: We're holding a beauty contest. We're going to pick your brains and then downsize everyone we decide we don't like.

ManagementSpeak: I know we've empowered you, but that doesn't mean you can say no.

Translation: Too bad.

ManagementSpeak: I want a member from each of the teams to work on resolving this conflict.

Translation: How do I benefit by getting in the middle of this?

ManagementSpeak: The project team has been working diligently on the release and has made significant progress.

Translation: The project is behind schedule.

ManagementSpeak: Quality is an overhead expense and must be reduced.

Translation: Management is an unnecessary expense but we'll keep funding it.

ManagementSpeak: That's a good start, let's see what else you come up with.

Translation: I need some time to find the flaws.

ManagementSpeak: It's a good suggestion, but we don't have time to develop the perfect system.

Translation: It's too hard for me, it's out of my league, and I sure don't want my subordinate taking the lead!

ManagementSpeak: A number of innovative approaches are currently under consideration.

Translation: We're still spitting in the wind.

ManagementSpeak: This was the most successful project I've ever participated in!

Translation: Everyone liked the report. Even better, the company changed direction before we had to make it work.

ManagementSpeak: This will be a long process.

Translation: This will never be finished.

ManagementSpeak: The procedure which you have referenced is the correctly referenced procedure for the procedure which you referenced and which I am referencing in my reply about the procedure in which your original inquiry was referenced.

Translation: Yup.

ManagementSpeak: For an IS individual he appears to have decent people skills.

Translation: No translation needed.

ManagementSpeak: This upgrade is a drop-in.

Translation: Get out the aspirin and No-Doz.

ManagementSpeak: This assignment will be a good learning experience for you.

Translation: It's a crappy, thankless job that no one wants any part of.

ManagementSpeak: We have made some changes to our benefits package I think you will be very excited about.

Translation: Pull my finger.

ManagementSpeak: I understand that you feel you are overloaded. To help me get a handle on your workload, please keep a daily record of everything you do and how long each task takes. I will evaluate this and see what suggestions I can offer.

Translation: If you have time to do the list, you're not too busy. If you don't have time to do the list, it'll get you off of my back.

ManagementSpeak: The good news is that the system is flexible. The bad news is that the system is flexible.

Translation: The system doesn't even come close to doing what is needed. In fact, we don't know what it does.

ManagementSpeak: We didn't budget for that.

Translation: It's a great idea. Wish I'd thought of it.

ManagementSpeak: I want you to be proactive on this.

Translation: I want you to take the blame if there's any heat.

ManagementSpeak: "Can't you just…?"

Translation: I need it solved, and I can't afford a complicated solution.

ManagementSpeak: That violates our standards.

Translation: We don't know how to do that.

ManagementSpeak: Remember, your career is a marathon, not a dash.

Translation: We no longer provide a real career path, and we're overstaffed besides. With luck, enough employees will quit that we can avoid any severance costs.

ManagementSpeak: Let's take that offline.

Translation: Shut up. (Or, I don't want to deal with you.)

ManagementSpeak: I don't see any reason we can't do this. What do you think?

Translation: Here's what I've decided to do. Disagree with me at your peril.

ManagementSpeak: I'd like to see a more cooperative effort between our groups.

Translation: Do what I tell you.

ManagementSpeak: I talked with the Director about your promotion and he is warm to the idea.

Translation: It will be a cold day in hell before you see your promotion.

ManagementSpeak: He's not a team player.

Translation: He's not a grinning yes-man.

ManagementSpeak: We are not interested in helping the users here. We are only interested in clearing the help desk queue.

Translation: None needed.

ManagementSpeak: You have the unique ability to describe technology in an easy-to-understand format.

Translation: We had no idea you were such a simpleton when we hired you.

ManagementSpeak: We have a personality conflict.

Translation: You have a personality and I'm the only person in this company allowed to have one.

ManagementSpeak: We're doing the same thing, but in a different way.

Translation: We've completely changed our minds.

ManagementSpeak: This person is a loose cannon with our system!

Translation: This person actually tries to really use the technology!

ManagementSpeak: I will personally steward that process.

Translation: I'm betting you'll forget about it within a month.

Alternate Translation: I'm betting this will be a great career builder.

ManagementSpeak: We don't have time for solutions, I need an answer!

Translation: Tell me what I want to hear, immediately!

ManagementSpeak: People are our greatest asset.

Translation: People are our biggest expense item.

ManagementSpeak: You have to apply common sense to this problem.

Translation: You have to think like me.

ManagementSpeak: We've learned our lesson and we'll never make that mistake again.

Translation: Shut up. Shut up! SHUT UP!

Alternative Translation: We have an entirely different mistake in mind for next time.

INDEX

mcp.com
The Authoritative Encyclopedia of Computing

Resource Centers
Books & Software
Personal Bookshelf
WWW Yellow Pages
Online Learning
Special Offers
▶ Choose the online ebooks
that you can view from your   Site Search
personal workspace on our site.   Industry News

About MCP   Site Map   Product Support

Get the best information and learn about latest developments in:

■ Design

■ Graphics and Multimedia

■ Enterprise Computing and DBMS

■ General Internet Information

■ Operating Systems

■ Networking and Hardware

■ PC and Video Gaming

■ Productivity Applications

■ Programming

■ Web Programming and Administration

■ Web Publishing

Turn to the *Authoritative* Encyclopedia of Computing

You'll find over 150 full text books online, hundreds of shareware/freeware applications, online computing classes and 10 computing resource centers full of expert advice from the editors and publishers of:

- Adobe Press
- BradyGAMES
- Cisco Press
- Hayden Books
- Lycos Press
- New Riders
- Que
- Que Education & Training
- Sams Publishing
- Waite Group Press
- Ziff-Davis Press

mcp.com
The Authoritative Encyclopedia of Computing

When you're looking for computing information, consult the authority. The Authoritative Encyclopedia of Computing at mcp.com.

Other Related Titles

Pure JFC Swing
Satyaraj Pantham
0-672-31423-1
$19.99 US/ $28.95 CAN

Database Access with Visual Basic 6
Jeffrey McManus
0-672-31422-3
$39.99 USA/ $57.95 CAN

Doing Objects in Visual Basic 6
Deborah Kurata
1-56276-577-9
$49.99 USA/ $71.95 CAN

Database Developer's Guide with Visual Basic 6
Roger Jennings
0-672-31063-5
$59.99 USA/ $85.95 CAN

Delphi 4 Developer's Guide
Steve Teixeira and Xavier Pacheco
0-672-31284-0
$59.99 USA/ $84.95 CAN

Building Enterprise Solutions with Visual Studio 6
G. A. Sullivan
0-672-31489-4
$49.99 USA/ $71.95 CAN

Java Distributed Objects
Bill McCarty and Luke Cassady-Dorion
0-672-31537-8
$49.99 USA/ $71.95 CAN

Microsoft SQL Server 7.0 DBA Survival Guide
Mark Spenik and Orryn Sledge
0-672-31226-3
$49.99 USA/ $71.95 CAN

Developing COM/ActiveX Components with Visual Basic 6
Dan Appleman
1-56276-576-0
$49.99 USA/ $71.95 CAN

SAMS
www.samspublishing.com

All prices are subject to change.